RICHARD BEACON
SOLON HIS FOLLIE
(1594)

MEDIEVAL & RENAISSANCE

TEXTS & STUDIES

VOLUME 154

RENAISSANCE ENGLISH TEXT SOCIETY

SEVENTH SERIES

VOLUME XVIII (FOR 1993)

SOLON HIS FOLLIE,

OR

A POLITIQUE DISCOURSE

TOUCHING THE

Reformation of common-weales
conquered, declined or corrupted.

BY RICHARD BEACON

An Annotated Edition by
Clare Carroll
and
Vincent Carey

MEDIEVAL & RENAISSANCE TEXTS & STUDIES
Binghamton, NY
1996

Library of Congress Cataloging-in-Publication Data

Becon, Richard.
    Solon his follie, or, A politique discourse touching the reformation of
common-weales conquered, declined or corrupted / by Richard Beacon; an
annotated edition by Clare Carroll and Vincent Carey.
        p.   cm. — (Medieval & Renaissance Texts & Studies; v. 154)
    Includes bibliographical references and index.
    ISBN 0–86698–194–2 (alk. paper)
        1. Ireland—Politics and government—16th century. 2. Munster (Ireland)—
Politics and governemnt. 3. Land tenure—Ireland—Munster—History—16th
century. 4. British—Ireland—Munster—History—16th century. I. Carroll, Clare,
1955– . II. Carey, Vincent, 1961– . III. Title. IV. Series.
DA937.B43   1996
325 '.3142 '0941909031—dc20   95–41147
                                                                              CIP

This book is made to last.
It is set in Palatino, smyth-sewn,
and printed on acid-free paper
to library specifications.

Printed in the United States of America

Table of Contents

4/6/96

In Memory of

John Blake Carroll
(1913–1962)

and

Thomas G. Carey
(1969–1991)

ACKNOWLEDGEMENTS

In our research in the field of early modern tracts on Ireland, we were greatly helped by the work and advice of fellow historians and textual scholars. We would especially like to thank Brendan Bradshaw who from the earliest stages of the project advised us about the important differences among the various New English authors. Nicholas Canny also gave us useful criticism from the outset. Roger Deakins, Hiram Morgan, and Michael MacCarthy-Morrogh deserve special thanks for sharing their unpublished work with us, much of which was crucial to our interpretation of Beacon's text and context.

We have benefitted from the encouragement and inspiration of our teachers Karl Bottigheimer, James V. Mirollo, and the late Helena Shire, as well as from colleagues Steven Ellis and Margaret MacCurtain. Thanks are also due to John Williams for his seminar on imperialism, Jill Kraye for her advice on research, Amy Mandelker for the use of her office, and Fred Nichols for help in identifying some of the Latin quotations.

We would also like to thank Richard McCoy and the Folger Institute for making it possible for us to do research at the Folger and to participate in Arthur Kinney's seminar on Tudor Literary History. The librarians and staff at the Bodleian Library, the British Library, the Cambridge University Library, the Folger Library, the National Library of Ireland, the Public Record Office, London, the Trinity Library, and the archivist Malcolm Underwood at St. Johns College were all unstinting in their efforts to answer questions and to provide us with the necessary materials for our research.

Two trips to England and Ireland were funded by grants from the Professional Staff Congress of the City University of New York, and the National Endowment for the Humanities.

These research trips were also made possible by the generosity and hospitality of our families—the Careys in Ireland, the Freemantles in England, Charles Carroll and Margaret Creedon in New York, Kate Cox in California, and especially Margaret Carroll and Margaret O'Connor in Washington, D. C.

The publication of the text would not have been possible without the initial interest of Mario Di Cesare, and the expertise in textual editing of Arthur Kinney and Speed Hill. Thanks also to Tracy Youells for her care in guiding this book through the press.

This has been a collaborative work in more ways than one; our companions Jennifer Creedon and Daniel Scanlon played an important part, even though at times they wished that they didn't. Our gratitude to them goes beyond anything we could say here.

Clare Carroll
Vincent Carey
New York City, 1993

ABBREVIATIONS

Acts Privy Council	*Acts of the Privy Council of England*, 1542–1631. 46 vols. London: Eyre and Spottiswoode for H. M. Stationary Office, 1890–1964.
BL	British Library, London
Bodin, *De Republica*	*De republica libri sex, Latine ab autore redditi: Multo quam antea locupletiores*. London: Iacobum DuPuys, 1586.
Bull	Niccolo Machiavelli. *The Prince*. Trans. George Bull. Harmondsworth: Penguin, 1975.
Cal. P. R. Ire., Eliz.	*Calendar of patent and close rolls of chancery in Ireland, Henry VIII–Elizabeth*. 2 vols. Dublin: Thom & Sons for H. M. Stationary Office, 1861–1862.
Cal. Salisbury MSS.	*Calendar of the Manuscripts of the Marquis of Salisbury at Hatfield House*. 24 vols. London: Historical Manuscripts Commission, 1883–1976.
Cal. S. P. Domestic	*Calendar of State Papers, Domestic Series, of the Reigns of Edward VI, Mary, Elizabeth, and James I, 1547–1625*. Ed. Robert Lemon. Reprint, 12 vols. Nendeln: Kraus, 1967.
Cal. S. P. Ire.	*Calendar of the state papers* relating to *Ireland, 1509–1603* [etc.] 11 vols. London: Longman [etc.], 1860–1912.
DNB	Leslie Stephen and Stephen Lee, ed. *Dictionary of National Biography*. 1885–1901. Reprint, 22 vols. Nendeln: Kraus, 1968.
Discorsi & Principe	Niccolo Machiavelli. *Il Principe e Discorsi sopra la prima deca di Tito Livio*. Ed. Sergio Bertelli. Milano: Feltrinelli, 1983.

Discursus	Niccolo Machiavelli. *Disputationum de republica quas discursus* [etc.]. Mompelgarten, 1591.
Fenton, *Historie of Guicciardin*	Francesco Guicciardini. *The Historie of Guicciardin* conteining the warres of Italie and other partes, continued for many yeares under sundry kings ... with a table at large. Reduced into English by Geoffrey Fenton. London, 1579.
Fiants Ire., Eliz.	"Calendar to fiants of the reign of Henry VIII ..." [etc.] Reigns Henry VIII to Elizabeth in *Seventh* to the *Twenty-Second Report of the Deputy Keeper of the Public Records in Ireland*. Dublin, 1875–1890.
Geneva Bible	*The Geneva Bible, A facsimile of the 1560 edition.* Ed. Lloyd E. Berry. Madison: University of Wisconsin Press, 1969.
IHS	*Irish Historical Studies: the joint journal of the Irish Historical Society and the Ulster Society for Irish Historical Studies.* Dublin, 1938–.
Knolles	Jean Bodin. *The Sixe Bookes of a Commonweale.* A facsimile reprint of Richard Knolles's English translation of 1606, corrected and supplemented. Ed. Kenneth Douglas McRae. Cambridge, Mass.: Harvard University Press, 1962.
Lipsius, *Pol.*	Justus Lipsius. *Politicorum sive civilis doctrinae libri sex. Editio altera, quam Auctor pro Germana fide agnoscit.* London: George Bishop, 1590.
NHI	T. W. Moody, F. X. Martin and F. J. Byrne, eds. *A New History of Ireland.* 10 vols. Oxford: Oxford University Press, 1976– .
NLI	National Library of Ireland, Dublin
North, *Plutarch's Lives*	*The Lives of the Noble Grecians and Romanes, Compared together by that grave learned Philosopher and Historiographer, Plutarke of Chaeronea: Translated out of Greeke into French by Iames Amyot ... and out of French into English by Thomas North.* Boston and New York: Houghton Mifflin, 1928.
OCD	*The Oxford Classical Dictionary.* Ed. N. G. L. Hammond and H. M. Scullard. 2d ed. Oxford: Clarendon Press, 1970.

PRO SP
Public Record Office, State Papers, London followed by shelf number of series and volume number.

Solon
Richard Beacon, *Solon His Follie or A politique discourse, touching the reformation of common-weales conquered, declined or corrupted.* Oxford: Joseph Barnes, 1594.

Stat. Ire.,
10 Hen. VI–14 Eliz.
In this volume are contained all the statutes [10 Hen. VI–14 Eliz.] *made in Ireland.* fol. Dublin: R. Tottle, 1572.

Telius
De Principe libellus … ex Italiano in Latinum per Sylvestrum Telium. Basil: Petrus Perna, 1560.

Tudor Ire.
Steven G. Ellis, *Tudor Ireland: crown, community and the conflict of cultures, 1470–1603.* London: Longman, 1985.

Walker
The Discourses of Niccolo Machiavelli. Ed. with an introduction by Bernard Crick and trans. by Leslie J. Walker. Harmondsworth: Penguin, 1988.

All references to classical texts, unless otherwise indicated, are to the Loeb Classical Library editions.

INTRODUCTION

Richard Beacon's Irish Experience

Richard Beacon and *Solon His Follie* (1594) are rooted in the establishment of an English settlement in Munster in the 1580's and early
1590's. Beacon's career parallels the development of the Munster plantation from its inception in the aftermath of the rebellion (1579–83)
and the death and attainder of the Old English lord Gerald Fitzgerald,
the 14th earl of Desmond, to the climax of instability which resulted
in Beacon's discharge and the outbreak of the Nine Years War (1594–
1603). The Old English, descendants of the twelfth-century Anglo-
Norman settlers, are to be distinguished from Beacon's New English
compatriots who came to prominence as a consequence of the
renewed English intervention in Ireland in the sixteenth century. Beacon's participation in this process, and his difficulties as a colonist
and legal administrator during this period, provide the background to
Solon His Follie.[1]

The suppression of the Desmond rebellion allowed for English settlement in the largest confiscation of Irish land that century. In order
to plant Munster successfully, the English administrations in both
Dublin and London endeavored not to repeat the failures of earlier
efforts at colonization in the Midlands and Ulster.[2] The government

---

[1] See Brady 1980–81; *Tudor Ire.*, 237, 250–54, 262–66, 279–84; and below, *Solon*
I, notes 84 and 85.

[2] Much of our understanding of the development of the Munster plantation
is based on the work of Michael MacCarthy-Morrogh. He kindly provided essen-
tial information on Beacon's landholding in the area. For the definitive work on

stipulated that all settlers be English-born (thus excluding the older colonial elite, the Old English), that lands be granted to settlers who would "undertake" to farm their estates with specified numbers of English tenants, that the "undertaker" provide a specific component of militia based on the size of his "seigniory," and that all of these conditions be met within a seven-year period. By establishing a model of English "civility" and providing a bulwark on the southern coast of Ireland against a possible Spanish invasion, the government hoped to advance its program of control and reform.[3]

Richard Beacon's *Solon His Follie* is a justification of these goals. It was not, however, his sole contribution to this mission. Beacon would devote almost a decade of his life (1586–1595), to the cause of the plantation in Munster. His preparation for this task included a B. A. (1567–1571) and an M. A. (1575) from St. John's College, Cambridge. While it is not clear how Beacon spent the period 1577 to 1586, the fact that he completed his studies at Gray's Inn (1577), and that he served as a barrister in the brief period from 1585 to 1586, suggest legal employment. Otherwise it would be hard to account for his initial Irish appointment as attorney general for the council and province of Munster in 1586.[4] Later correspondence with Lord Chancellor Sir John Puckering (1592–6) suggests a possible patron, but it is not clear how Beacon got the post. This legal experience and training could hardly have prepared the attorney general for the confusion of the first settlement efforts in the devastated province of Munster.[5]

Beacon was appointed to the commission for the allocation of the

---

the Munster plantation, see MacCarthy-Morrogh 1986; for a brief overview, *Tudor Ire.*, 291–99; and for a discussion of the failure of the plantation schemes in Ulster and in the Midlands, Canny 1976.

[3] MacCarthy-Morrogh 1986, 30–37.

[4] *Fiants Ire., Eliz.*, 4949; *DNB* under Becon; Judson 1947, 165–68; Quinn 1976, 85–87.

[5] "Richard Beacon to the Lord keeper of the Great Seal," 21 Jan. 1595 (PRO SP 63/178/13), where Beacon thanks Puckering for his opinion on his "late labors," more than likely a reference to the by now published *Solon* (March-April, 1594), and declares that he "shall rest forever more bounden than [he] may well express by letters." He concludes this letter, which is replete with classical and contemporary Continental references reminiscent of *Solon*, with an expression of gratitude for "sundry honorable favors."

confiscated lands of Desmond and the Old English rebels to the New English settlers in 1586. The commission surveyed the escheated lands, measuring, dividing and allotting them to the undertakers. The commission also examined disputed titles and claims of the former owners, and appointed replacements.[6] Despite the opposition of some former inhabitants and their tenants, the commission's work was sufficiently successful that by September 1587 most of the undertakers were in possession of their holdings.[7] This did not bring peace to the region, however. Since both the government and the settlers attempted to plant Munster on highly inadequate legal claims, the former landowners and their tenants responded with an intense campaign of litigation and intimidation to regain their holdings. In addition, many of the settlers added to the legal confusion by instigating legal proceedings against each other over disputed boundaries to their new holdings.[8]

In the latter half of 1587, Beacon arbitrated two prominent disputes. In October he served on a commission to settle the dispute between New English settler Sir Edward Phyton and Old English claimant Richard Power, and in December of the same year he had to decide on rival claims between two New English settlers, Sir William Herbert and Denzel Holles.[9] Later, in February 1589, he was one of the commissioners appointed to inquire into and deal with the extravagant land claims of Sir Walter Ralegh.[10]

More significantly, Beacon participated in the government's efforts to suppress the claims of many native and former tenants who asserted that they had been unjustly dispossessed. From serving on the commission appointed to settle these claims in 1588, Beacon gained insight into the problems of colonizing lands where the native population still resided. Only claims based on official court records

---

[6] MacCarthy-Morrogh 1986, 56–57.

[7] MacCarthy-Morrogh 1986, 58–63.

[8] MacCarthy-Morrogh 1986, 70–102; and Sheehan 1982–83.

[9] "Thomas Norris, Jessua Smythes and R. Becon, . . . to Walsingham," 17 Oct. 1587 (PRO SP 63/131/61), and "Same to Hatton and Walsingham," 2 Dec. 1587 (PRO SP 63/132/25).

[10] *Fiants Ire., Eliz.,* 5297.

were admitted, insuring that those who had held their land by Gaelic custom or who had imperfect documents were not heard. Although the 1588 commission decided in favor of the settlers, many former landholders continued to press the privy councils in Dublin and London for redress, and refused to move from their lands.[11]

Beacon's reflections on these problems formed the background to his views on colonization in Book III of *Solon His Follie*, as did his own experience as a landholder. By May 1589, he was granted lands in the counties of Cork and Waterford and became a settler.[12] Beacon joined others in inheriting a series of legal and more physical problems as they attempted to settle in the face of local opposition. His lands in Cork, the seigniory of Clandonnell Roe, had originally been granted to a group of English settlers (Edward Rogers, Roger Warre and Robert Baynard), but in July 1587, the powerful previous owner and Gaelic lord, Domhnaill MacCarthy Mor, had the confiscation reversed.[13] This order was reversed again in London in the summer of 1588 and the land once again granted to the English settlers. The proprietors Rogers, Warre, and Baynard soon left, taking with them a settlement group of more than sixty, and in early 1589 the lands were assigned to one more ill-fated English settler (Alexander Clarke). Beacon acquired the land by May 1589 because Clarke, like the others before him, could not handle the area's barren and remote nature and the intimidation by MacCarthy Mor, the Earl of Clancare.[14]

---

[11] "Book of the proceedings in Munster by the lord chief justice Anderson, . . . etc.," 3 Sept. 1588 (PRO SP 63/136/21–22); MacCarthy-Morrogh 1987, 97–100; *Tudor Ire.*, 294–96.

[12] For details of Beacon's land, see *Fiants Ire., Eliz.*, 5536; *Cal. P. R. Ire., Eliz.*, 2:266; and "An abstract or brief particular of all the names of the undertakers . . . the quantity of their lands, and their yearly rents," 31 Dec. 1592 (PRO SP 63/167/44, enc. iii), where Beacon is recorded as holding 6,000 acres and owing 16L.13s.4d per annum from Michaelmas 1591. Although these grants were not issued until 29 Feb. 1591, there is evidence that Beacon held these lands as early as 15 May 1589. See "Petition of Gerrot Fitzrichard to the lord treasurer" (PRO SP 63/144/46).

[13] MacCarthy-Morrogh 1986, 82–86.

[14] Information on the complexities of these Munster land disputes was kindly supplied by Michael MacCarthy-Morrogh from unpublished research on the subject. Some of the Beacon material is summarized in MacCarthy-Morrogh 1986, 86–87. For more specific detail, see *Cal. P. R. Ire., Eliz.*, 2:175; *Cal. S. P. Ire., 1588–*

Beacon's Abbey of Bantry was sacked by the earl's illegitimate son Domhnaill. In response, Beacon challenged both the earl and his son, through the law and on the ground in Clandonnell Roe. In meetings with the earl, Beacon "did use his lord unreservedly and pronounced great thretenings against his bast[ard] son [Domhnaill]."[15] This dispute informs Beacon's condemnation of the nobility that figures prominently in Book III of *Solon*, where the Irish "over-mighty" subject and his "grievous exactions" are held responsible for the decline of English rule in Ireland. Beacon characterizes the oppression of the Gaelic tenants by their Gaelic and Old English lords through duties and exactions as "the very nurse, and teate, that gave sucke and nutriment to all disobedience, rebellions, enormities, vices, and iniquities of that realme" (K3). Beacon's depiction of the Gaelic lords' claims to sovereign authority derives from his acrimonious dealings with a prominent member of that group.

Beacon faced a similar challenge from the Old English, in this case to his ownership of the lands near Dungarvan in County Waterford. By 1594, the attorney was "forcibly dispossessed of the said lands by the strength of 50 kerne armed & [his] house & servants robbed and spoiled."[16] The previous Old English owner Gerrot Mac Thomas Fitzgerald was behind the assault on Beacon's Waterford property. Fitzgerald also utilised legal channels to have the new settler's title overturned, claiming that his family's dispossession was a mistake. Mac Thomas asserted that his brother, Richard, who had been attainted as a supporter of Desmond, was not the legitimate owner; Richard as an illegitimate son should be ruled an intruder on the lands. Gerrot Mac Thomas, who claimed to be the loyal and proper heir, wanted the lands restored to him and campaigned to keep Beacon from profitably holding them.[17]

92, 130–31, 198, 208; and especially, "Answer of Alexander Clarke ... to the articles given in charge to the commissioners," [ ] May 1589 (PRO SP 63/144/67); "Sir Warham St. Leger to Burghley," 22 June 1589 (PRO SP 63/145/19).

[15] "Sir Thomas Norris to Burghley" 27 Aug. 1591 (PRO SP 63/159/63); "Docquet of Irish suitors," [ ] Feb. 1595 (PRO SP 63/178/64).

[16] "A true answer to the unjust complaint of Gerald FitzJames alias McThomas," 31 Aug. 1594 (PRO SP 63/171/78).

[17] "Abstract of the title of Gerrot McThomas," "Petition of Gerrot Fitzrichard

Beacon also had to confront the issue of the legality of the plantation itself. The problem arose from the uncertain title to the
Gaelicized earl of Desmond's lands and the sweeping and imprecise
claims of overlordship that the local Gaelic and Old English lords
asserted. Through Gaelic and feudal custom, Desmond's rule had
extended over a vast area of Munster, and included authority over
many who were not his legal tenants. Often this overlordship was
asserted in terms of "chargeable" lands where specified services—for
example, victuals, lodging, and maintenance for his soldiers—were
owed to the earl as a form of customary duty or exaction. These lands
over which Desmond had only claimed lordship were not freehold
and therefore not technically forfeit to the crown.[18] As queen's attorney in Munster, Beacon assisted in the task of arbitrating claims to the
lands that the crown had confiscated, and in 1591 he served on a
commission to settle the issue of the "chargeable" lands in County
Cork.[19] These issues were not finally settled for the province as a
whole until October 1592.

In Book III of *Solon His Follie*, the proposed solution to these problems of land tenure and taxation is "composition."[20] Under "composition," duties that had been exacted from the tenants by the Gaelic
lords are converted into an annual payment to the crown. Successful
composition had already been instituted in 1585 by Lord Deputy Sir
John Perrot and implemented by the Provincial President of Connacht, Sir Richard Bingham.[21]

In effect, composition replaced the diffuse and customary overlordship of the nobility with the centralizing sovereignty of the Tudor
state. Beacon claimed that "composition" aimed to "restraine and

---

alias McThomas to the privy council," "Petition of Gerrot Fitzrichard to
Burghley," "Petition of Gerrot Fitzrichard to Walsingham," "Petition of Gerrot
Fitzrichard to the lord treasurer," 15 May 1589 (PRO SP63/144/41, 42, 43, 44, 45,
and 46).

[18] MacCarthy-Morrogh 1986, 71–76; *Tudor Ire.*, 293.

[19] *Fiants Ire., Eliz.*, 5561.

[20] "Lord deputy Sir William Fitzwilliam to the privy council," 21 Oct. 1592
(PRO SP 63/167/8, enc. i–viii); *Cal. S. P. Ire., 1592–96*, 2–12.

[21] Brady 1986, 22–49; Cunningham 1984–85, 1–14; *Tudor Ire.*, 268–74, 284–88;
for more detail, see *Solon* III, note 41.

suppresse the ambition of the nobles and ... defende the people from oppressors" (K4v). This could only be accomplished if the nobles, whom he often represents in the text as "Caesar," were disarmed by revoking their customary exactions and eliminating their bands of armed retainers.[22] Beacon did not, however, want the native Old English or Gaelic aristocratic elite destroyed. On the contrary, he advocated that, once they were disarmed, they should be granted official responsibilities and "due regard of their merites and services towardes the state" to prevent their alienation (L2v). To insure these results, Beacon insisted that composition include the "cesses" or taxes necessary to maintain the English garrison, so that instead of frequent and extortionate levies

> payment ought to be made at the common charge of the subject, but convenient it were that this charge were drawne to a contribution certaine; for where the contributions are altogither uncertaine ... there the people are usuallie oppressed (L4).

It would appear that the commission on composition in Munster, which completed its report in October 1592, proceeded along these very lines. The success of this commission, however, did not advance Beacon's career.[23] By December 1591, Beacon had suffered a severe setback in his career, and, as a result, had been forced to resign his government position.[24]

Beacon's fall must be seen in the context of political disputes among the New English settlers in Munster as well as constant infighting among various factions which dominated the upper echelons of English administration in Ireland. Beacon had hoped to advance

---

[22] "if we shall cut off all exactions, and tributes, which *Caesar* leavieth uppon the people; if we shall cut of all that infinite number of retainers, followers and men which follow *Caesar* (L1v)."

[23] "Lord deputy Fitzwilliam to the privy council," 21 Oct. 1592; "Declaration of the proceedings of Sir Thomas Norris, Sir Robert Gardener and the Commissioners for making the composition in Munster," 14 Oct. 1592; "An answer to the additions," 14 Oct. 1592; "Chief Justice Sir Robert Gardener and Solicitor Roger Wilbraham to Burghley," 31 Dec. 1592; "Burghley to Gardener and Wilbraham," 19 Nov. 1592; and "Gardener and Wilbraham to Burghley," 31 Dec. 1592; *Cal. S. P. Ire., 1592–96*, 2–13, 44–55.

[24] *Fiants Ire., Eliz.*, 5692.

into this elite. His efforts included the short reports he sent to the administration in London in early 1589,[25] in which he demonstrated his command of local politics and his approach to governing Ireland.[26]

These letters reveal that Beacon favored the same approach to government in Munster that he outlined in *Solon His Follie*. This approach was also reflected in Beacon's letter of support for his fellow settler and justice of the peace, Sir William Herbert. Beacon defended Herbert as a settler conscientious in his dealings with the native population, and one who managed, because of "general affection towards him in Desmond and Kerry" to bring them into a "quiet and loyal disposition."[27] As *Solon His Follie* and Herbert's tract *Croftus Sive De Hibernia Liber* attest, Herbert and Beacon advocated similar strategies for the reformation of Ireland. They were both strong supporters of composition and colonization. They both allowed for coercion or extra legal force in dealing with a restless population, but only under specific circumstances. They frequently defended the practice of law and argued for its impartial application to the native population.[28]

Beacon's praise of Herbert came at a time when the latter was under attack by his New English rivals, who ridiculed him for conciliatory dealings with his Irish tenants. Herbert complained,

I have drawn upon me the evil will of some of mine English neighbours ... they cannot brook my course, so contrary unto theirs, by the which if it be not redressed I foresee they will make themselves and this action [the planting of Munster] (which they undiscreetly use) odious and hateful unto this

---

[25] "Richard Beacon to Sir Francis Walsingham," 24 Feb. 1589 (PRO SP, 63/141/40); "Justice Jessua Smythes and Richard Beacon to Sir Francis Walsingham," 3 Mar. 1589 (PRO SP 63/142/3).

[26] "Richard Beacon to Sir Francis Walsingham," 24 Feb. 1589 (PRO SP 63/141/40).

[27] "Justice Jessua Smythes and Richard Beacon to Sir Francis Walsingham," 3 Mar. 1589 (PRO SP 63/142/3).

[28] See *Croftus sive de Hibernia liber*, ed. Keaveney and Madden 1992, xii–xiii, xxxix–xli; MacCarthy-Morrogh 1986, 93–96; Brady 1986, 24–25. Herbert's support for composition, impartial justice, and his criticisms of his fellow New English Munster settlers can be seen in his shorter tracts, *Cal. S. P. Ire., 1586–88*, 527–47.

people, "wherehence" very great inconveniences in time may grow, whereby they think to gain much, but without Her Majesty's excessive charge are more like to lose all.[29]

Herbert had recently criticized the greed and extortionate actions of certain New English settlers, advocating instead his policy of equity before the law for the native population and his scheme for the spread of Protestantism through the medium of the Gaelic language.

Although concern for the natives was a frequent rhetorical ploy in letters of complaint to London against fellow English settlers, its assertion by Herbert seems to have been genuine enough.[30] Beacon's praise of Herbert placed them both in opposition to those settlers who advocated a harder line. They were certainly associated with this approach when the two were condemned in a July 1589 letter from Herbert's chief New English rival, Sir Edward Denny. Denny argued that "perswasion" could never bring the Irish "to god or to her majestie, but justis with out mercie must first tame and com[m]and them."[31] Furthermore, he suggested the conciliatory approach was a pretense to enrich its proponents at the expense of the natives. Beacon and Herbert were singled out for appointing native "thefes, robers and murderers" as their constables and, in particular, as extreme abusers of the law for their own monetary gain:

yet did he and Beakon caus[e] the people to be pilled by a statut[e] most unconcionable beyond all measur[e], if statut[e]s and
lawes of good effect and fit for this time wear as well folowed
for her Majesties good, as this was to fill Mr. Beacons pilling
purse, upon the extortion of the poorest begars ... it were
good.[32]

These charges of corruption stuck. Herbert left Ireland later in the summer of 1589, and would not return after 1590; although Beacon continued to serve as attorney for another two years, these charges

---

[29] Sir William Herbert, "The Description of Munster," *Cal. S. P. Ire., 1586–88*, 533.
[30] For a discussion of accusations of "abuse" by settlers, and a modern assessment of Herbert's sincerity, see MacCarthy-Morrogh 1986, 93–96.
[31] "Sir Edward Denny to Walsingham," 25 July 1589 (PRO SP 63/145/78).
[32] Ibid.

surfaced again in the late summer of 1591.[33] At that time Sir Thomas Norris, the powerful Vice-President of Munster, accused Beacon of levying excessive fines for minor offenses and using the proceeds for personal profit. Norris portrayed Beacon as an official who carried out his duties with such a zeal that his victims were forced to "live in the woods, apt to take every occasion for mischiefe that shall be offered."[34] Norris had Beacon imprisoned, and petitioned the lord deputy in Dublin and the Privy Council in London to have him punished. Under the council's direction and Lord Deputy Fitzwilliam's authority, Beacon was removed from his Munster official post.[35] This blow was evidently devastating. In December 1591 Beacon surrendered his post, and by May 1592 sold off some of his lands in Cork.[36] Shortly before or after this date, Beacon left for England with the goal of reacquiring his position in the colonial administration.

The publication of *Solon His Follie* was Beacon's intended way out of political exile, by angling for a patron through his literary endeavors.[37] Accorded the privileges of an Oxford degree in 1594, Beacon had *Solon His Follie* published at the university press the same year. Dedications in *Solon His Follie* by the Trinity College scholars John Budden and Robert Wright confirm Beacon's stay at Oxford and his associations there (¶¶ 2, ¶¶2v). The patronage connections of these academics may also point to the route Beacon hoped would rehabilitate his reputation. Wright and Budden shared the patronage of Sir Henry Unton, whose prestige was rising through his association with the royal favourite Robert Devereux, Earl of Essex. Wright later edited a volume of Latin elegies, *Funebria* (Oxford: Joseph Barnes, 1596), to which Budden also contributed a poem, written on the death of Sir Henry Unton.[38]

---

[33] "Privy Council [England] to the lord deputy," Sept.–Dec. 1591 *Acts Privy Council, 1591–92,* 94.

[34] "Sir Thomas Norris to Burghley," 27 Aug. 1591 (PRO SP 63/159/63).

[35] As above, note 39; *Fiants Ire., Eliz.,* 5692, 5707.

[36] *Fiants Ire., Eliz.,* 5692. For the sale of these lands see Chatsworth, Lismore MSS, "Boyle Patent Book," 377–79. We are grateful to Michael MacCarthy-Morrogh for this reference from his unpublished research.

[37] Judson 1947, 165–68.

[38] See *DNB* under Budden, Unton and Wright, and below, *Solon* I, notes 20,

Beacon hoped that these associations would advance him, yet "The booke unto the Reader" suggests an even more influential recipient for his text than Sir Henry Unton. A reading of his "Circe" and "wise Ulysses" allegory implies that Beacon aimed to flatter the Earl of Essex, Elizabeth's most prominent courtier at the time (¶¶iv).[39] While Unton hoped with Essex's backing to acquire a diplomatic posting on the Continent, Beacon himself hoped to gain the earl's patronage and assistance in changing Irish policy.[40] *Solon His Follie* was published at Oxford in 1594, precisely at the time when Essex was seriously attempting to have one of his candidates replace Sir William Fitzwilliam as Lord Deputy for Ireland.

Fitzwilliam's administration (1588–1594) was characterized by personal corruption and bitter attacks on the preceding Lord Deputy, Sir John Perrot, resulting in Perrot's trial for treason in April 1592. Motivated by private political concerns, Fitzwilliam overturned Perrot's policy in Ulster and purged his allies from the Irish administration.[41] Possibly Richard Beacon was a victim of such a purge, since his removal in the summer of 1591 came in the midst of the conspiracy to bring down Perrot which had been initiated by Fitzwilliam in February 1590 and would culminate in Perrot's imprisonment in the Tower in March 1591.[42] Fitzwilliam's sweep of the Irish administration and his "minimalist" style of government (in which local officials were given extensive autonomy) did not bring stability to Ireland, however, and by the end of 1593, Ulster and certain other parts of the country were on the verge of rebellion.[43] Charges of corruption aside, Fitzwilliam was being blamed at the end of 1593 for the circumstances

---

25. Wright was Sir Henry Unton's chaplain. Budden was the translator for Sir Thomas Smith's *De Republica Anglorum* (1610).

[39] *Solon* I, note 15.

[40] For Unton's expectations of Essex, see *DNB* under Unton; for Beacon's aspirations, see *Solon* I, notes 16–18.

[41] This interpretation of Fitzwilliam's administration is based on Morgan 1986, 40–68.

[42] Evidence for the purge of the Irish administration of Perrot's supporters is drawn from Morgan 1987, 42–45, where it is noted that even minor officials such as Stephen Seager, the Constable of Dublin Castle, and Rice Ap Hugh, the Provost Marshal, were imprisoned.

[43] Morgan 1987, 45.

which had led to a complete destabilization of the Irish situation.[44]

At this moment between January and April 1594, when the clamor to recall Fitzwilliam was at its height and the pressure was on at court to appoint his successor, Beacon published his text. The publication date of 1594, the allusion to the "wise Ulysses," and the consistency of the allegory, where Epimenides (Beacon) advises Solon (Russell) as he is about to depart for Salamis (Ireland), all suggest that the text was published to coincide with the appointment of the accomplished veteran of the war in the Netherlands, Sir William Russell, to the Irish lord deputyship. Praising Russell directly, Beacon described his deeds in the future tense:

> Therefore provident were the counsel of *Athens* in committing this of the reformation of *Salamina*, ... into the handes of *Sir William Russell* as unto another *Iacomine*, by whose rare skill and knowledge in militarie discipline, the *Pisans* have and will be forced at the last to obey the *Florentines* (F2–F2v).[45]

The immediacy of publication is reinforced by the end of the text where Epimenides hears "the great noise and clattering of the weapons, and armour of the soldiers" as they depart with Solon to fight the Megarians. Russell's appointment as deputy in April 1594, and receipt of his official instructions in May make publication before May 1594 certain.[46] This dating and the Russell-Solon identification are further confirmed by Beacon's return to Ireland in 1594 with the

---

[44] "An information of certain disorders continued in Ireland since Sir William Fitzwilliam's last government until this time," [ ] 1593 (PRO SP 63/172/50); "Lord deputy to Burghley," 30 Jan. 1594 (PRO SP 63/173/9); "Same to Sir Robert Cecil," 30 Jan. 1594 (PRO SP 63/173/10); "Sir Geoffrey Fenton to Burghley," 17 Feb. 1594 (PRO SP 63/173/40); "Queen Elizabeth to the lord deputy and council," 14 Mar. 1594 (PRO SP 63/173/85).

[45] *Solon* II, note 66.

[46] "Sir Edward Conway to his Father Sir John Conway," 12 Apr. 1594, *Cal. S. P. Domestic, 1591–94*, 482; "Sir Geoffrey Fenton to Burghley," 13 Apr. 1594 (PRO SP 63/174/14); and "Note of the necessary things desired for the despatch of Sir William Russell," 27 Apr. 1594; "Memorial for Ireland at the going of Sir William Russell," 28 Apr. 1594; "Queen to the lord deputy Fitzwilliam and council," 3 May 1594; "Instructions for Sir William Russell," 3 May 1594 (PRO SP 63/174/27, 28, 34, 35).

new lord deputy and his letter of January 1595 from Dublin in lavish praise of his champion's efforts.[47]

Russell certainly, and Beacon perhaps, benefited from Essex's exertions at court and in the privy council in London. Russell's attachment to the earl dated from the period when both served with Leicester in the Netherlands. This connection was corroborated in December 1591, when Russell wrote to the earl confirming his loyalty and asserting his willingness to serve him.[48] Essex repaid this loyalty in March 1594, when he supported the hardened campaigner Russell for the Irish post. Essex chose Russell over his other supporter Unton, informing Unton in these words:

> Sir William Russell I have commended, to him I have given my word to stand only for him, and to him the Queen seems to be the most disposed. If he give over or be refused I am free, and being free will do as much for you as yourself can ask or wish for; which is as much as my wit and credit, both set on tender hooks, can stretch to.[49]

Richard Beacon had also extended his "wit and Credit" in 1594. His means of doing so were *Solon His Follie* and his return to Ireland under Russell. He explained himself in the text:

> I did first aime and shoote at the publique good and profit, according to the trust reposed in me, and now as one that hath lost his arrowe, and missed the marke, I have at al adventures discharged the seconde time, to the ende that my second labours may drawe home my first losses (¶¶i).[50]

---

[47] "Beacon to the lord keeper [Sir John Puckering]," 21 Jan. 1595 (PRO SP 63/178/13). Russell formally took up his position in August 1594, "Fitzwilliam to Burghley," 11 Aug. 1594 (PRO SP 63/175/43).

[48] *DNB* under Russell; "Russell to the earl of Essex," 10 Dec. 1591, *Cal. Salisbury MSS.*, 4. 162.

[49] "Earl of Essex to Sir Henry Unton," Mar. or Apr. 1594, *Cal. Salisbury MSS.*, 4. 499.

[50] *Solon* I, note 14.

The Text, Its Sources, and Traditions

Solon His Follie is an important document for English and Irish history. This text sheds light on both the sixteenth-century debate over how to colonize Ireland and the more recent historiographical debate over how to interpret the texts that record this controversy.[51] Throughout the sixteenth century, as English activity in Ireland fluctuated between political reform and military campaign, so too did the policies recommended in these tracts. Written on the eve of the Nine Years' War (1595–1603), the widespread rebellion that was at that time the greatest threat to English power in Ireland, Beacon's tract steered a middle course between two "plottes for reformacion": (1) "by Conqueste and by peoplinge of Contres with english inhabitantes" and (2) "by publique establishment of Iustice."[52] As D. B. Quinn notes, legal reform as opposed to military conquest was a characteristic strategy in writing by the Old English of the Pale, who wanted to protect their property and secure their positions in the Crown's government.[53] Some New English tracts—including Beacon's *Solon* and Herbert's *Croftus*—shared the aims of the Old English tracts to extend common law throughout Ireland and to protect the interests and lands of Old and New English alike from the exactions and incursions of the "mere" Irish. New English soldiers and settlers, rivals of the Old English for positions and land, staked their claim to power in Ireland upon the exercise of arms and appropriation of land;

---

[51] Among the most important tracts from this period are: Richard Stanyhurst, "Description of Ireland" (Holinshed 1577, 1587); John Derricke, *The Image of Ireland with a Discoverie of Woodkarne* (1581); Sir William Herbert, "Croftus sive de Hibernia Liber" (1588); Edmund Spenser, "A View of the Present State of Ireland" (1596); Barnabe Riche, *Allarme to England* (1578), *A Short Survey of Ireland* (1609), *A New Description of Ireland* (1610); Sir John Davies, *A Discovery of the True Causes why Ireland was never entirely Subdued* (1612). For the recent debate on Spenser's "A View" in relation to the tracts of Beacon and Herbert, see: Canny 1983, 1988; Brady 1986, 1988; and Bradshaw 1988.

[52] "A treatise of Irelande" (ca. 1588), NLI, MS 669, fol.55, as cited in Quinn 1947, 303.

[53] Quinn 1947, 303. Old English tracts include: "Edward Walsh's 'Conjectures' Concerning the State of Ireland (1552)"; "Rowland White's 'Discourse touching Ireland,' (c. 1569)"; "Rowland White's 'The Dysorders of the Irisshery' (1571)". Richard Stanyhurst, "Description of Ireland" (Holinshed 1577, 1587).

hence, conquest and colonization were their preferred policies.[54] As a result of reverses suffered in the Nine Years' War, the New English proposed even more extreme measures. Edmund Spenser's *A View of the Present State of Ireland* (1596, published 1633) recommended a war against the entire people, which would entail forced relocation, starvation, and mass extermination. The anonymous New English author of "The Supplication of the blood of the English" (c. 1598) echoed Spenser's characterization of the Irish as an "evil race":

> they are all of one disposition. There is no difference of sex, of age, of conditions: It is a nature engraffed in them ... Malitious, hatefull, bloody: a fitter brood to fill hell, then to people a country.[55]

Beacon, however, eschewed this demonization of the Irish and struck a balance between Old English legal reform and New English military conquest. Whereas Spenser rejected the common law in Ireland because of its ill-suitedness to the "degenerate" Irish, "it is vaine to prescribe lawes where no man carethe for keeping them,"[56] Beacon promoted the strict implementation of already existing English law in Ireland: "the more often princes shal acquaint their subjects with the discipline of the lawe the more great obedience shall the subjects yeelde (B4)." Like Spenser, Beacon advocated martial law and severe penalties for traitors and rebels, but he stopped short of endorsing "the sworde" rather than "good ordinances" and directly promoting policies that would result in "famine."[57] Instead, Beacon argued that the governor might well take advantage of such conditions as "famine, plague, pestilence" if they were found to "advaunce this action of reformation (G4v)." It was only after the publication of *Solon* and its author's successful return to Ireland that he would write in a letter to Lord Puckering, Keeper of the Great Seal:

---

[54] New English tracts in this category, despite internal differences, include those by Spenser, Riche, Davies, and Derricke (see above, note 51); Captain Thomas Lee's "A brief declaration of the government of Ireland (1594)"; and the "Dialogue between Pergryne and Sylvanus, c. 1598" (PRO SP 63/203/119, fols. 283–357).

[55] Spenser 1949, 120; BL Add. MS 34, fol. 114r.

[56] Spenser 1949, 147.

[57] Spenser 1949, 158, 148.

Leave therefor no matter in the body of this commonwealth for
the pestilent humour or the Spanish physician to work upon
but with sword and famen remove the same for so shall her
majesty uphold the body of of this our kingdom in safety.[58]

By January 1595, Beacon had witnessed Russell's campaign against
Feagh Mac Hugh and had begun to worry over the impending outbreak of the Earl of Tyrone's rebellion, or the Nine Years' War.

Spenser's ethnography of the Irish, deployed to justify his rejection
of the common law in Ireland, is missing from Beacon's tract.
Beacon's approach is political, historical, and legal. Rather than focus
on the Irish as a race or ethnic group, Beacon approaches them as a
political entity—if only that of a conquered people, still one capable
of incorporation into the republic or commonweal. Historical analogy
between the present state of Ireland and ancient Greece and Rome as
well as Renaissance Europe takes the place of Spenser's ethnography
as Beacon's means of argument. If Spenser's ethnography is as old as
the twelfth-century Anglo-Norman *Topographia Hibernia* of Giraldus
Cambrensis, Beacon's use of classical precedents for colonization may
be traced back to the Old English Edward Walshe's "Conjectures"
(1552), Sir Thomas Smith's promotion of the Ardes plantation (1571),
and Sir William Herbert's "Croftus sive de Hibernia liber" (1588).[59]

Because Beacon's tract is a dialogue it has been compared to Herbert's *Croftus* and Spenser's *A View*, rather than to the many position
papers, descriptive topographies, and occasional historical accounts of
the same period.[60] In form, Beacon's *Solon* adheres more closely than

---

[58] PRO SP 63/178/13.

[59] *Topographia Hibernia* in *Giraldi Cambrensis Opera*, Vol. 5, ed. J. F. Dimock
1867. For Walsh, see note 74; for the broadsheet promoting Smith's colony, see
*The offer and order given forth by Sir Thomas Smith Knight . . . for the inhabiting some
parts of the North of Ireland*, cited in Mary Dewar 1964, 157; see also "A Letter sent
by T. B. Gentleman . . . wherein is contained a large discourse of the peopling
and inhabiting the Cuntrie called the Ardes . . . taken in hand by Sir Thomas
Smith," in G. Hill 1873, 405–514; for Herbert see above, note 28. On this aspect
of the tracts see Quinn 1945, 1947, 1976 and Jardine 1990.

[60] Among occasional polemical pieces are: A. M., *The Successe God Gave unto.
Souldiours* (1581); Thomas Gainsford, *The True Exemplary, and Remarkable History
of the Earle of Tyrone* (1619). Some appreciative descriptions of Ireland include: Sir
John Harington, "A Short View of the State of Ireland written in 1605"; Robert

either Herbert's or Spenser's tract to the conventional order of the Italian humanist dialogue, which according to Carlo Sigonio in his *De Dialogo* (1561) should provide a *vestibule* describing the time and place of the speakers' meeting, followed by a *proposition*, and an argument or *contention*.[61] Beacon's *vestibule* presents Solon as "now heere landed for the repossessing and reforming of *Salamina*" (A1v). He is introduced to his interlocutor Epimenides by Pisistratus, who relates that Solon "hath now for his better recreation withdrawne himself into a pleasaunt and solitary garden neare unto the temple of *Venus*, whereunto if your leasure serve, I wil readilie conduct you" (A2). The exact location (Salamina, standing for Ireland) and time (the arrival of the Lord Deputy in Ireland), and the emphasis on the context of the dialogue in the space of "leasure" make Beacon's introduction conform to the traditional *vestibule*.[62] By contrast, Spenser's dialogue begins abruptly without such an introduction, and Herbert's tract omits the convention of two speakers.

Although *Solon* closely follows the dialogue form, its philosophical content is less dialogic than that of either Herbert's *Croftus* or Spenser's *View*. Such aspects of Beacon's text as the theoretical opposition between Rome and Athens as exemplary governments, and the organization of the text into three books—suggesting thesis, antithesis, synthesis—indicate its adherence to "dialectic" in Rudolf Agricola's sense of "the art of arguing about probable propositions employing probable rather than certain arguments."[63] In *Croftus*, the author pre-

---

Payne, "A Brief Description of Ireland: 1590"; John Dymmok, "A Treatise of Ireland (c. 1590)."

[61] Carlo Sigonio, as cited in Roger Deakins 1980, 11. Sigonio's *De dialogo liber* (Venice, 1561) is one of the very few Renaissance theoretical works on the dialogue. While we cannot be certain that Beacon knew this work, he could have, and he certainly would have known dialogues, such as Thomas Starkey's *Dialogue between Pole and Lupset* (written 1529–32) that conform to the tradition which Sigonio describes. Although Deakins reckons that only five out of the two hundred thirty-odd Tudor dialogues extant exactly meet Sigonio's requirements, both Deakins and K. J. Wilson cite Sigonio, as a point of reference for their discussions of the Tudor dialogue. See Deakins 1964, 16, and K. J. Wilson 1985, 11–13.

[62] See Deakins 1980, 12.

[63] Rudolf Agricola, as cited in Deakins 1980, 6.

sents objections and rebuttals to every proposition, and in *A View* two distinct perspectives on Ireland are embodied in the personae of Eudoxus, the reformer, and Irenius, the veteran. *Solon* also has two interlocutors, who according to the trope of *prosopographia* are based on historical figures with distinct roles; their views, however, are the same. Unlike the Ciceronian dialogue which calls for "discussing both sides of every question," Beacon's interlocutors move from point to point, refining each issue, but never disagreeing with one another.[64]

If there is no debate within Beacon's *Solon*, the text itself was part of a larger political debate: the tracts of the 1580's and 1590's on how the English should govern Ireland attempted to influence policy. Beacon's *Solon*, Spenser's *View*, and Herbert's *Croftus* are all in this sense dialogues of counsel, meant to influence the decisions of the English Queen, her Privy Council, and her Lord Deputy.[65] The implied reader for all three texts is someone making decisions about the administration of the law, use of an army, and the deployment of resources. Whereas Spenser complains about the Queen's recall of his former superior in Ireland, Lord Grey, Beacon and Herbert praise Elizabeth. Herbert calls her "administration for Ireland ... perfect in every detail," and Beacon hails her for her "hav[ing] ... brought [Ireland] for the most part to be obedient, gentle and civill" (¶4–¶4v).[66]

Beacon is also addressing potential political patrons including "Ulysses" (a figure for Essex, then a Privy Councillor)[67] and the incoming Lord Deputy, William Russell, who was closely connected with the Essex circle. Solon the lawgiver is an apt figure for the chief officer of the law in Ireland, and Epimenides, who counseled Solon, is a figure for Beacon himself. Even more than Herbert, Beacon devotes attention to the necessity of a strong magistrate and to the failures of previous governors. Beacon wrote to commemorate Russell's appointment and to solicit a position in his adminstration.[68]

---

[64] See K. J. Wilson 1985, 35–39, for a discussion of Cicero's *Tusculan Disputations* 2.9.

[65] See Ferguson 1965, 162–99.

[66] Spenser 1949, 159–60; Herbert 1992, 116–19.

[67] See *Solon* I, note 16.

[68] See *Solon*, F2v.

Despite Beacon's five years in Ireland as Attorney General for the province of Munster (1586–91), the text itself relies more heavily on textual sources than it does on experience. While Spenser refers frequently to contemporary events, Beacon does so rarely, content rather to cite the *Acts and Statutes* to illustrate a point of policy. Even more frequently cited are Sir Thomas North's translation of Plutarch's *Lives* and a Latin version of Machiavelli's *Discorsi*.[69] Unlike Herbert's Latin treatise, Beacon's text is largely written in English; however, large portions of the text are quotations from Latin translations of the *Discorsi* and of Jean Bodin's *République*.[70] While Herbert often cites ancient Greek and Latin authors, Beacon quotes from contemporary Continental texts, never naming their authors or titles.

Unique among the tracts on Ireland, Beacon's text is an extended allegory based on Plutarch's story of Solon. Beacon adapts the legend of Solon's "follie" of political speech in defiance of the law as an analogy to the writing of his own tract. According to Plutarch, Solon feigned madness in order to transgress an Athenian law forbidding, upon pain of death, discussion of the colonization of Salamis. To Plutarch, Solon's folly is a heroic action in which he risks his life to counsel war against Athens's colony Salamis for the glory of the home country and its defense against its colonial rival Megara. In Beacon's text, England is Athens, Ireland is Athens's colony Salamis, and Spain is Athens's colonial rival Megara, and its author Solon dares to counsel how the colony is to be ruled.

By invoking Plutarch's "Life of Solon," Beacon signals his controversial subject matter. Through the allegory of Solon's transgression, Beacon may be obliquely referring to the Queen's displeasure with earlier Irish tracts. Sir Thomas Smith's 1571 "discourse for the peopling and inhabiting the county called Ardes ... in the North of Ireland," for example, was published without the Queen's consent, and angered her.[71] Not all writing about Ireland was necessarily

---

[69] North, *Plutarch's Lives* (London, 1579). Machiavelli, *Discursus* (Mompelgarten, 1591).

[70] For Machiavelli, see note 90; Jean Bodin, 1586.

[71] For Elizabeth's anger at the unlicensed publication of this book, see Dewar 1964, 159.

controversial. But to criticize current policy (as Beacon did the former lord deputies), or to vindicate those who had been censured in the past (as Beacon praised Grey, Lord Deputy in 1580–82), however, could make a tract politically opprobrious.[72] A sensitive issue for Beacon was his own recall from Ireland, which is repeatedly figured in *Solon* through Plutarch's story of Camillus.[73]

Beacon criticizes Old English and New English alike through allegorical figures from Plutarch. Caesar sometimes stands for the strict executor of the law but just as often for Beacon's rivals the Old English.[74] *Solon* portrays the corruption of the Old English and of past English lord deputies as one of the main causes of Ireland's decline. The latter discussion was risky enough to demand allegorical disguise. Sir John Perrot's policy of composition (a fixed rent to replace feudal duties) would seem to qualify him as one of Beacon's heroes, but unlike Bingham and Grey, he is never mentioned by name.[75] Instead, the figure of the dead Phocion cloaks the identity of Perrot, who had been brought to trial for treason and died in prison in 1592.[76]

Beacon's use of Plutarch also affiliates his text with the patriotism of Sir Thomas North's popular translation. Like North's English version of François Amyot's French translation of Plutarch, Beacon's text is prefaced by a flattering dedication to the Queen. Beacon's *Solon* portrays Plutarch's heroes as moral exemplars for Elizabeth's subjects, as does North's dedication to the Queen:

> I hope the common sort of your subiectes shall . . . be animated to the better service of your Maiestie. For among all the profane bookes . . . there is none . . . that teacheth so much honor, love, obedience, reverence, zeale . . . and devocion to Princes, as the lives of Plutarke does.[77]

---

[72] Criticism of Lord Deputies: *Solon*, K4, M1v; praise of Grey: *Solon*, B3, F2v.

[73] On Camillus, see *Solon*, B3, B4, G4, I1v, I2, M2v.

[74] For Caesar as the Old English, see *Solon*, C4–C4v, G1v, G4. For Caesar as a New English hero, see *Solon*, B1–B1v, I3, M2.

[75] On Bingham, see *Solon*, A4v, B4v, M2; on Grey, see *Solon*, A4v, F2v.

[76] See *Solon*, N2; see Morgan 1987, 42–44, on how Fitzwilliam set in train the conspiracy which was to bring down not only Perrot but also his allies in the Irish government.

[77] North, *Plutarch's Lives*, 1928, x.

The portrayal of Beacon's ideal counselor as Solon connotes the loyal service of the author and the moral instruction of the reader.

The political argument of *Solon His Follie* is mediated not only by Plutarchan allegory but also by dream vision. Beacon was drawing on a tradition reaching back to Cicero's *Somnium Scipionis*, known through Macrobius's commentary.[78] Excerpted from Cicero's *Republic*, the text was important to Neoplatonic and Hermetic concepts of the cosmos. In the Renaissance, both Erasmus and Florence Wilson, a Scots humanist and friend of Thomas More, wrote commentaries on the *Somnium Scipionis*.[79] Wilson also wrote an allegorical dream vision dialogue, *De animi tranquilitate dialogus* (1539), which Beacon may well have known, since both dream visions end with the dreamer awaking to the sound of battle.[80]

In such visions, the dreamer is led by a psychopomp, or spiritual guide, on a mental journey towards understanding, upon which he awakes sadder but wiser. Although Epimenides, the Rip Van Winkle of ancient Greece, awakes at the end of *Solon His Follie*, at the outset he appears to guide the dreamer Solon. Epimenides plays the role of psychopomp by interpreting Solon's dream and leading the discussion which follows. According to Macrobius's classifications, Solon's dream is a *somnium*, a dream which presents the truth in fictional form and so "requires an interpretation for its understanding."[81] Epimenides's exegesis of Solon's dream adds to the text's complexity.

In particular, Epimenides's decoding of "the threatening Diana" as the "people of Salamina" is a provocative reading for an icon usually associated with Queen Elizabeth (A2v). This unexpected reading of Diana is further complicated when the Queen herself is referred to as "Circe," a distinctly non-virginal image usually associated with the corrupting power of both Italy and Ireland.[82] The metaphor of the "golden Dove" as "the pleasaunt countrie of Salamina" suggests the

---

[78] Macrobius, *Commentary on the Dream of Scipio*, trans. and ed., Stahl 1952. See Kruger 1992, for a recent study of this genre.

[79] M. T. Cicero, *Somnium Scipionis*, ed. Erasmus 1557; ed. Wilson 1535.

[80] Wilson 1751. I am indebted to Helena Shire for this reference.

[81] Macrobius, 1.3.10.

[82] *Solon*, ¶¶iv. Cf. Roger Ascham, *The Scholemaster* (1570), 1967, 24: "Some Circes shall make him, of a plaine English man, a right Italian." On the image of Circe in tracts by Stanyhurst and Davies, see Carroll 1993.

wealth that may be amassed through colonization. The ambivalent image of Diana at once arouses the dreamer's "love" and "ardent desire" and threatens "the losse of [his] hande" (A2v). There is a possible allusion to the myth of Actaeon in Book 3 of Ovid's *Metamorphoses*, where Diana causes the hunter to be attacked by his own hounds as a punishment for seeing her naked. The vision suggests an erotics of attraction and repulsion, fascination and fear, directed at a powerful female sovereign and feminized, unruly subjects.

At the end of the text, when Epimenides awakes, the entire dialogue—presumably including Solon's dream—is revealed as Epimenides's dream. As often in the dialogue form, the relationship between the interlocutors is unstable. Solon and Epimenides are both dreamers and both guides. This form encloses a narrative of the dreamer's and the reader's enlightenment about the solution to the crisis in Ireland, while allowing for movement back and forth in space and time, in the course of which examples from ancient Athens and Rome and early modern Ireland and Florence can all be portrayed side by side and interpreted in terms of one another.

Solon was also familiar to Beacon's audience as an example of the wise counsellor. The text's subtitle, *a Politique Discourse, Touching the Reformation of common-weales conquered, declined or corrupted*, together with Beacon's use of the word "common-weale" to designate the governments of Ireland and England signaled that the text was a commonweal dialogue. As G. R. Elton has pointed out, there were two meanings of commonwealth in the sixteenth century: "a political structure," and more commonly the "welfare, the well being, of all members of the community."[83] In both Sir Thomas Smith's *Discourse of the Commonweal This Realme of England* (written 1549, published 1581) and Thomas Starkey's *Dialogue between Pole and Lupset* (written 1529–32), Solon appears as a counsellor concerned with the second sense of commonweal, specifically with the economic well-being of the country.[84] At the outset of Starkey's *Dialogue*, Solon is cited as an example of such a public-spirited individual:

---

[83] Elton 1973, 5–6. See *Solon* I, note 34.

[84] See the modern edition of Smith, Dewar 1969; and of Starkey, Mayer 1989.

al men are borne & of nature brought forth, to commyn such gyftes as be to them gyven, ychone to the profyt of the other, in perfayt cyvylyte ... I nede not reherse ... the example of Solon, by whose wisdom and pollycy <dyverse> cytes cuntres & natyouns were brought to cyvyle ordour & polytyke lyfe.[85]

Starkey defines "civility" as living according to the common good, with an awareness of its etymology in *civilis*, Latin for the political rights of citizens, whereas Spenser defines it as what is English rather than Irish.

Starkey's sense of civility as citizen government, while absent from Spenser's *View* (where civility is Englishness), is deployed throughout Beacon's *Solon*. Beacon's text sometimes seems to echo Starkey's. One of the first principles in Starkey's argument against overly strong power in the hands of the monarch, "lawys are made for the pepul ... & not the pepul for the lawys," is restated in the first chapter of *Solon*, where Epimenides praises Solon: "you framed your lawes to the subject and matter, and not the matter and subject unto your lawes" (A3v).[86] This principle is contradicted by Spenser's Irenius, a veteran of the colonization of Ireland, who protests: "sithens We Cannot now applie Lawes fitt to the people as in the institution of Common wealthes it ought to be we will applie the people and fitt them to the Lawes."[87] While Beacon recommends "absolute and thorough reformation" rather than "reformation of particuler mischiefes," his discourse is framed in more conservative terms than Spenser's (A3). As Nicholas Canny argues, Spenser proposes a radical restructuring of Irish society; Beacon argues conversely for a stricter enforcement of already existing laws.[88] Epimenides calls his reformation "an happie restitution unto his first perfection," a translation of "*ricorso,*" a concept Beacon takes from Machiavelli's *Discorsi*, one of the best known texts in the Italian republican tradition.[89]

---

[85] Starkey, Mayer 1989, 1–2.
[86] Starkey, Mayer 1989, 74.
[87] Spenser 1949, 199.
[88] Canny 1983.
[89] *Solon*, P1; *Discorsi* 3.1.

Beacon's handling of Machiavellian political theory reveals significant differences between the politics of *Solon* and that of the commonweal tradition.[90] Whereas both Smith and Starkey base their view of
the common good of the citizens in the polity on a Christian-
Aristotelian concept of natural law, Beacon bases his recommendation
for the commonweal on the more secular politics of Machiavelli's analysis of power in classical and Renaissance states. A Machiavellian
analysis of power is nowhere more evident than in Beacon's praise of
Numa, recalling that in *Discorsi* 1.11.[91] Beacon praises Numa's manipulation of the Roman people through the state religion, analogous to
the new fusion of church and state in Tudor England, symbolized in
the substitution of the monarch's coat of arms for the crucifix in the
Tudor church.[92]

Beacon's praise of Solon as the wise civic-minded lawgiver is significantly qualified by Machiavelli's criticism of Solon's political error.
Beacon translates and interprets *Discorsi* 1.2:

> For this cause the institution of Athens being merely popular
> and corrupt and unperfit coulde never after by any lawes made
> for the reformation thereof be defended from the tyranie of
> such as did aspire unto the principalitie (A3v).

According to Beacon, Solon's "Follie" is both his feigned madness
and his error in instituting what Machiavelli calls "a merely democratic form of government," which Beacon notes, quoting *Discorsi* 1:
"non eam tamen conservare supra centessimum annum potuerunt"
(which did not retain it [i.e., liberty] for more than a hundred years)
(A3v). Not only does Beacon envision his reformation as a Machiavel-

---

[90] On Beacon's use of Machiavelli, see Anglo 1990. Unlike Spenser, Beacon
never names Machiavelli; at the same time, Beacon never distances himself from
"the slanting roundabout ways of counterfeit," as Herbert does. See Spenser
1949, 229; Herbert 1992, 75. Perhaps this is because Beacon's Machiavelli is
largely that of the *Discorsi* rather than *Il Principe*. Greenlaw (1909) argues that *Il
Principe* was a greater influence on Spenser than the *Discorsi*. On the manuscripts
and editions of Machiavelli's works, see Gerber 1962; for those produced in
England see Orsini 1937.

[91] *Solon*, E1–E1v, E3v.

[92] See Collinson 1988, 9.

lian *ricorso*, but he also favors a mixed constitution, "formed of the three sortes and formes of government, after the maner and institution of Rome," as Machiavelli does (A4).[93]

Beacon deploys the language of Machiavellian republicanism to make the strong magistrate, whom he recommends, *seem* like a man of political virtue rather than mere violence. Beacon often cites Machiavelli's example of Brutus's execution of his sons as an example of the strict execution of justice that it would take to reform the state; as institutor of republican reform, Brutus had to take extreme measures.[94] The English colonial governors of Ireland are made analogous to Roman republican heroes. Cicero's "severe course and manner of proceeding in cases of extremity" are the model for "Sir R. Binghame Provincial Governor of Salamina['s]" delivering "traitors and rebels to be put to death without lawful indictment or condemnation" (B4v). Lucius Junius Brutus, Renaissance humanist hero of Republican liberty, is held up as an example of "vertue and severitie" to the incoming governor, William Russell, for whom Beacon wrote *Solon* (F2). And Beacon's ideal counselor is exhorted to act as the anti-imperial "Cato" to "resist here the proroging of Caesar his government" (C4v).

A departure from the commonweal tradition is Beacon's discussion of Roman colonies, which he takes from both the *Discorsi* and *Il Principe*. If Beacon admires Rome as empire rather than republic, he allows for a more assimilative version of colonial expansion than Spenser does. Paraphrasing *Il Principe* 3, Beacon proposes the Romans' colonial practice of supporting the weaker and crushing the stronger powers: "Therefore in Salamina, and in the common-weales gained by conquest, ... providently shall we favour and deliver the people in such estates from oppression" (L1v). The "mere" Irish are

---

[93] There are analogies to Beacon's source in *Discorsi* 1.2, in Aristotle's classification of constitutions (*Politics* 3.6; *Nichomachean Ethics*, 8.10) and praise of Sparta's mixed constitution (*Politics* 2.6). For commentary on *Discorsi*, 1.2, see Walker, vol. 2, 9–13. While Beacon's source is Machiavelli, Aristotle is a source for such Tudor discussions of England's mixed constitution as those by Sir Thomas Smith, and Sir Thomas Elyot. See Michael Mendle 1985, 42–59, and Janel Mueller, 1995.

[94] *Solon*, A4, H2, N2v.

portrayed as "the people ... oppressed by the ambition of the mighty," i.e., Beacon's enemies, the Old English and Gaelic lords (L1). Beacon's advice for a long-lived empire is that of his Florentine mentor: to "restrain and suppresse the ambition of the nobles" (K4v).[95]

The few instances in which Beacon contradicts Machiavelli show that the republican rhetoric of *Solon* is at times more an attempt to impress the reader with the author's erudition than to express policy. When Beacon praises Lord Grey's and Sir Richard Bingham's reformation of Salamina's government, he cites Machiavelli's praise for the city of Paris "which always hath most severly punished offendors" (A4v). The republican Machiavelli, however, had not praised Paris for its strict ruler but for its parliament, "whenever it takes actions against a prince of this realm or in its judgment condemns a king."[96] One reason why Beacon departs from Machiavelli is the incommensurability of this republicanism with Beacon's colonial context. Another reason for apparent inconsistencies in Beacon's argument is his eclectic use of a variety of sometimes conflicting sources. Many passages from the *Discorsi* in a republican vein are set alongside quotations from authors who favored monarchy: Justus Lipsius, Francesco Guicciardini, and Jean Bodin.

The source of quotations from such authors as Seneca, Pliny, Cicero, and St. Ambrose is Lipsius's *Politics*.[97] Quotations from Guicciardini's *Historia d'Italia* in the 1579 translation by Geoffrey Fenton, *The Historie of Guicciardin*, are also woven into Beacon's text. Like North's translation of Plutarch and Beacon's *Solon*, Fenton's translation of Guicciardini was dedicated to Queen Elizabeth.[98] For Beacon,

---

[95] *Principe* 19.

[96] *Discorsi* 3.1.

[97] The *Politics* was published both in Latin by Bishop in 1590 and in English in 1594 by Spenser's printer, Ponsonby. That the text's English translator was W. Jones, who later became Chief Justice of Ireland, and that the dedicatee of his works was John Puckering, Lord Keeper of the Great Seal, to whom Beacon wrote from Ireland about the publication of *Solon*, suggest a common audience for the two works.

[98] The success of Fenton's work gained him an appointment in Ireland (1580), where, in 1587, he would rise to the position of principal secretary of the Irish Council. It is likely that Beacon (Attorney for Munster, 1586–91) had met Fenton.

Fenton's Guicciardini would have been ideologically compatible because of the Italian author's support for monarchy and criticism of the abuses of the papacy.[99] In *Solon*, the pope is represented as "Polycarphon" who bribed "his flattering orators the Jesuits" (N2). Beacon and Guicciardini also agree on the need for a well-paid and well-disciplined army to ward off the discontent of the people and political decline. The only modern writer whom Beacon names, Matthew Sutcliffe, was another admirer of Guicciardini's advice on warfare.[100]

Beacon quotes Bodin as well to stress the need for a strong force and centralized power. Beacon gleans from Bodin's *République* recommendations on a system of taxation, adequate pay for soldiers, and land division. Bodin is enlisted to support Beacon's argument against perpetual garrisons, as alienating the people,[101] and for limiting the colonists' land tenure. While Spenser recommends the expropriation of the natives ("all the Lands I will geve unto Englishe men"), Beacon proposes limitations on settlers ("we shall wisely make them proprietors of the landes during life only") (O4).[102]

Beacon's use of commentary from the Geneva Bible for his millenarian allegory in Book III, however, conflicts with this voice of moderation. As the editor of the facsimile edition of the Geneva Bible points out, the marginal notes were its most important and controversial feature.[103] The particular passages which Beacon cites and his application of them to contemporary history ally him and his text with the Elizabethan Puritan movement.[104] One of the three most

---

The incoming Lord Deputy William Russell's staff, of whom Beacon was a member, would have worked closely with Fenton in Dublin.

[99] See Gottfried 1940; Fellheimer 1945.

[100] *The practice, proceedings and laws of arms* (London 1593). For Sutcliffe's views of Machiavelli and colonization, see Quinn 1976, 86–87.

[101] *Solon*, O2.

[102] Spenser 1949, 179.

[103] "Introduction" by Lloyd E. Berry, in *The Geneva Bible, a facsimile of the 1560 edition*, 1969, 15.

[104] The Geneva Bible had been translated by the Marian exiles—some of whom would return to St. John's College, Cambridge, during Beacon's time there—who formed a congregation in Geneva headed by John Knox. The influence of Knox on the Geneva Bible can be seen in its commentary on the

important sources for Protestant apocalyptic tradition, the Book of Daniel is also the major source of Beacon's apocalyptic allegory of history in Book III.[105] Beacon's description of "The times wherein commonweales do usually fall and decline" is taken from the prophecy of the four kingdoms in Daniel 11, and the Geneva Bible's commentary on how these kingdoms stood for the "enemies to the Church of God, as of Persia, of Grece, of Egypt, of Syria and of the Romanes."[106] Some Protestant exegetes connected the four kingdoms with the rise and fall of the four empires from Babylon to Rome.[107] The Geneva commentary connected the four monarchies of Daniel with the four heads of the beasts in Revelation, the last head and the last empire both signifying the papacy.[108]

For Beacon, as for John Knox, the Bible was what Katharine Firth has called "a handbook for the judgement of God upon nations and powers of the world."[109] That Beacon saw the struggle of the New English against the Irish and Old English as the struggle of the elect against the Anti-Christ is verified by a letter to Sir Francis Walsingham, signed by Beacon and dated 24 February 1588/9:

> These people further so farre abhorre the service of God, established by her Majestie ... uppon the hearinge thereof theye stoppe theire ears and hasten so faste out of the church as if theye shoulde flye from some common plague or pestilence ... They entertain Jesuites secretlie in ther houses, which as

---

Book of Revelation, and the identification of the Papacy as the Anti-Christ (which had been resisted by Tyndale). Through the Geneva Bible, this version of the apocalyptic tradition influenced English Calvinism.

[105] The other two sources of the apocalyptic tradition are the Book of Revelation and the Prophecy of Elias, (which originated in Midrash and, though not directly cited in British texts, did influence Continental works). See Firth 1979, 5; Bauckham 1978, 277–87. Bradshaw (1988) was the first to draw attention to the Calvinist apocalyptic character of Beacon's text.

[106] Chapter heading to Daniel 11, *Geneva Bible*, 363.

[107] Firth 1979, 3, 17.

[108] Influences upon the Geneva Bible commentaries include: Philip Melanchthon's *Carion's Chronicle* (English trans. London, 1550) in which the last empire, that of the Turk, stands allegorically for the Roman Church (Firth 1979, 17–18), and John Bale's *Image of Both Churches* (1548) (Firth 1979, 51).

[109] Firth 1979, 125.

overthrowers of the state, they hate the light and the night they reserve for their recreacion.[110]

Even though the official purpose of this document was to advise Walsingham of the need for garrisons in Connaught, the larger part of the letter was devoted to an anti-Catholic tirade.

The New English had a real need to be concerned, however. Spanish intervention was a threat to the English domination of Ireland, especially in the years between the Armada and the Nine Years' War. Another of Beacon's letters, dated 21 January 1594/5, and written at Dublin after his return to Ireland under Russell, complained about the danger of Hugh O'Neill and openly equated religious practice with politics: "hath he not by commanding the Mass there to be used throughout all the parts of Ulster by maintaining Jesuits manifested a confederation with the Pope and Spaniards."[111] In the same letter, Beacon foresaw the Nine Years' War as a conflict in which religion would play a crucial role: "both factions of the Ancient English and mere Irish will march under the colours of the Pope and Spaniard for both remain discontented with the state."

If the allegorical content of *Solon* is grounded in the Protestant tradition, Beacon's method is that of Ramism. Walter Ong described the effect of Ramist diagrams as "thinking . . . in terms of spatial models," the loss of dialogue from dialectic, and the conception of the world as a collection of physical objects.[112] Ramism renders the world as an outline, and Beacon's discourse can be outlined as such a Ramist tree. It may also be significant that the principle of the discreetness of categories in Ramist logic is called "Solon's law."[113] Beacon's text abounds with examples of Ramist distribution, objectifying and enumerating reality:

In all mutations made of auncient lawes and customes, three matters especially fall into deliberation: first the meanes; sec-

---

[110] PRO SP 63/141/40.

[111] PRO SP 63/178/13.

[112] Ong 1958, 8–9. Similarly characterized by Ramist method are the Italian dialogues of the late sixteenth century, as discussed by Virginia Cox 1992, 112–13.

[113] Ong 1958, 280–81.

ondly the form and maner; lastly the subject and matter. The meanes are in mumber five: the first is authority; the goodwill and consents of the people, the second; the thirde perswasions; a sufficient power and force, is the fourth; the fifth and the last is a magistrate, of rare and excellent vertues (C3v).

There is also no feature of speech or point of view that distinguishes Epimenides's lines from Solon's; the interlocutors are virtually interchangeable. People often disappear from Beacon's language altogether, as when Starkey's "laws ... fit for the pepul" is rendered "laws framed to the subject and matter." "Pepul" have been replaced by "subject and matter" as though people were abstract categories without real existence. The Ciceronian ideals of the language of everyday speech and the flavor of real conversation are missing from this text laden with quotations and abstract outlines, the conventions of monologic textuality rather than dialogic orality.[114]

Beacon's style makes *Solon His Follie* open to ambiguous readings, which may have been part of what allowed for its publication despite the sensitivity of its matter. The form of a dialogue expresses Ramist dialectic rather than dialogic thought. Patriotic praise of the Queen exists side by side with criticism of her previous Lord Deputies of Ireland and their policies. A discourse of a commonweal allegorized as democratic Athens, *Solon* recommends England's expansion into empire on the model of Rome. The text appears to counsel both a conservative *ricorso*, or return to first principles—"without bloodshed and spot of tyranny"—and a strict regime under martial law (P1). All of this decorative erudition—commonweal discourse, allegorical conceit, Machiavellian gloss, Ramist dialectic—might seem to make it difficult to determine what Beacon's proposals for Ireland were. When, at the end of *Solon*, Epimenides awakes from his "follie" to the "great noise and clattering of weapons, and armour of the souldiers," it would appear that Beacon is arguing for a military solution no less extreme than Spenser's (P1v). The battle here, however, is not against the inhabitants of Salamina but the "Megarian army." Beacon advises a strong defense against the threat of Spanish invasion, not a war

---

[114] See Cicero, *De Oratore* 1.12, and K. J. Wilson, 39–45; Cox, 21, 103–13.

against the Irish. Both the moderation of his plan and its potential for violence are well expressed through an allusion to Cicero in the last chapter: "where *sanandi medicina* may not prevaile, there *execandi* is rightly used" (P1). Cicero had written to Atticus: "a remedy which cures the diseased parts of the State should be preferable to one which amputates them."[115] Beacon champions the cure that he believes strict adherence to the law can achieve, but he is also willing to amputate in cases where the law has proven ineffective. Beacon negotiates a way between law and war. This edition will allow the readers to see this complex process mediated through the layers of sources, allegorical figures, and traditions that create a "follie" or an act of the imagination.

---

[115] Cicero, *Letters to Atticus* 2.1. See *Solon* III, note 138.

TEXTUAL INTRODUCTION

In *The Early Oxford Press: A Bibliography of Printing and Publishing at Oxford 1468–1640*, Falconer Madan indicates that in 1594 Joseph Barnes printed *Solon His Follie, or a Politique Discourse, Touching the Reformation of common-weales conquered, declined or corrupted* by Richard Beacon. Based on the reference to Lord William Russell in the text and Beacon's presence in Ireland with him in 1594, we can assume that the publication of the text occurred before May 1594, when Russell received his official instructions as Lord Deputy of Ireland (see introduction, pp. xxiv–xxv). Although it is clear that Beacon was incorporated at Oxford and had associations with scholars there, we have no clear evidence that he oversaw the publication of the text.

We have used the University of Michigan Microfilm of the Huntington Library copy for our transcription of the text and compared it to nine other copies of the text.

Hn: Huntington Library C1653, 60261 the copy-text for this edition.
Title: SOLON HIS FOLLIE, | OR | **A POLITIQVE DIS-** | COVRSE, TOVCHING THE | Reformation of common-weales conque- | red, declined or corrupted. | _BY_ RICHARD BEACON GENT. STV- | *DENT OF GRAYES INNE, AND SOME-* | times her Maiesties Attor- | ney of the province | *of Mounster in Irelande.* | *⁺* | [arms of Queen Elizabeth] | *AT OXFORD,* | Printed by IOSEPH BARNES, Printer to the Vniversitie. | *Anno Domini,* 1594.
Collation: 4°: ¶⁴ 2¶² A–O⁴ P² [\$4 signed (–¶2, –P2; D4 signed 'C4'; ¶1v, ¶2v, C1v, P2, P2v blank)]
Pagination: 64 leaves, pp. *i–xii, 1,* 2–114, *115–116* (misprinting 42 as '32')

Paper: 20 x 14.5 cm.

Contents: ¶1 borders, ¶1v blank, ¶2 title, ¶2v blank, ¶3–¶4v The Epistle Dedicatorie, 2¶1 The Author to the Reader, 2¶1v The booke vnto the Reader, 2¶2–2¶2v dedicatory poems in Latin by Robert Wright and John Budden, A1–A2v preface, A3–P1v text, C1v blank, P2 blank, P2v blank

Notes: old limp vellum; lower margin of O1 torn; Bridgewater copy

Fo1: Folger Library STC 1653

Collation: identical with Hn

Pagination: 64 leaves, pp. *i–xii, 1,* 2–114, *115–116* (misprinting 41–42 as '31–32'; 9–16 misbound after 56 [leaves B1–B4 misbound after G4])

Paper: 20 x 16.1 cm.

Contents (differing from Hn): 2 blank pages following 2¶1v.

Notes: owned by Christopher Harvey; contains marginalia: Latin passages translated into English in an early seventeenth-century hand.

Fo2: Folger Library STC 1653.2

Collation: identical with Hn

Pagination: 62 leaves, pp. *iii–xii* (¶1 lacking), *1,* 2–114 (P2 lacking) (misprinting 41–42 as '31–32')

Paper: 17.9 x 13.6 cm.

Notes: owned by Christopher Grymeston; inscribed on fly-leaf "ex dono authoris"; referred to as "Harmsworth copy"; paper covers; stained.

BL1: British Library G5779.

Collation: identical with Hn

Pagination: identical with Hn

Paper: large paper copy, each page ruled in red; a small hole in the center of the margin at the top of each page; 21.5 x 15.5 cm.

Notes: brown leather volume with seal in gold of Right Honorable Thomas Grenville on cover and again inside front cover; notes on fly-leaf suggest this was a presentation copy. Variant readings from Hn on pp. 87 and 88.

BL2: British Library 100.K.10
Collation: identical with Hn
Pagination: 63 leaves, pp. *iii–xii* (¶1 lacking), *1*, 2–114, *115–116* (misprinting 41–42 as '31–32')
Paper: 19.5 x 14 cm.
Notes: modern linen binding in red.

BL3: British Library 523.g.25.
Collation: identical with Hn
Pagination: 63 leaves, pp. *iii–xii* (¶1 lacking), *1*, 2–114, *115–116* (misprinting 42 as '32')
Paper: 17.5 x 13 cm.
Notes: dark brown leather, black cover engraved in gold, "Cedric Chivers Bath 1987."

Cam: Cambridge University Library Syn, 6.59.20
Collation: identical with Hn
Pagination: identical with Hn
Paper: large paper copy, each page ruled in red; 21.5 x 15.5 cm.
Notes: on fly leaf, "Sum Ex Libris Tho. Rowe ... M. Templi, 1686." On ¶2v, a bookplate with the motto "Munificentia Regia, 1715"; head crowned with laurel; on lower margin "Georgius D.G. MAG. BR. FR. ET HIB. REX. F.D."

Ox: Oxford, Bodleian Library 4° G20Art.BS.
Collation: identical with Hn
Pagination: 64 leaves, pp. *i–xii*, 1, 2–114 (misprinting 41–42 as '31–32')
Paper: 20 x 14.5 cm.
Notes: a bookplate inside front cover reading "Alex Thistlewayte Esq."; on fly leaf "Wm Herbert 1775."

TR: Dublin, Trinity Library, p.11.43.No.11
Collation: 4⁰: ¶⁴ A-O⁴ P² 2¶² [$4 signed (-¶2, -P2; D4 signed 'C4'; ¶1v, ¶2v, C1v, P2, P2v blank)]
Pagination: 64 leaves, pp. *i–x*, 1, 2–114, *115–116*, *xi–xii* (leaf 2¶2 appears after P2 misprinting 42 as '32')

Notes: bound last in a collection of seventeenth-century texts (theological and political texts, book catalogues); leather spine, marbled paper covers.

Ire: National Library of Ireland L.O.1.848.
Collation: identical with Hn
Pagination: 64 leaves, pp. *i–xii*, 1, 2–114, *115–116* (misprinting 41–42 as '31–32')
Paper: 19.5 x 14 cm.
Contents (differing from Hn): ¶1 blank
Notes: on 3rd leaf in ink: M. C.

The present edition includes one substantive change indicated in ink by hand in the Huntington copy, explained in the textual notes of the present text. In (L4v), line 3 of the copy text, the words "his wives" in the phrase "other his wives charges" are overscored in ink. BL3, Fo2, Ox, and Ire are identical with the Huntington copy. BL2, Cam, Fol, and TR read "other charges due" rather than "other his wives charges" in (L4v), l.3. This variant indicates that the Huntington copy and those identical with it are corrected by hand—possibly the author's. The copies with the reading "other charges due" indicate in-press correction, incorporating the handwritten correction. Other changes made in the present edition, such as those in punctuation, capitalization, spelling, page numbers, and signatures, are also explained in the textual notes. The punctuation of the copy-text is followed except in cases of obvious error.

Styling: Italics and capitals have been preserved. Signatures are indicated in brackets. The typesetting reflects the typeface of titles, ornamental initials, and running heads. Headpieces and tailpieces have been ignored, excepting facsimile plates reproduced here. Marginal references to the *Acts and Statutes* have been placed in brackets within the body of the text. Hyphenation is determined by the typesetting process.

Orthography: For the most part, the spelling of the copy-text has been retained since such spelling is significant in connecting Beacon's text with other texts of the period. (Many passages are quoted Verbatim out of other contemporary texts.) Long s has been changed to short s, i to j, v to u, and vv to w to conform with modern printing conventions.

Latin and Greek: For the Latin quotations, i has been left unaltered, as in *Iusticia* and *Iulius* (since j is not a Latin letter), but the Renaissance convention of making the second i a j when doubled has not been followed. V and u have been silently altered to conform to standard Latin usage. There is no consistency in the differentiation of u and v in the copy-text, where, for example, both *ut* and *vt* appear. The one Greek word printed in Greek characters in the copy-text is rendered the same in the present text: Σεισάχθεια (Seisachtheia).

Abbreviations, accents, compound words, spacing: Tildes are expanded to include the subsequent m or n, and abbreviated Latin words are expanded (repub. to respublica, q; to que). Words that are commonly joined, such as another (an other), otherwise (other wise), myselfe (my selfe) and itself (it self), but which are printed as separate in the copy-text, are all silently joined. Word spacing has been regularized. Chapter headings are italicized (as in the copy-text) but uniformly centered.

Explanatory notes: The commentary appears in footnotes, numbered serially, each book starting note 1.

SOLON HIS FOLLIE,

OR

A POLITIQVE DIS-
COVRSE, TOVCHING THE
Reformation of common-weales conquered, declined or corrupted.

BY Richard Beacon GENT. STV-
DENT OF GRAYES INNE, AND SOME-
times her Maiesties Attorney of the province
of Mounster in Irelande.

✳ ✳
✱

AT OXFORD,
Printed by Ioseph Barnes, Printer to the Vniuersitie,
Anno Domini, 1594.

TO HER MOST SACRED
MAJESTIE.

f all the actes and monumentes[1] of former ages, most mighty and renowned Queene, and Empresse,[2] which might recommend this action of reformation unto all posterities, were committed to oblivion, yet the recordes and monumentes of your Majesties most happy governement, may sufficiently revive the same: where it is saide, that your Highnes hath atchieved unto that which is most rightly tearmed the greatest magnificence of a Prince, which doth not onely consist in high bloud, hauty progenie, aboundance of private riches and substance, wherewith your Majestie is every way plentifully adorned, but it resteth chiefely in populous and wel governed regions, & in beautiful Cities and Townes; [*The act of attainder of Shane Oneile, Ann. 11. Elizab.*][3] al which being impaired in your Realme of Ireland, by the iniquitie of former times, nowe as well the one as the other, by your Majesties most godly and careful course of governement, are recontinued,

---

[1] Cf. John Foxe, *Actes and Monuments* (1563, 1570, 1576, 1583).

[2] "Empresse" refers to the royal supremacy over the church and state adopted by Henry VIII. See "Act of Appeals" (1533: 23 Henry VIII, c.12): "this realm of England is an empire ... governed by one supreme head and king having the dignity and royal estate of the imperial crown of the same" (Elton 1982, 353). See also the initial C of the dedication to the first edition of Foxe (1563), which portrays Elizabeth as the Emperor Constantine.

[3] *The act of attainder*: this and all subsequent references to the *Statutes* within brackets are printed in italics in the margins of the 1594 edition.

"Act of attainder of Shane Oneile and thectinguishment of the name of Oneile and thintitling of the Queenes Maiesty ... to the countrey of Tyrone" in *Stat. Ire., 10 Hen. VI–14 Eliz.*, fols. 156–65. Shane was the son of Conn Bacach O'Neill (1519–59), who through surrender and regrant gave up the Gaelic title O'Neill and swore allegience to the crown in return for the English title Earl of Tyrone. The English system of primogeniture pitted Shane against his alleged illegitimate half-brother, Matthew, the designated successor. Despite Shane's claim in both English and Gaelic law, Lord Deputy Sussex (1556–64) supported Matthew for the earldom. Shane had Matthew killed (1558) and then asserted traditional O'Neill rights and control over much of Ulster. He was a threat to English rule on the borders of the Pale until his death in 1567. See *NHI*, 9:142; *Tudor Ire.*, 238–42.

amended, and augmented.[4] What more? Have you not reformed all exactions grievous [¶3v] unto that people? Have you not reformed that horrible and most detestable custome of Coiney and Livery,[5] that fretter of the peoples lives and substaunce, that Nurse and teate which sometimes gave sucke and nutriment unto all disobedience, rebellions, enormities, vices and iniquities of that Realme, over foule and filthie heere to bee expressed? Have you not in place of sorrow, famine, howling, and cursing, brought joy, jolitie, plentie, and everywhere blessings of so gratious a Queene? Have you not reformed that daungerous custome of Captaineshippe, which by factions did dismember the state of Irelande? for all which if wee should bee founde unthankefull, yet the statutes and recordes of that lande, would witnes the same against us. [*Anno 11. Eliz. cap.7. fo.168.*][6] Great is the honour which is due unto Robert FitzStevens, which first opened the waie of Irelande to the Earle of Stranguile: and great is the honour due unto the Earle, which opened the same unto Henry the King: & great is the honor which is due unto the King, which opened the way unto John his Sonne:[7] greatly is he to bee praised, that first

---

[4] *Stat. Ire., 10 Hen. VI–14 Eliz.*, fol. 156: "thone well amended, and the seates, signes, plattes and places of thother recontinued to the quiet protection of your most excellent maiestie, aswel by the death and finall destruction of that caitife and miserable rebel Shane Oneile, as also by other godly carefull trade and government used by your Maiesties deputie Sir Henry Sidney, which rebell to the perpetuell damage and infamy of his name and linage, refusing the name of a subject, and taking upon him as it were the office of a Prince, hath proudly, arrogantly and by high and perillous practices enterprised great sturres, insurrections, rebellious horrible treasons against your Royall Maiestie."

[5] "Coiney and Livery": a Gaelic system of billeting and maintaining mercenaries which as early as the fourteenth century had overflowed into Old English areas. At its simplest it was the exaction of food and lodging without payment. By the sixteenth century it had expanded into the widespread maintenance of mercenary soldiers. Old and New English alike saw it as an example of the tyranny of the Gaelic Irish lords. The text indirectly refers to Sir Henry Sidney's unsuccessful efforts in the 1569 parliament to revive legislation outlawing coyne and livery. *NHI*, 2:84; Empey and Simms 1975, 250–64.

[6] "Captaineshippe": See *Stat. Ire., 10 Hen. VI–14 Eliz.*, fols. 168–69, "An Act for taking away Captaineships, & all exactions belonging there unto from the lords and great men of this Realme." This act outlawed any titles to authority and land except those granted directly from the crown through surrender and regrant. See Treadwell 1966, 55–89. Beacon's reference to this particular folio provides convincing evidence that he made use of the 1572 edition of the Statutes inspired by Sir Henry Sidney and printed in Dublin by Richard Tottle.

[7] Beacon bases his account of the origins of the Norman invasion of Ireland

so boldlie began; and woorthy of greater praise is he, that after the beginning so nobly came to exe-[¶4]cute the thing so well begun; but most of all he is to be praised, that shall perfect and finish the same; which praise by Gods divine providence is light on your Majestie; for so the subject of Irelande in the act of Attainder of Shane Oneile doeth liberallie confesse: [*Anno 11. Elizab.*] therefore goe forwarde Brutus,[8] for thy glory in reforming, is farre greater then the glory of Romulus in building and instituting of the citie of Rome. All nations with the Romaines shall honour your presence, as another Time-sitheus,[9] for reforming and restraining the Lyparians from their accustomed robberies and spoiles; all nations shall rightly honour you with the Ladies of Rome, which sometimes offered their jewels to be solde for the furtherance of publike services;[10] for huge be the charges already imployed by your Majestie, for bringing to passe so great things tending to the sound & universall reformation of this your Realme of Ireland, as in the acte of subsidie more at large may appeare. [*Act of subsidie Ann. 11. cap.1. fol.148.*[11]] What further

---

on the "Act of the attainder of Shane O'Neill," *Stat. Ire., 10 Hen. VI–14 Eliz.*, fols. 156–65, where Giraldus Cambrensis is cited as a source. Robert FitzStevens and Richard FitzGilbert were leading figures in the 1167 Norman intervention in Ireland. Their Angevin king, Henry II, personally intervened in Ireland in 1171 not so much to extend his kingdom but rather to impose control on his free-booting Anglo-Norman nobles who threatened to become an independent power in their own right. In order to counteract these elements Henry appointed his youngest son John as Lord of Ireland in 1177 in the hope that the latter's personal rule would solve Henry's problem of governing this complicated and war torn island. John visited Ireland in 1185, and, after he became King of England in 1199, instituted the first effective royal administration of Ireland; Frame 1981, 1–62.

[8] Lucius Junius Brutus reformed Rome when he avenged the rape of Lucretia by Lucius Tarquinius Superbus by exiling the Tarquins and by instituting the consuls (Livy 1.58–60; Plutarch, "Life of Publicola," 1–9).

[9] Timasitheus, a native of Lipari who defended the Roman legates against Liparian pirates (Livy, 5.28.4), is praised by Machiavelli for acting "as if he were a Roman" (*Discorsi* 3.29). See North, *Plutarch's Lives*, vol. 1, "Life of Camillus," 358.

[10] "Ladies of Rome": see North, *Plutarch's Lives*, vol. 1, "Life of Camillus," 357, which tells how the women of Rome gave their jewels in order to make the offering to the gods promised by Camillus before the taking of Veies.

[11] See *Stat. Ire., 10 Hen VI–14 Eliz.*, fols. 148–52. This subsidy act cites sub-duing coyne and livery as the reason for renewing the "subsidie of thirteene shillings four pence of every plough land, originally enacted in the reign of Philip and Mary."

honour now remaineth due unto your Majestie, for the accomplishing
of so great & worthy actions, if not that which was sometimes given
unto Janus?[12] for that you have chaunged the life of man which
before your time was rude, cruell, and [¶4v] wilde, in Ireland, and
brought it for the most part to be obedient, gentle, and civill, in such
sort as we may truely say with the subject of Irelande, this is the
favour which your Majesty hath found in the sight of God to augment, strengthen, and honour your imperiall crowne of Englande, by
the thorough reformation of this your Realme of Ireland. All which
considering with my selfe, I could not suffer so honourable actions to
bee buried in oblivion, without leaving some speciall remembrance to
all posterities, but have made this plat & counterfet, the which I here
present unto your Majesties sacred handes, in baser coulours then
princes doe usually beholde, or so weighty matters may require: but
I hope that your Majesties accustomed clemency will impute this to
Solon his follie and lunacie,[13] which now for his boldnes craveth
pardon, rather then commendation.

Your sacred Majesties

most humble and loyall subject

RICHARD BEACON.

---

[12] "Janus ... civill": see North, *Plutarch's Lives*, vol. 1, "Life of Numa," 195.
[13] Solon's folly: Ibid., vol. 1, "Life of Solon," 220.

1

The Authour to the Reader.

ENTLE Reader, with the unskilful archers of our times, I did first aime and shoote at the publique good and profit, according to the trust reposed in me, and now as one that hath lost his arrowe, and missed his marke, I have at al adventures discharged the second time, to the ende that my second labours may drawe home my first losses,[14] if my hande be fortunate to pearce the secret partes of thy tender and kinde affections, and move in thee a friendly acceptaunce of these my rude labours; if not, looke no more for my returne to accompany the pleasaunt fieldes, and meddowes, for henceforth I take up my habitation amidst the rockes and deserts, where my arrowes may not pearce, nor the strength of my bowe withstand the bitter windes, and the harde and hoary frostes, where I shall no more play the foole with *Solon* in the market-place, but the wilde man in the desertes. But if thou shalt vouchsafe to recall so unskilfull an archer againe into the fieldes, I may perhaps winne a bet, that shall pay for the losse of a rubber.[15] Receive then, *Solon* his folly, not as a testimony of his skill, but rather of the goodwil he beareth unto thee, and his country, whereof if thou shalt make acceptaunce, the same is thy honour, and not his: which with thy bounty and goodnes, hast now overcome as well the giver, as the gift. But if thou shalt censure it by his owne proper woorth, he hath fore-tolde thee the valewe thereof, and before thy face hath now waighed the same in equall ballance, with *Solon* his follie, but not with his wisedome.

---

[14] "my first losses": Beacon is referring to his failed first tour of duty in Ireland as Attorney General of the province of Munster (1586–91). He was recalled from office for exacting excessive fines, keeping the extra money for himself, and imprisoning people on trumped up charges (*Acts Privy Council*, 27:94). He was also engaged in land disputes with both Gaelic Irish and Old English residents. Beacon's conflicts should be seen in the larger context of land disputes between the tenants of the Old English magnate the Earl of Desmond, whose rebellion had been defeated in 1583, and the New English settlers. Beacon served on the 1588 commission to determine land claims which arose as a result of the Munster settlement. See: MacCarthy-Morrogh 1986, 97–106; and Quinn 1966. The imagery of archery recalls Roger Ascham, *Toxophilus, The Schole of Shootinge Conteyned in Two Bookes* (London: Edward Whytchurch, 1545).

[15] A rubber is a set of three games, the last of which is played to decide between the parties when each has gained one.

The booke unto the Reader.

S ITH Circe *at the instance of* Ulysses *hath once againe graunted unto dumbe creatures liberty of speech, I may not but complaine, for that she hath brought us from our former rest & silence, now to speake before that wise* Ulysses, *who havinge not tasted of the sweetenes and pleasure of this our solitary life, since which time* Circe *first chaunged us* Græcians *into the habite of mute and dumbe creatures, may fortune to advance his wisedome, and to holde our former silence and rest as contemptible.*[16] *And againe of the other side, we beeing long deprived of the use and arte of subtill speaking, shall much discontent wise* Ulysses, *with our homely discourses. But O* Circe, *hath the love of* Ulysses, *and the cuntry of* Greece, *drawn thee unto this indignation against us, as with* Epaminondas,[17] *naked and unarmed, I must oppose myselfe against the scornes and reproches of al ages, as against a* Græcian *army? And with the fonde lover in* Petrarke *must thou of force make me a sorrowfull minister thereof? And with the silly birdes fast tied and bounde, must I represent the face of thy loving thoughts?*[18] *Then what comfort remaineth, If I may not say with them, though here we remaine fast tyed and bounde, subject to all scornes and reproches, and bereaved of our former liberty and delightes, yet this one Joy resteth, that the Author of these our Calamities,*[19] *is falne more deepely*

---

[16] In this allegorical address to the reader the story of Circe's turning Ulysses's men into swine and then restoring them to their former state as men (Homer, *Odyssey* 10) is used to represent Elizabeth's reluctance to hear arguments for campaigns in order to promote the conquest of Ireland that would require large expenditures of both money and men. Ulysses most likely represents the young and influential Robert Devereaux, 2nd Earl of Essex, Elizabeth's favorite in the early and mid 1590's. Elizabeth had appointed Essex as a member of the Privy Council in 1593. He would later lead a disastrous expedition to Ireland in the spring of 1599. See *DNB*.

[17] Epaminondas was the Theban general who delivered Thebes from servitude to the Spartans. For his valor in battle and self-defense against the charges brought against him, see Plutarch, "Life of Epaminondas" (not part of the 1579 edition of North's translation, but added to the 1603 edition). For Epaminondas as an opponent of tyranny and defender of republican government, see *Discorsi* 1.17.5; 1.21.3.

[18] "The fonde lover in Petrarke," and "the silly birdes fast tied and bound" allude to the Elizabethan courtiers' practice of writing Petrarchan verse to the Queen. These allusions strengthen the likelihood that "Ulysses" is the chief courtier of this period, Essex. Beacon, as an experienced colonist, likens himself to the general Epaminondas and contrasts himself with the effeminate and fawning courtiers.

[19] "The Author of these our Calamities" is Sir William Fitzwilliam (Lord

then ourselves therin, in such sort as with us he must tast the bitternesse of disdaine and contempt, with the which comfort, I heere present myselfe unto your most friendly viewe, hoping that this my naked and innocent simplicity shall have your leave if not your likinge.

Deputy 1588–94), who was responsible for having Beacon briefly imprisoned and then dismissed from office for the exacting of excessive fines (see above note 14). "Our calamities" include the gathering storm that was the Nine Years War (1594–1603), the last great Gaelic Irish rebellion, which was occasioned by the development of the power of Hugh O'Neill, Earl of Tyrone. Fitzwilliam aroused the ire of the New English as a group because of his indecisiveness in the face of Tyrone, his conciliatory policies toward the Old English, and his financial corruption. See *Tudor Ire.*, 297–99, and, Nicholas Canny 1987, 109–13.

2

In reformatam ornatissimi Beaconi Rempublicam:
seu simulatam Solonis Insaniam, Carmen.

Insidias fugiens, & lætum cæde tyrannum,
   Brutus, nobilium gloria prima patrum,
Prudens desipuit; quantum O fuit utile Brute
   Desipere, ingenio qui periturus erat.
Crede mihi gratus furor est, & amabilis error,
   Ut teipsum serves negligere ingenium.
Insignem simili fama est usum arte Solonem,
   Amissam patria dum Salamina petit.
Illum quippe furor, præcepsque insania mentis,
   Effrenis rabies, & vagus error agunt:
Illi barba impexa, comæ sine lege fluentes,
   Et loca sola placent, & sine teste nemus.
Sic ambo insani sunt, sed cum dispare laude,
   Hic furit, ut seipsum servet, & hic patriam.

Robertus Wright Bacc: Theol.[20]

---

[20] Robertus Wright is probably the person of this name (1560–1643) who was a fellow of Trinity College, Oxford (1581), M. A. (1584), B. D. (1592), *DNB* . He wrote Latin elegies and edited a collection of them called *Funebria* (Oxford, 1596), printed by Joseph Barnes, the printer of Beacon's *Solon*.

On the reformation of a commonwealth by the brightest Beacon:
or, on the Feigned Folly of Solon, A Poem.

Leeing snares, & exulting in the tyrant's slaughter,[21]
Brutus, of noblest forefathers first in glory,
Feigned folly wisely; O beneficent Brutus,
As great your feigning as the wit which devised it.[22]
Believe me, furor is sweet, & a loveable error,
So that you should take care to make light of your wit.
With similar art, great Solon uses his fame,
When fatherland attacks abandoned Salamis.[23]
Thus wherever furor and headlong insanity,
Drive forward unbridled rage and wandering error:
Therein an uncombed beard, hair flowing without law,
A solitary place, & field without a brick are pleasing.
So both are insane, but with unequal praise,
One rages to serve himself, & the other his country.[24]

Robert Wright, Bachelor of Theology

---

[21] The allusion is to Brutus' assumption of leadership as he withdrew the sword from the breast of Lucretia who had committed suicide, and to his vow to seek revenge upon the family of Lucretia's rapist, Lucius Tarquinius Superbus (see Livy, 1.59.1–13).

[22] Livy describes how Lucius Junius Brutus pretended to be a simpleton and accepted the title Brutus (literally "dullard") to protect himself from the injustice of the king: "so that behind the screen afforded by this title the great soul of the Roman people might bide its time unseen" (Livy, 1.56.4–9). See also *Discorsi* 3.2.

[23] Plutarch recounts the Athenians' response to Solon's feigned madness in order to sing elegies in favour of the conquest of Salamis: "This Elegie is intituled SALAMINA, and containeth a hundred verses, which are excellently well written. And these being songe openly by *Solon* at this time, his friendes incontinently praysed them beyond measure, & specially *Pisistratus:* and they went about persuading the people that were present, to credit that he spake. Hereupon the proclamation was revoked, and they beganne to followe the warres with greater furie then before, appointing Solon to be generall in the same" (North, *Plutarch's Lives,* vol. 1, "Life of Solon," 221).

[24] The contrast is between the "insanity of mind" of those like Brutus and Solon, here standing for Beacon as author, that was feigned for the greater good of the country and the "unbridled rage and error" of the Gaelic Irish. "With uncombed beard and hair flowing without law" recalls the common descriptions of the Irish in English sixteenth-century texts, especially in Spenser's *A View.*

Viro verè politico, civique patriæ benevolentissimo,
Richardo Beacono Salutem.

Qualis in Euboico Salamis fuit Insula ponto,
  Quâ freta vicinas interlabuntur Athenas:
Talis ad occiduum, pelagi propè marmora, Solem,
Agnovit (Regina) tuos Hybernia fasces.
Cincta mari Salamis, cincta est Hybernia utrisque,
Ardua per medios consurgunt mœnia fluctus.
Quàm bene munitum, fati haud ignara futuri
Composuit natura locum, tàm docta tueri
Si foret, & dubiis si consulat Anglia rebus;
Non te Hispane ferox, populi prædator Eöi,
Dira per insolitos minitantem prœlia motus,
Non lectos iuvenes, non robora gentis Iberæ,
Non volucrem in tumido salientem gurgite pinum,
Fluctus cum gemitu, ventosque labore prementem,
Hàc primùm attonitus spectaverat Anglus in ora.
Nunc ubi quisque sibi sapere, & succurrere malit,
Quàm patriæ, videatque aequis securus ocellis
Labentem, & valido tibicine sustentandam,
Prona ruit tacito sensim respublica casu.
At tibi pro meritis tantis, pro tam benè factis,
Proque hoc in patriam officio, pietate, fideque
Contingat (Beacone) decus post fata perenne.

Iohannes Budden Magist. Artium.[25]

---

[25] Iohannes Budden is John Budden (1566–1620), scholar of Trinity College, Oxford, who studied civil law at Gloucester Hall (1587–c. 1601) and later (1609–18) became king's professor of civil law at Broadgates Hall. Budden probably met Beacon when he was writing *Solon* at Oxford. See *DNB* under Budden.

Greetings to a man truly political, and a most benevolent
citizen of his country, Richard Beacon.

As an island in the Euboean sea was Salamis
Where straits fell between it and neighboring Athens:
So is Hibernia set towards the sun, in a marble sea,
She (the Queen) has acknowledged as hers your fasces.
As Salamis is girt by water, so is Hibernia on all sides.
Amid towering ramparts disturbances arise.
How strongly fortified, hardly ignoring future fate,
Did nature, so skilled in defense, fashion the place
If it is told, & if England looks to doubtful matters;
Not you ferocious Spain, predator of Eastern people,
Threatening dire battles through unusual agitations,
No youthful biers, no bulwark of the Iberian nation,
No swift ship bounding over swelling waters,
Flowing with a groan, and pressing winds with labor,
Had the astonished Englishman first seen on this coast.
Now when everyone hastens to aid and prefers to know
His own country, and a fearless man with level eyes sees
A strong pillar must sustain the tottering commonweal,
Lest declining it fall, silently, slowly, by chance.
For such services, for such honorable deeds,
And for this duty, piety and loyalty to country
Glory befalls you, Beacon, after everlasting fate.

John Budden, Master of Arts.

A BOOKE INTITULED, SOLON

his follie and lunacie, made for the better reformation of
common-weales, conquered, declined or
corrupted, by R. B.

PIMENIDES PHÆSTIAN.[26] Wel met good Sir *Pisistratus,*[27] in this holy place of the temple of *Venus,*[28] where though the sacrifices bee finished, yet notwithstanding your devotion is highly to bee commended. *Pisistratus.* You also are happely well saluted right wise and famous *Epimenides,* and this devotion which you have friendly now com-mended, is but a duety first unto the Gods, and next unto my friendes, amongst whom I enumber you not the least. *Ep:* I am the least in power I must confesse, that is worthy of *Pisistratus,* but not in goodwill: but what matter of importaunce hath

---

[26] Epimenides was a religious leader and prophet who flourished in Athens around 500 BC (see *OCD*). See North, *Plutarch's Lives,* vol. 1, "Life of Solon," 226: Epimenides Phaestian was "reckoned the seventh of the wise men ... He was a holy and devoute man, and very wise in celestiall things, ... When he was come to *Athens,* and growen in friendshippe with *Solon:* he dyd helpe him much, and made his waye for establishing of lawes." Beacon represents himself in this discourse as the new Epimenides in order to assist the new Solon (Sir William Russell, L. D. 1594–97), who as Lord Deputy would go to Salamina (Ireland) to reform its laws and defend it from the Megarians (Spanish).

[27] Pisistratus was the tyrant of Athens who flourished in 560–527 BC. He distinguished himself in the war against Megara for the control of Salamis. See North, *Plutarch's Lives,* "Life of Solon." Pisistratus' active military role in this conflict would seem to rule out the possibility that he represents Elizabeth I in Beacon's dialogue, as suggested by Canny 1991, 203. A more likely figure would be the hero of Cadiz and leading courtier Robert Devereux, Earl of Essex (above, note 16, and the introduction, where the connections among Beacon, Russell and Essex are explored).

[28] The temple of Venus was the sanctuary of the Roman goddess of love. As Venus Genetrix (mother of the gens Iulia) she was prominent in the Roman Imperial cult (see *OCD*). For a fuller discussion of classical allusions in support of the Elizabethan imperial cult, see below, *Solon* 1, note 32.

caused your arrivall so unexpected upon this coast and haven? *Pisistratus*. We leade heere a strong army by the commaundement of the councell of *Athens* unto *Salamina*,[29] for the better repossessing and reforming thereof. *Ep:* What? contrary to their former decrees and proclamations, which were so streight, and that upon paine of death, that no Citizen of *Athens* should be so hardy, as once to moove the question to the counsell of the Citie, for the repossessing and reforming of *Salamina*? *Pisistratus*. Yes verily: for when the *Athenians* did once beholde that their long and troublesome warres, the which they had now sustained against the *Megarians*,[30] for the repossessing and reforming of *Salamina* did arise unto them, not from the nature of the people, nor from the difficultie of that action; but rather that [A1v] they received all their advertisementes for the advauncement of those affaires, from such as gave counsel therein, more for their private profit then for the publicke good, but chiefly for that sundry governoures there placed, were found either negligent, or ignorant in the managinge of publicke affaires, they willingly revoked their publicke proclamations, and made choice of *Solon*, a most wise and expert governour for leading and conducting their armies, now heere landed for the repossessing and reforming of *Salamina*. *Ep:* But who perswaded this first unto the Counsell of *Athens*? *Pisistrat: Solon* that faithfull counsellour of *Athens*. *Ep:* But how durst *Solon* the wise offende their publicke lawes and proclamations? *Pisistrat: Solon* holding it for an open shame the which woulde bee left unto all posterities, if the Citie of *Athens* should not be able to repossesse and reforme *Salamina*, now commaunding the most partes of *Greece*, fained

---

[29] Salamis (of which Salamina is the accusative case) was an island in the Saronic Gulf between the western coast of Attica and the eastern coast of Megarid (Megara). Colonized by Aegina, and temporarily occupied by Megara (c. 600 BC), Salamis came under Athenian occupation during the rule of Solon and Pisistratus (see *OCD*). Salamina stands for Ireland.

[30] Megara, a town on the isthmus of Corinth, engaged in considerable colonizing activity between 730–550 BC. Sometime after it fell prey to Athenian advances and lost important lands, including Salamis (see *OCD*). The analogy is as follows: Megara = Spain, a great power and serious threat to Athens = England, must soon give way to the latter's power. Beacon characterizes himself as Solon who urged the Athenians to renewed effort in Salamis when they despaired of success. As a result of Solon's efforts, including his direct military involvement, Megara lost its footing in Salamis and was eventually defeated by the Athenians. See North, *Plutarch's Lives*, "Life of Solon."

himselfe to bee out of his wittes, and caused it to be given out that *Solon* was become a foole: and soone after on a day, cloathed with the habite, gesture, and countenaunce of a foole or man possessed with lunacy, hee ran sodenly out of his house with a garland on his heade unto the market place, where the people streight swarmed like bees about him, and raising himselfe upon the stone where all proclamations were made, did so effectually perswade the repossessing of *Salamina* unto the people, as what with the weight of his reasons, and the laud and praise everywhere spreade by his friendes of his proceeding therein, their former proclamations were revoked, & the wars for the repossessing and reforming of *Salamina* with greater furie then before were followed, they giving unto *Solon* as I saide before, the leading of the army, and the whole managing of that action. *Ep:* After this manner did *Brutus* by a fained frency and lunacie, not onely reforme the mighty Citie of *Rome,* but wisely acquited himselfe thereby, of the suspition and jelousie of *Tarquine,* by the which manner of proceeding, hee delivered as well the Citie of *Rome,* as his own person from perill & danger, so as this common proverbe did first arise, *Simulare stultitiam nonnunquam sapientis est.*[31] But where remaineth *Solon* my deare and familiar friende, that I may salute him, and give him the best comfort I maie, in this [A2] worthy action of reformation? *Pisistrat.* Hee is newly landed with his whole army, and hath nowe for his better recreation withdrawne himselfe into a pleasaunt and solitary garden neare unto the temple of *Venus,* whereunto if your leasure serve, I wil readilie conduct you. *Ep:* I readily followe you. *Pisistratus.* Sir I goe before as the best guide, and not the best man, and beholde *Solon* in the most solitary place of the garden. *Solon.* Thrise welcome my deare and familiar friende *Epimenides,* beholde, this solitarie and pleasaunt place, as also the times, hath even newly conspired with my thoughtes and desires to impose a great and weighty labour upon you. *Ep:* No labour may bee thought ever so greate as shall exceede the greatnesse of my goodwill I beare unto *Solon.* But what may the same be? Tel it unto me. *Solon.* As you have of late most friendly lent unto mee, your faithfull councell, and best advise for the reformation of the Citie of *Athens,* greatly to the

---

[31] "To feign folly is often wisdom." *Discursus,* 427; *Discorsi* 3.2.

advancement of that estate, in like manner now I am earnestlie to entreate your most friendly advise for the better reformation of *Salamina. Ep:* This labour and travell, I must confesse is due unto *Solon*, if there wanted not wisedome, which shoulde give strength for the performaunce thereof: but I have chosen at this time, for our olde familiarity and friendshippe, to give you just cause rather to reprehende my skill, then to accuse any parte of that office and duety, which in the highest manner belongeth unto *Solon;* so as when the faulte appeareth, you shall acknowledge the same to bee imposed by yourselfe, and not received by mee without your commandement. *Solon.* Then friendly *Epimenides*, before we enter into this large discourse for the reformation of *Salamina*, I will declare unto you a dreame, which this last night amazed my thoughts. *Ep:* I pray thee tell it unto me. *Solon.* This night I seemed to beholde faire *Diana*[32] with a beautiful Dove[33] glistering like golde, placed upon her shoulder, slyding and wavering everywhere, in such sorte, as it seemed to me to be in great jeopardy of falling, but forthwith mooved with compassion I stretched foorth my right hande, to better and reforme the place of her standing: wherewith I might beholde *Diana* with a sharpe and sowre countenaunce to threaten the losse of my hand where-[A2v]at being

---

[32] Diana, virgin goddess of the hunt in Roman antiquity, also associated with the Greek goddess Artemis, was frequently used by Elizabethan poets and writers in allegorical reference to the Queen. As patroness of chastity, Elizabeth as Diana became the focus of a cult which emphasized her virginity and constancy as symbols of her "universal imperium" and of Protestant and national independence. See the Dutch engraving of the bare-breasted Diana defeating the Pope, reproduced in Yates 1975, l.11a. See also King 1989, 182–267. Spenser's portrayal of Elizabeth as Cynthia (one of Artemis' names) in the *Faerie Queene* is widely known; see Wells 1983.

[33] Beacon's dream of Diana's threatening the mutilation of Solon is explained by Epimenides as a lesson in the dangers of attempting reform in Ireland. The "difficulties and dangers" inherent in this endeavour are portrayed as Diana's attempted mutilation of Solon. Beacon's imprisonment while on service in Ireland might suggest a more immediate and personal reference on the author's part. Solon's mutilation by Diana may represent the failed careers and the alienation experienced by the New English government officials in Ireland who favoured an aggressive English policy in Ireland but were frustrated and hindered by a more conservative and parsimonious monarch. On colonial alienation, see Canny 1987, 159–212. The complex and at times multilayered nature of Beacon's text allows for more than one interpretation of this allegory. See the introduction (pp. xxxiii–xxxiv) on this unusual depiction of Ireland as Diana and the more common symbol of Diana as Elizabeth I.

amazed, I did awake out of my drousie sleepe. *Ep:* The people of *Sala-mina,* is the threatening *Diana,* hating all reformation: the golden Dove, is the pleasaunt countrie of *Salamina:* the wavering of this Dove from place to place, is the frailty and mutability, whereunto this coun-trie of *Salamina* hath ever beene subject: the compassion which you have taken of this golden Dove, is the love you beare unto *Salamina:* the moving of your body and hande, to succour this golden Dove, is the ardent desire now newly kindled in you for the reformation there-of: the losse of hande threatned by *Diana,* is the difficulties and dangers, which shall from time to time, oppose themselves against you in this action of reformation. *Sol.* Describe therefore unto us, first, what you intende by this word reformation, and then the difficulties and daungers that followe the same, and lastly the waies and meanes, whereby we may readily eschewe those daungers and difficulties.

CAP. 1.

OF THIS WORD REFORMATION, AND A
generall description thereof, and howe the same is
devided into two severall parts and
members.

 REFORMATION of a declined common-weale,[34] is nothing els but an happy restitution unto his first perfection: this worde Reformation being thus described, may in like sorte be devided into two parts and members: the one may bee termed an absolute and a thorough reformation of the whole bodye of the common-weale, namely of the ancient lawes, customes, governementes and manners of the people: the other may be termed a reformation of particuler mischiefes and inconveniences onely, which like unto evill and superfluous humors dailie arise to the annoyance and disturbance of this politicke body.[35] For like as in our naturall bodies, saith the

---

[34] "Commonweale," as defined by Beacon, is used in the sense of a state or a community (including its laws, customs, government and people) or the whole body of the people constituting a nation or a state. For Beacon the body or substance of a commonweal includes laws, customs, government, and people. See introduction, pp. xxxiv–xxxvii).

[35] "Politicke body" is used in the sense of the nation and state in its corporate character and also has the more specific sense of the body as directed by the "headship" of the sovereign. The Tudor conception of the greatness of their "imperial" crown, based on the royal supremacy of the church, envisioned "a reconstruction of the body politic which depended for its validity on the notion of national sovereignty embodied in the head and king" (Elton 1982, 338–78). This understanding of the body politic is encapsulated in the preamble to the Act of Appeals (1532–33): "governed by one supreme head and king having the dignity and royal estate of the imperial crown of the same, unto whom a body politic, compact of all sorts and degrees of people divided in terms and by names of spirituality and temporalty, be bounden and owe to bear next to god a natural and humble obedience" (as above, 344). This English state and body politic was to be an independent organic unit consisting of the ruler and the body of subjects, both related to and dependent on each other. See Elton 1982, 215–35.

Phisitian, so in common weales there daily ariseth that, *Quod curatione indiget, & nisi tollatur, inde morbos læthales parit.*[36] This maner of reformation of particuler mischiefes and accidents consisteth of two partes and members: the one by the profitable laws, which are framed to meete with such mischiefs and inconveniences, which doe or may arise to the annoyance of the common-weale: such was the law called Σεισάχθεια,[37] which pacified the poorer sort of people called *Hectemarii*,[38] then in armes against the rich and better sorte of *Athens*: the other is the true discipline and execution of lawes so made and established. This manner of reformation of particuler mischiefes and inconveniences by good and profitable lawes, was mightily endevoured [A3v] by yourselfe, when as the *Athenians* made choice of you as their general reformer of their lawes and common-weale. For you did not change the whole state thereof, but altered only that which you thought by reason you might perswade your Citizens unto, or els by force you ought to compell them to accept; and framed your lawes to the subject and matter, and not the matter & subject unto your lawes, as sometimes *Lycurgus* did in his reformation of *Sparta*.[39] *Sol:* You

---

[36] *Discursus*, 421, *Discorsi* 3.1.2: "that which requires a remedy, and unless it is destroyed, produces fatal diseases" (trans. Carroll). Machiavelli quotes a corrupt Medieval Latin trans. of Avicenna: "Quod quotidie aggregatur aliquid, quod quandoque inidget curatione" (Bertelli, 380), "every day it absorbs something which from time to time requires treatement" (Walker, 386).

[37] "Seisachtheia": literally the shaking off of burdens; the disburdening ordinance of Solon for the debt relief. As a result of his role in the Salamis campaign Solon was elected archon of Athens for the year 594–593 BC and was given sweeping powers. The problem that most seriously threatened Athenian social stability was the question of the debtors and their land. Solon's law "Seisachtheia" cancelled all debts but did not substantially alter the substance of the creditors' wealth. His law forbade all future loans on the security of a person so that never again could a man, or his wife and family, be enslaved for debt. See, Ehrenberg 1968, 60–62; North, *Plutarch's Lives*, "Life of Solon."

[38] Hectemorii were the common people "so sore indetted to the riche, that either they plowed their landes, and yelded them the sixt part of their croppe: (for which cause they were called *Hectemorii* and servants) or els they borrowed money from them, at usurie, upon gage of their bodies to serve it out" (North, *Plutarch's Lives*, vol. 1, "Life of Solon," 228).

[39] Machiavelli, in *Discorsi* 1.2., praises Lycurgus for instituting a mixed constitution that combined all three forms of government: "prudent legislators, aware of their defects refrained from instituting any one of these forms [principality, aristocracy, democracy] and chose instead one that shared in them all ... Lycurgus ... assigned to the kings, to the aristocracy and to the populace each its own

have saide the truth, for if I should have attempted to turne uppe side downe the whole government, & to have changed the whole state thereof, I might afterwardes never have beene able with that smal power and forces then granted unto me, to settle and establish the same againe. Againe, I did not thinke, but that *Athens* then declined, might well have beene restored by this kinde of reformation.

CAP. 2.

What common-weale may be restored unto his first perfection by applying thereunto this manner of reformation.

E pi: No verily: for *Quæ primis institutis omninò corrupta fuerit, ea nunquam in tales casus incidet, propter quos novis legibus institui queat.*[40] For this cause the first institution of *Athens* being meerly popular, corrupt, and unperfit, coulde never after by any lawes made for the reformation thereof, be defended from the tyrannie of such as did aspire unto the principalitie, or from the ruine first conceived in the corrupt institution thereof. For notwithstanding they established many lawes for the reformation of the insolencie of the noble men, as also to restraine the libertie of the people, *non eam tamen conservare supra centessimum annum potuerunt.*[41] But such common-weals as have their first institution and foundation good,

---

function, and thus introduced a form of government which lasted for more than eight hundred years to his very great credit and to the tranquility of that city" (Walker, 109). Sixteenth-century English writers, such as Sir Thomas Elyot in *The Book of the Governor* (1531), William Harrison in the "Description of England" in Holinshed's *Chronicles* (1577), and Sir Thomas Smith in *De republica Anglorum* (1583), praised England for being a mixed state. See Michael Mendle 1985, 42–49.

[40] *Discursus*, 12. *Discorsi* 1.2. "For it is by no means possible in such cases in which [a state] is entirely corrupt in its first institutions for it to be set right [literally, stopped or cut out] through the institution of new laws" (trans. Carroll).

[41] *Dicursus*, 19; *Discorsi* 1.2. Beacon omits Machiavelli's comparison of Solon to Lycurgus: "It was not so in the case of Solon, who drew up laws for Athens, for he set up merely a democratic form of government, which was so short-lived that he saw before his death the birth of tyranny under Pisistratus; and though, forty years later, Pisistratus' heirs were expelled, and Athens returned to liberty because it again adopted a democratic form of government in accordance with Solon's laws, [here Beacon's quotation begins] nevertheless they were not able to conserve this for more than one hundred years" (Walker, 110).

though not altogether perfit and complete, at any time declining from the first state and perfection, may by this manner of reformation (made by profitable laws as occasion shal them require) be not only restored to their first perfection, but the happie estate thereof may thereby be long continued and augmented: such was the [A4] common-wealth of *Rome,* whose first institution and foundation was so wel laid by *Romulus & Numa,*[42] as that after by new laws made for the reformation thereof, as the necessity of that commonweale did require, the same was rendered long, happy, and prosperous, in somuch as it attained at the last an happy temper and forme of governement, compounded of three sortes and kindes of governement, namely the *Monarchia, Aristocratia,* and *Democratia:* so that wee maie conclude, that those common-weales which have their foundation good, though not perfit and complete, *ex iis quæ subinde occurrunt, emendari & perfici queant ad exemplum Romæ:*[43] for it is saide, *non prima illa Romanæ reipublicæ: institutio tantum a recta via aberrabat, ut perfici non posset.*[44] Lastly such common-weales which in al the parts thereof are found corrupted and declined from their first institution, maie not by profitable lawes made and established as occasion shal them require, be reformed; whereof sometimes the Citie of *Rome* and nowe the state of *Salamina* may be unto us an example: sith neither the one after her finall declination, which did chiefely growe by a general corruption of manners in the people, could be reformed by the lawes against *Captainship,*[45] against *Coyney,* and *Lyvery,*[46] or against the unlawefull custome of supporting and maintaining of rebels or any other new lawe whatsoever; nor the other by their lawes *sumptuarii ambitus,*[47] and such like, the reason whereof shall more at

---

[42] Romulus: mythical founder of Rome; Numa: the second king of Rome (715–673 BC), founder of the priestly colleges (see *OCD*).

[43] *Discursus,* 12, *Discorsi* 1.2: "For these [states] which withstand these things are able to improve and be perfected according to the example of Rome" (trans. Carroll).

[44] *Discursus,* 20; *Discorsi* 1.2: "if Rome did not get fortune's first gift, it got its second. For her early institutions, though defective, were not on wrong lines and so might pave the way to perfection" (Walker, 110).

[45] See above, *Solon* I, note 6.

[46] See above, *Solon* I, note 5.

[47] *Discursus,* 98; *Discorsi* 1.18.2: "the sumptuary law, a law concerning ambition" (Walker, 161).

large appeare in this discourse following. *Sol:* There remaineth nowe
the discipline of lawes as the second parte and member of this particuler reformation not as yet consulted of.

CAP. 3.

Of a reformation made by the discipline of lawes.

E *pi:* This maner of reformation is nothing els but a feare to
offende, bred in the hearts of the people by the true discipline
of lawes, after which manner the Citie of *Rome* was sometimes
reformed *per supplicium de Bruti filiis sumptum pœnam Decemviris impo-
sitam, Spurii Mœlii cædes, & similia, post captam urbem Manlii* [A4v] *Tor-
quati pœnam*ª *de filio sumptam, eò quod pugnasset contra Imperatoris man-
datum, Fabii Magistri equitum accusationem a Papyrio cursore institutam,
eò quòd præter Dictatoris imperium pugnam commisisset, Scipioni diem
dictam,*[48] all which beeing most memorable and feareful examples,
did admonishe all others of their duty and obedience unto lawes and
magistrates.[49] *Sol:* Therefore wisely saith a learned writer, *In conser-
vandis imperiis regnisque faciendum est, ut antiquæ leges & consuetudines
in usum reducantur, ex earum præscripto vitia puniantur.*[50] After this
maner by a severe discipline of lawes, did the *Lorde Gray*[51] in times

---

[48] *Discursus*, 423; *Discorsi* 3.1: "Notable among such drastic actions ... were
the sacrifice of the sons of Brutus, the punishment imposed upon the ten citizens,
the execution of Spurius Maelius. After the taking of Rome there was the death
of Manlius Torquatus' son, the action taken by Papirius Cursor against Fabius his
master of the horse, and the charge brought against the Scipios" (Walker, 387,
rev. Carroll).

[49] This last is a continued translation of Machiavelli into English by Beacon.

[50] *Discursus*, 426; *Discorsi* 3.1: "In conserving kingdoms, it is necessary that the
ancient laws and customs be reduced to their starting points, and according to
the law abuses must be punished" (trans. Carroll).

[51] Arthur Grey, 14th Baron Grey De Wilton (1536–1593), an accomplished
commander and committed Protestant, did not welcome appointment to the
potentially career-damaging post of Lord Deputy of Ireland in July 1580. Grey
was simultaneously faced with two of the most serious rebellions against Tudor
rule in Ireland prior to the Nine Years' War, one led by Gerald Fitzgerald, 14th
Earl of Desmond, in Munster, and the other by James Eustace, 3rd Viscount
Baltinglass, in the Pale. Grey's early efforts to suppress the rebels in the Pale met
with near disaster at the hands of Feagh MacHugh O'Byrne at Glenmalure (25
Aug. 1580). Both rebellions drew encouragement from a small Continental force

past, and now *Sir R. Bingehame*,[52] mightily reforme and advance the government of *Salamina*, so as wee may truely say, by such governours must this nation be reformed. By this manner of reformation hath *France* in times past, mightily advanced their government, and especiallie the Citie of *Paris*, which alwaies hath most severely punished offendours.[53] *Sol:* But what order of times in this reformation

---

which had landed at Smerwick on the southern coast with Papal blessing and assistance. Grey successfully rushed to this fort, and under disputed circumstances, supervised the massacre of the entire garrison after they had surrendered. Convinced of a widespread Irish Catholic conspiracy, Grey had the leading Anglo-Norman lords of the Pale arrested on his return there in December 1580. He had the remaining Pale rebels relentlessly pursued, and summarily executed many of the sons of prominent Pale merchants and gentry. Grey added to his excesses by his brutal policy of destroying the Munster rebels. By the end of 1582 he had succeeded, at an enormous cost in relations with the Old English and Gaelic Irish, in subduing the country. His repressive policies eventually resulted in his recall in August 1582; see *Tudor Ire.*, 278–86, and *DNB* under Grey. Grey's severity and unapologetic Protestantism were received more positively by the New English colonial elite in Ireland, most notably by Spenser in *A View.* Beacon shares the poet's admiration for Grey, but his praise for him in *Solon* is more qualified. Although Beacon favors Grey's use of severe exemplary justice in order to enforce the discipline of laws, he does not advocate outright extermination.

[52] Sir Richard Bingham (1528–99), successful diplomat and soldier on the Continent, became president of Connacht in 1584. He had first seen service in Ireland in the suppression of the Desmond rebellion in 1579, when he took part in the massacre of the Continental force at Smerwick in 1580. He was knighted and appointed to the Connacht post by the Lord Deputy Sir John Perrot (1527–92). Bingham's most significant impact on the province came as a result of his and Perrot's implementation of the "Composition of Connacht." The Lord Deputy compounded with the Anglo-Norman and Gaelic lords of the province to commute their traditional feudal dues and exactions in return for a regular rent from their freeholders. They also agreed to a composition rent from their territories, which would be raised to maintain the President and his garrison. Composition aimed at reducing the arbitrary powers of the local lords, while in return guaranteeing them a regular income, and at the same time insuring that the responsibility for law and order would shift toward a financially secure English President and garrison. Despite the success of "composition" in Connacht, Bingham ruled the province with an iron fist. Those who resisted, like Mahon O'Brien and the MacWilliam Burkes, were met with the utmost brutality, best exemplified in the case of the massacre of 2,000 Scottish mercenary allies of the Burkes at Ardnaree in September 1586. Bingham's severity, however, led to conflict with Perrot, who disapproved of his methods and attempted to have him removed from office. Their conflict lasted until the latter's death in 1592. For further discussion of Beacon's reflections on Bingham's methods, see below, *Solon* I, notes 81 and 82; *Tudor Ire.*, 288–91; and *DNB* under Bingham.

[53] Beacon's example of the military actions of Grey and Bingham differs significantly from the example of the French parliamentary procedures in *Discorsi*

made by profitable lawes and discipline thereof is rightly observed?
Ep: This manner of reformation is made after two sorts: either by
lawes limiting the times certaine for this reformation; or accidentally
thereunto led and provoked by occasions: for so the Citie of *Rome*
after the overthrowe given by the power of the *Gaules* did reforme
their common-weale and all disorders[b] formerly by them committed.[54] The *Athenians* also after the *Megarians* had recovered from
them the Ile of *Salamina,* and the haven of *Nicœa,* reformed that
common-weale.[55] And not long after the sedition betwixt the people
of the mountaines, the valleies, and sea coasts, did occasion a generall
reformation to be made of our Citie and common-weale of *Athens.*
Againe, the *Romaines* to give an ende of many contentions raised
betwixt the senators & people, sent *Spurius Posthumius Albus, A. Manlius,* and *Sulpitius Gamerinus,* as legates unto *Athens,* that they might
the better be enformed of the laws which you *Solon* had established
for the reformation of *Athens,* that thereby as by a line, they might the
better reforme the Citie of *Rome;* and further made choice of their
Decemviri to perfit this their intended reformation by profitable
lawes.[56] *Sol:* Now you have declared to us the reformation which is
made accidentally: there remaineth nowe the other reformation,
which is made by [B1] force of laws & at times certaine, wherin I
would willingly understand the reason, that should limit the times
certaine of our reformation, and that by lawes certaine in that behalfe
established, sith the accidents, and occurrants in al common-weales,

---

3.1. Whereas Machiavelli praises the *parlement* of Paris for punishing the offences
of the nobility, Beacon believes that military means are needed to check the
offences of the Old English nobility.

[54] See *Discorsi* 3.1: "This return to its original principles in the case of a
republic, is brought about either by some external event or by its own intrinsic
good sense. Thus, as an example of the former, we see how it was necessary that
Rome should be taken by the Gauls in order that it should be re-born and in its
rebirth take on a new vitality and a new virtue, and also take up again the
observance of religion and justice, both of which had begun to show blemishes"
(Walker, 386).

[55] The examples of occasions for reform here, by the Romans "after the
overthrowe given by the power of the Gauls" and by the Athenians "after the
Megarians had recovered from them the Ile of Salamina," suggest the need for
reform by the English faced with the threat to their power in Ireland by the
Spanish.

[56] *Discorsi* 1.40: The appointment of the Decemvirate in Rome.

which doe occasion this reformation made by profitable laws, be in themselves uncertaine, and accidentall. *Epi:* This manner of reformation made of particular accidentes at times certaine, and that also by lawes and statutes certaine, established in that behalfe, is founde more profitable then the other which is made accidentally. For lawes are required herein, *Ne opus sit per vim peregrinam idem præstare,* and time herein is also to be respected, *ne si impunit ac longo tempore concedatur, usque adeò augeantur vitia, ut sine periculo publico deinde nec puniri nec extirpari, queant:*[57] and for these causes especially, the rulers and governours of *Florence* were accustomed to say, *Singulis quinquenniis redintegrare formam reipublicæ oportere,*[58] otherwise the discipline of law may not be wel preserved. And therefore it is said, that if *Roome, singulis decenniis, secundùm leges, aliquod magnum exemplum in delinquentes statuissent, nunquam tanta morum corruptela potuisset civium animos occupare; sed quia tandem rara esse capit, aucta est tantopere morum corruptela, ut remdium nullum adhiberi potuerit.*[59] In like maner may we truely say, that so great a corruption could never have possessed the mindes of the people of *Salamina,* if there the exact discipline of lawes had in good time beene applied. *Sol:* Now sith you have declared at large the order and time, which is rightly observed in this manner of reformation, proceede unto the dangers and difficulties, which do usually accompany the same.

---

[57] *Discursus,* 426–27, *Discorsi* 3.1.5: "between one case of disciplinary action and the next there ought to elapse at most ten years, because by this time men begin to change their habits and to break the laws; and unless something happens which recalls to their minds the penalty involved and reawakens fear in them, there will soon be so many delinquents that it will be impossible to punish them without danger" (Walker, 388).

[58] *Discursus,* 424; *Discorsi* 2.1.6.: "It was necessary to reconstitute the government every five years" (Walker, 388).

[59] *Discursus,* 425; *Discorsi* 3.1.5: "If then effective action [according to the laws] together with this setting of good example, had occurred in that city at least every ten years, it necessarily follows that it would never have become corrupt" (Walker, 388).

CAP. 4.

The sundrie difficulties and dangers that followe this maner
of reformation.

E pi: The difficulties which herein arise, may lively appeare by the question, which *Cæsar* propounded sometimes unto *Pompey*, and *Crassus*, when he was Consul preferring then unto the Senate, the law for division of landes, called *Agraria*; doe [B1v] you *Crassus* and *Pompey*, saith he, give your consents unto the laws which I have now propounded? They answered, yea; then he prayed them to stande by him, against those that threatened him with force of sworde to let him. It may appeare also by that action of *Pompey*, when as he filled the market-place with souldiers, and by open force established the lawes, which *Cæsar* made in the behalfe of the people.[60] The same also was sometimes lively expressed in the person of *Lycurgus*, which for the better establishing of profitable lawes, gaged the losse of his eie;[61] and you *Solon* the losse of your credite and reputation with the people of *Athens*; when as by the law Σεισάχθεια, otherwise called discharge, you incurred the generall displeasure and hate, as well of the poore as of the rich: all which sometimes you lively expressed after this maner.

Even those which erst did beare me friendly face,
And spake full faire where ever I them met:
Gan nowe beginne to looke full grimme of grace,
And were like foes in force against me set:

---

[60] Caesar utilized his consulship in 59 BC to attempt an agrarian reform law in the face of stiff aristocratic opposition to his increasing power and ambition. This law, the "Lex Agraria," which aimed at the distribution of government land among the people, was delayed in the senate by an aristocratic coalition and, in particular, by the actions of his colleague Bibulus who claimed the omens were unfavourable. Caesar, forming an alliance with Crassus and Pompey, forced his legislation through, and, in the name of the people, used Pompey's forces to drive Bibulus from the forum. See *OCD*; North, *Plutarch's Lives*, vol. 5, "Life of Julius Caesar," 281–83; *Discorsi* 1.37.

[61] "Yet also, he used more persuasion than force, a good witness thereof, the losse of his eye: preferring a lawe before his private injurie, which hath power to preserve a cittie long in union and concorde, & to make cittizens to be neither poore nor riche" (North, *Plutarch's Lives*, vol. 1 "Life of Solon," 234).

As if I had done them some spite, or scorne,
Or open wrong, which were not to be borne.[62]

Sol: You have nowe revived the memory of my former sorrowes, the which I labour rather to forget. Proceede therefore unto other difficulties, or rather tell me, why such dangers should arise and follow these actions, which are found so profitable for the common-weale. *Epi:* They arise, partly from the contrarietie of humours, and opinions, lodged in the brests even of the wisest; partly from the insolency of the multitude. *Sol:* It is most true: for *Cæsar*, *Crassus*, and *Pompey*, allowed the division of landes, and established the lawe *Agraria*; but *Calphurnius*, *Bibulus*, *Cato*, *Considius*, and other Senators rejected the same: the people allowed therof, but the nobility condemned it, and the ambition of *Cæsar*.[63] In another assembly also the Senate of *Rome*, *Crassus*, *Appius*, and *Nepas*, prayed the Senate to proroge the government of *Cæsar* for five years longer, and to deliver money unto him out of the common treasure to pay his army, but others impugned the same; especially *Phan-*[B2]*nius*.[64] *Sol:* For these causes (be you remembred) I helde it a matter very difficult and dangerous, to deale betwixt the poore and the rich, whereunto I was required sometimes by the City of *Athens*, fearing the covetousnesse of the one, and the arrogancy of the other; the poore desiring, that the lande might againe be devided; the rich also of the contrarie, that their bargaines and covenantes might a newe be confirmed. But what waies and meanes may be found that may avoide these difficulties and daungers?

---

[62] North, *Plutarch's Lives*, vol. 1, "Life of Solon," 234.

[63] See above, *Solon* I, note 60.

[64] While Caesar campaigned in Gaul, Pompey, Crassus, Appius (the praetor of Sardinia) and Nepos (Proconsul in Spain) attempted to insure that he was supplied and he had authority for his campaign. Cato, the triumvirate's main opposition, had been sent to campaign in Cyprus, thus leaving only his ally Phanius to stem the growth of Caesar's power. Phanius, failing in the senate in this endeavour, attempted to appeal to the people, but they ignored him. See North, *Plutarch's Lives*, vol. 5, "Life of Julius Caesar," 292–93.

CAP. 5.

The readie waies and meanes to avoide these
difficulties and daungers.

E PI: Such Princes and governoures, which will avoide the difficulties and daungers, which commonly arise in establish-ing of profitable lawes and ordinaunces; by reason of diversitie of humours, opinions, and factions, they must of necessitie remove for a time, or otherwise imploy the leaders and heades of all such factions, as may give any waies impediment unto their proceedings; imitating herein *Cæsar*, *Pompey*, and *Crassus*, who purposely sent *Cato* unto *Cipres*, knowing assuredly, that he would otherwise give imped-iment unto their lawes and proceedings, especially for the proroging of *Cæsar* his governement, and allowance for his army; or otherwise, with *Cæsar*, they shalbe forced to suppresse them by authoritie, and to put *Cato* to silence by imprisonment, the which may fortune to displease as well the nobles, as the people.[65] *Ep:* Or otherwise, we are to delude either faction by faire promises and sweete wordes, the which subtletie you *Solon* sometimes used (as *Phanias* the *Lesbian* writeth) when as you secretly promised the poore to devide the lande againe, and the rich also to confirme their covenantes and bargaines; when as you used these wordes and sentences; namely that æquality did breede no strife; by which æquivocation of wordes, you did winne as well the poore as the rich, unto a reformation of disorders; the one supposing that all thinges shoulde bee measured according to the [B2v] quality of the men, and the other tooke it for their purpose, that you would measure thinges by the number, and by the poule only, whereby you did safely proceede, and mightily further your law called Σεισάχθεια,[66] and did therein overcome all difficulties, by the which, the mighty sedition, which was then entertained betwixt the poore and the rich, was appeased. *Sol:* You saie truelie: and for the

---

[65] Ibid., 293.

[66] "Yet *Phanias* Lesbian writeth, that he used a sutiltie, whereby he deceived both the one and the other side . . . for he secretly promised the poore to divide the lande againe: and the riche also, to confirm their covenants and bargaines" (Ibid., vol. 1, "Life of Solon," 229). See also *Principe* 18.

better justifyng of this manner of proceeding herein, you shall understande, that in a publike magistrate, the same is rightlie tearmed pollicie, but in private persons, the same is not unjustly condemned by the name of deceite. *Ep:* We have remembred the same, not as condemners, but as approvers of the fact, and therefore needelesse you have justified yourselfe herein. *Sol:* Be it so: proceede then further unto other difficulties and daungers, which arise herein from the insolencie of the multitude, whereof you made mention in this former treatise but did not at large discourse thereof. *Ep:* Many daungers and difficulties arise from the insolencie of the multitude, as I have saide, for that never with one consent of minde, they doe admit or obey any new lawes or ordinances, untill they plainly understande the same to bee necessarie; but the necessitie of lawes never appeareth without daunger to the common-weale, which often falleth to his last ruine, before the lawes can bee perfitly established, which might support the same. The *Athenians* first received the evill and mischiefe, even into the bosome of that common-weale, before they sought to withstand the same by profitable lawes, yea they suffred the sedition, & uproares, betwixt the issue of *Megacles & Cylon,* still fighting & quarrelling, before they could be perswaded to chuse you *Solon,* as the reformer of there commonweale.[67] *Sol:* You maie best witnesse the same, for they suffered the invasion of the *Megarians,* they lost the haven of *Nysea,* and the Ile of *Salamina,* before they sent unto you *Epimenides* into *Creta,* by whose advise they then reformed there common-weale, greatlie to your laude and praise.[68] *Ep:* But more greatly *Solon* to your commendations, were the mighty factions long entertained betwixt the people of the mountaines, vally, & sea coasts,

---

[67] "Megacles (governour of the cittie of Athens) dyd with fayer words handle so the confederates of the rebellion of Cylon," his political rival (North, *Plutarch's Lives,* vol. 1, "Life of Solon," 225).

[68] When Athens was, once again, threatened with the loss of Salamis it sent "into CRETA for *Epimenides Phaestian,* whom they reckoned the seventh of the wise men ... He was a holy and devoute man, and very wise in celestiall things, by inspiration from above: by reason whereof, men of his time called him the newe *Curetes,* that is to saye, Prophet: and he was thought the sonne of a Nymphe called Baltè. When he was come to ATHENS, and growen in friendshippe with *Solon:* he dyd helpe him much, and made his waye for establishing of his lawes." (North, *Plutarch's Lives,* vol. 1, "Life of Solon," 226.) See above, *Solon* I, note 26.

quenched and pacified to the great good of *Athens. Sol:* they suffered the [B3] factions betwixt the poore and the rich, so long to fester in the bowels of the common-wealth, as the poorer sort did rise in armes with a purpose to chuse unto themselves a captaine, and to subvert the whole state of that common-weale, before they coulde be perswaded to make a generall reformation of their lawes and common-weale: they suffred many uproares and braules, before they condemned the excommunicantes.[69] The state of *Florence* also may with their perill and danger witnes the same: which contended not to suppresse the corruptions in the *Aretines*, before they well neere tasted of their rebellions.[70] In like manner, the *Athenians* could not be induced, either by my auctoritie, or els by the vehement perswasions which then I used, to withstande the tyrannie of *Pisistratus*, before they endured the weight thereof so heavily, as they could neither cast the same from their shoulders, neither yet endure the burden thereof.[71] *Ep:* This did occasion you sometimes to write and speake after this manner,

---

[69] Here Beacon draws on Plutarch's life of Solon to highlight the general Tudor lesson of faction as the major cause of societal collapse. Solon "stepped in betweene them [the factions], with the chiefest men of Athens, and did so persuade and intreate those whom they called the abjects and excommunicates, that they were contented to be judged" [the factional struggle between Megacles and Cylon]. And Solon had "the mighty factions long entertained betwixt the people of the mountaines, valley and seacoasts, quenched and pacified to the great good of Athens" (North, *Plutarch's Lives*, vol. 1, "Life of Solon," 226–28). These Athenian factions could allegorically refer to the ongoing and longstanding dispute between the Butlers and the Geraldines in Ireland. For a comprehensive discussion of faction in sixteenth-century Ireland, see Brady 1980–81, 289–312.

[70] Florence's suppressing rebellion of Arezzo: *Discorsi* 2.23.

[71] "But in the ende, seeing the poore people dyd tumult still, taking *Pisistratus* parte, and that the riche fled here and there, he went his waye also" (North, *Plutarch's Lives*, vol. 1, "Life of Solon," 257). This dispute, in substance over whether Pisistratus should have a personal bodyguard appointed by the Athenian people, arose as a result of his growing power. Supported by the Athenian artisanal class, Pisistratus was able to take control of Athens as its tyrant and expel the faction of the rich. Although Solon's constitution was not overthrown, his political career effectively came to an end as a result. Beacon is using this narrative to refer to endemic faction fighting in Ireland, and its ability to undermine the best efforts of the English Lord Deputies. See the careers of Thomas Earl of Sussex (1558–62), Sir Henry Sidney (1565–71, 1575–78), and especially, Lord Arthur Grey de Wilton (1580–82). See Brady 1986, 22–50.

Ech one of you ô men in private actes,
Can play the fox for slie and subtell craft:
But when you come 'fore in all your factes,
Then are you blinde, dull-witted and be daft, & c.[72]

But if we suffer daungers and difficulties in the establishing of good and profitable lawes, how much greater shall these daungers appeare unto us, when wee shall use and apply the sharpe discipline of lawes? the same no doubt is great, and farre exceedeth the other; for at such time as *Claudius* was accused, and indited of high treason, by one of the Tribunes of the people, and by others of the nobilitie and Senate, the rude multitude and people, did so boldlie and stoutly maintaine his unlawfull factes, as the Judges for feare durst not proceede against him, whereby hee was discharged of his accusations:[73] after the like manner did they compasse the Senate house, & called for *Cæsar,* and willed the Senate to let him out at such time, as he was to answere sundrie accusations laid against him.[74] But what waies and meanes are now left unto us, whereby we may overcome these difficulties and dangers?

---

[72] Beacon omits two lines from North's version of Solon's verse: "For pleausaunt speache, and painted flatterie,/Beguile you still, the which you never spye." See North, *Plutarch's Lives,* vol. 1, "Life of Solon," 256–57, where Solon speaks against Ariston's proposal to grant Pisistratus a bodyguard and exhorts the Athenians to protect their liberty.

[73] Clodius: accused of profaning the sacrifices of the goddess Gynaecia, but later chosen as Tribune by Caesar. "There was one of the Tribunes of the people that did indite him, and accuse him of high treason to the gods. Furthermore, there were also of the chiefest of the nobilitie and Senate, that came to depose against him, and burdened him with many horrible and detestable facts, and specially with incest committed with his owne sister ... Notwithstanding, the people stowtly defended *Clodius* against their accusations: and this did help him much against the Judges, which were amazed, and affraid to stirre the people ... So *Clodius* was discharged of this accusation" (North, *Plutarch's Lives,* vol. 5, "Life of Julius Caesar," 278–79).

[74] "when *Caesar* went into the Senate, to cleere him selfe of certain presumptions & false accusations objected against him, & being utterly taunted amongst them, the Senate keeping him lenger then they were wont: the people came about the counsell house, and called out aloud for him, bidding them let him out" (North, *Plutarch's Lives,* vol. 5, "Life of Julius Caesar," 276).

[B3v]

CAP. 6.

The severall waies and meanes to overcome all difficulties and
daungers, which arise in this action of reformation,
made by profitable lawes and the
discipline thereof.

E PI: First we are to remove all occasions, which may move the
people or beholders, to pittie or favour offendours. For when
Manlius Capitolinus was sometimes accused as a mover of sedition in *Rome*, his case was no sooner pleaded, but the sight of the
Capitoll troubled his accusers, and the Judges also; when as pointing
with his hand, he shewed the place unto the Gods, and weeping ten-
derly, laide before them the remembrance of the hazarde of his life, in
fighting for the common liberty and safetie of *Rome*, and in defending
the Capitoll itselfe, and repulsing the Gaules; in such sort, as the
Judges moved with pittie, knew not what to doe, and therefore put
over the hearing of his cause unto another day, because the place of
his so notable good service was ever still before their eies: wherfore
wisely *Camillus* finding the cause of delay of Justice, did make the
place of Judgement to be removed without the Citie into a place
called the wood *Petelian*, from whence they coulde not see the Capitoll, where his accusers gave apparant evidence against him, and the
Judges considering all his wicked practises, conceived a just cause to
punish him as he had deserved, so as they gave sentence of death
against him.[75] Further no orator, or pleader of causes, is to be suffered to speake in the behalfe of offendors, either to move the Judges
to compassion, or to winne the offendors favour in the eie of the
beholders. The mischiefe which ariseth hereby, did sometimes
appeare, when as *Cæsar* was suffered to speake in the behalfe of *Len-*
tulus, and *Cethegus,* companions of *Catiline* in his conspiracie, by
whose eloquence the offendors had then beene delivered, or at the
least not committed to the handes of the officers to be put to death, if

---

[75] North *Plutarch's Lives*, vol. 1, "Life of Camillus," 396–97. See also Livy, 6.20;
and *Discorsi* 1.8.

the gravitie and authority of *Cato*, and vehemency of *Catulus*, had not dis-[B4]swaded the contrary.[76] Lastly, the more often princes shal acquaint their subjectes with the discipline of the lawe, the more great obedience shall the subjects yeelde, as well unto lawes, as magistrates, and the lesse difficultie and danger shall princes finde therin. For the right discipline of lawes, doeth admonishe men of their dutie, and doeth cause them to leade their lives agreeable to lawe, and from time to time doth suppresse the malice of the offendors. For proofe whereof, the *Romaines* so long as they used the just and exact discipline of laws, they punished the offendors without feare,[c] danger, sedition, or mutiny; yea farther, when as they condemned *Camillus* unjustly, there was found no friend, no souldier, the number whereof were many and great, that durst make any resistance in his behalfe: for when as hee called unto him his friendes and souldiers, which had served under him in the warres, or that had taken charge with him, which were manie in number, he earnestly besought them, that they would not suffer him thus vilely to be condemned, through false and unjust accusations laide against him, and to bee so scorned and defamed by his enemies: his friends having laide their heads togither, and consulted thereupon, made him answere, how that for his judgement they could not remedy it, but if he were condemned, they would al joine togither with a very good will for the payment of his fine.[77] But not long after, *Cum iote decennio nullum Romæ statuebatur exemplum pœnæ*[d] *delinquentium*, then could not the Senate examine *Cæsar*[e] with their safetie, neither yet coulde the Judges condemne

---

[76] Caesar, on achieving the post of high priest, used his new prominence to make a speech in the senate on behalf of Lentulus and Cethegus, co-conspirators of Catiline. Caesar, arguing against Cicero who demanded a summary death penalty, claimed that it was unjust to take away the lives of nobles without a fair trial. Catullus and Cato, however, were able to convince the senate to the contrary. Plutarch's narration of this event casts doubt on Caesar's motives (North, *Plutarch's Lives*, vol. 5, "Life of Julius Caesar," 275).

[77] Beacon has a personal reason for focusing on this aspect of Camillus' career. Like the author of *Solon His Follie*, Camillus was unjustly accused of corruption, and, rather than suffer the humiliation of a trial, chose to go into exile. Camillus was overthrown because his public policy, though appropriate, was deemed too severe for popular support. (North, *Plutarch's Lives*, vol. 1, "Life of Camillus," 362). See also *Discorsi* 3.23, 30.

Claudius without peril.[78] *Sol:* Therefore in such common-weales, where the manners of the people are altogether corrupted, for not applying in good time the discipline of lawes, it behoveth the Judges, and such as shall revive the force of auncient lawes by the exact discipline thereof, strongly to be garded, according to the example of *Cicero* being accompanied with a strong garde of lustie men, when as Consull he was to convict and execute *Lentulus,* and *Cethegus,* for their conspiracies with *Catiline.* But *Cæsar* unadvisedly refusing a garde in such cases for the safetie of his person, did eftsones with the losse of his life approve his follie: for *Brutus,* and others, finding him naked in the Senate, without any strength, or [B4v] garde did easilie execute their malice upon him.[79] *Ep.* In like maner, governours in cases of great extremities, for the avoiding of daungers and difficulties, may proceede against offendors, without observing the usuall ceremonies of lawe. After this maner did *Cicero* proceede against *Lentulus,* and *Cethegus,* when as upon proofe onely, in open Senate, without any lawful inditement or condemnation, he commanded their delivery into the handes of the officers to be put to death; for so much may be gathered out of *Cæsar* his Oration, who at that instant mightily inveyed against that maner of proceeding, saying, it was not lawfull, neither that the custome of *Rome* did beare it, to put men of such nobility to death, without lawful inditement or condemnation, but in cases of extremity. This severe course and maner of proceeding in cases of extremity, may not be deemed any part of tyranny, if either we wil give credite unto the opinion of *Cæsar,* or unto the fact of *Cicero,* and the Senate; or followe the custome of *Rome,* or deeme *Cato* to be milde and just, who then being in the Senate, did vehemently perswade the same, and whose heart was so farre from crueltie, as

---

[78] *Discursus,* 426; *Discorsi* 3.1: "After ten years when no example of punishment for transgressing was set up."

[79] "When some of [Caesar's] frends did counsell him to have a gard for the safety of his person, and some also did offer themselves to serve him: he would never consent to it, but sayd, it was better to dye once then alwayes to be affrayed of death" (North, *Plutarch's Lives,* vol. 5, "Life of Julius Caesar," 334). In this instance Caesar's folly is contrasted with the astuteness of Cicero who, in demanding the summary execution of Lentullus and Cethegus for their part in the Catiline conspiracy, always went about with a guard: "a company of young men which garded *Cicero* for the safetie of his person" (Ibid., 275).

beholding the dead bodies slaine in the campe of his enimies, in the last skirmishe betwixt *Pompey* and *Cæsar*, he covered his face and went away weeping.[80] *Sol:* I call to remembraunce one *Sir R. Binghame* provinciall governour of *Salamina*, in my time a most valiant and honourable Knight, and withall a most wise and grave governour, being given to understand of a generall rebellion, with an intention, not onely to overthrowe the state and governement, but also to make deliverance of principall rebels of the sect and nation of the *Burkes*, then in prison and safegard, did forthwith deliver those traitors and rebels to be put to death, without lawfull inditement or condemnation. For seeing himselfe fallen into these extremities, that either he must spare the lives of open and manifest rebels to the damage of the common-weale, or execute them without lawfull inditement and other ceremonies, like a wise governour, two mischiefes offering themselves at once, made choice of the least,[81] not beeing as then to learne that which *Cæsar* sometimes taught *Metellus*, *The times of warre and lawe are two thinges:* so as in this action and in all other partes of his governement, hee [C1] hath shewed himselfe to bee the person, which *Archilocus* describeth in these his verses

> *He is both Champion stout of* Mars *his warlike band,*
> *And of the Muses eke, the artes doth understand.*[82]

---

[80] See above, *Solon* I, note 76, for the proceedings against Lentulus and Cethegus in the Senate. Beacon uses this episode from Plutarch's "Life of Julius Caesar" to argue against Caesar's position on the necessity to observe due process for the Roman nobility. Beacon favors the argument of Cicero and Cato that in cases of extremity, where the state is threatened by rebellion, it is necessary to proceed without observing the normal legal conventions. In order to rebut the charges of excessive cruelty, he observes that Cato was so shocked by bloodshed during the Caesar-Pompey civil war that he fled the battlefield in tears.

[81] For Bingham's career, see above, note 52. This reference to Bingham's actions in Connacht, and above all else, his summary execution of imprisoned members of the Burke family, represents a crucial aspect of Beacon's overall argument. While he emphasizes that the new governor of Ireland should accomplish his reform of the commonweal through a strict and proper observance of the law, he also notes that recourse to extra-legal measures may be at times necessary. The point to note, however, is that Beacon is quite specific about the times when this can occur. Only in times of war or general rebellion, when the state is in extreme trouble, could this suspension of the law occur.

[82] The defense of Bingham's extra-legal measures is further reinforced by Caesar's distinction between the operation of law in times of war and peace

EPI: It seemeth also convenient for the better avoiding of difficulties and dangers, that such heads and leaders, as shall be found to give impediment unto this maner of reformation, be committed to some safe-gard or prison, and there detained; all which *Dionysius* advised *Dion* sometimes by his letters, wishing him thereby, not to set them at liberty, which hated him and the action which he had then undertaken of reformation.[83] *Sol:* If the Earle of *Desmonde* late of *Salamina*, committed to safe-gard & prison for his sundry rebellions against the Citie of *Athens:* had there beene safely detained, the warres of *Salamina* had neither beene chargeable nor troublesome unto the Citie of *Athens*,[84] and if *James FitzMorrice* in like maner being in safetie and custody of officers to aunswere all accusations of high treason, had not beene set at large by the Justices for the time beeing, he had not then wasted, burned and spoiled a great part of *Salamina*, neither had he put the Citie of *Athens* to so huge and mighty a charge, nor yet combined with the enemy to the great daunger of that estate.[85]

(North, *Plutarch's Lives*, vol. 5, "Life of Julius Caesar," 310). Caesar defends his taking treasure from the temple of Saturn from Metellus' criticism. The lines applied in praise of Bingham's actions and character are those of Archilochus (Greek iambic and elegiac poet, 753–716 BC) quoted by Plutarch to describe how Phocion decided to imitate Pericles, Aristides, and Solon: "To bee both Champions stowt, of Mars his warlyke band,/And of the Muses eke, the artes to understand" (Ibid., vol. 5, "Life of Phocion," 357).

[83] "Dionysius advised Dion": Brother-in-law and son-in-law of Dionysius I, tyrant of Syracuse (c. 430–367 BC), both friends of Plato (see *OCD*).

[84] The "Earle of Desmonde late of Salamina" is the powerful Old English lord Gerald Fitzjames Fitzgerald, 14th Earl of Desmond (c. 1533–1583), whose death in rebellion paved the way for the Munster plantation. Beacon refers to the many possibilities the crown had of avoiding the great expense and trouble of suppressing the rebellion since prior to its outbreak it had the earl at its mercy. The earl had even spent from 1566 to 1572 in the crown's hands, initially in the Tower and then eventually in the home of Sir Warham St. Leger. On returning to Ireland in 1572, Deputy Sir William Fitzwilliam imprisoned the earl, who eventually escaped. Beacon considers the government's failure to detain Desmond illegally a key factor in the outbreak of the second Munster rebellion, reluctantly led by the earl from 1579 to 1583. See Brady 1980–81; and *Tudor Ire.*, 237–44, 250–54, 262–66, 279–84.

[85] Similarly Beacon claims that the government should have imprisoned James Fitzmaurice Fitzgerald, landless cousin of the Earl of Desmond and captain general of the earl's forces, when it met with him on various occasions during his rebellious career. Desmond's imprisonment in the mid 1560's allowed Fitzmaurice to come to prominence, and colonization efforts under Sir Henry Sidney from 1566 to 1572 prompted him to lead a joint Gaelic and Old English resistance

Therefore it is a chiefe suerty unto Princes, and great furtherance unto actions of importance, to commit to safe-gard and prison, such as may give impediment thereunto: for the which cause king *Fredericke* did no sooner intend the warres against the *French,* but he apprehended and put in prison the Prince of *Bisignan* and the County of *Molotte,* as friends unto the *French.*[86] But now sith we have spoken at large of the first part and member of this reformation, let us descend unto the other, which you have tearmed a reformation absolute and universall.

---

coalition. When his first major rebellion, coinciding with a similar Butler outbreak in 1569, was cruelly repressed by Humphrey Gilbert and by Sir John Perrot as President of Munster, Fitzmaurice surrendered to the Lord President at Kilmallock in February 1573. Beacon argues that if Fitzmaurice had been dispatched or kept imprisoned on this occasion, the Crown might have avoided the rebellion occasioned by his return from the Continent in 1579, accompanied by Papal Legate Nicholas Sanders and a small Continental force. The eventual rebellion, despite Fitzmaurice's death later in the same year, brought in the Earl of Desmond and the utter desolation of the province of Munster under the supervision of Deputy Lord Arthur Grey de Wilton by 1582.

[86] "King *Federyk* . . . to make a cleare way to an actio[n] of so great importance (it is a chiefe suertie to Princes to cut of treasons in the beginning) he apprehended and put in prison, the Prince of *Bisignan* and the Count of *Melotte* accused affore him to have had secret intelligence with the *Count Caiezze* who was in the French armie" (Fenton, *The Historie of Guicciardin* 5, 257). A contemporary of Beacon's, Fenton for more than twenty-seven years was a leading government official in Ireland, where he served on the Irish Privy Council. He was the first to translate Guicciardini into English. See *DNB.*

THE SECOND BOOKE OF
Solon his follie.

CAP. 1.

A description of a reformation universall, and of the whole
state and bodie of the common-wealth.

PI: This reformation universall of the whole state and body of the commonwealth, is nothing els, but a thorough and absolute mutation and change, of auncient lawes, customes, and manners of the people, and finally of the common-wealth itselfe, unto a better forme of governement. *Sol:* It seemeth then, that this reformation respecteth three matters principally: first, the mutation of auncient lawes and customes; secondlie, the alteration and change of manners in the people; and finally, a new institution and a better forme of governement, then before, prescribed.

CAP. 2.

Of the reformation of auncient lawes and customes.

PI: You have well observed my meaning and purpose: and to this effect, a subtile writer making mention of this reformation generall and absolute, saith, that he which shall attempt the same, must alter and chaunge all the auncient [C2v] lawes and customes, *quia ne leges quidem, quæ in ipso ortu reipublicæ à bonis viris latæ sancitæque sunt, sufficientes utilesque sunt adeos cives frenandos, qui in eadem rempublicam à maiorum virtute degenerarunt, & pravi facti sunt,*[1]

---

[1] *Discursus*, 97; *Discorsi* 1.18: "Furthermore, situations and laws made in the early days of a republic when men were good, no longer serve their purpose when men have become bad" (Walker, 160–61).

for, saith he, where we finde, the times and people thoroughly changed, embracing now that which is found contrary to their former course and manner of living, wee ought also to chaunge the auncient lawes and customes: for, *contraria subiecta non debent eodem modo tractari*.[2] The *Romaines* may herein be unto us a lively example: for after they had subdued *Asia, Africa,* and in a manner had reduced under their governement al *Greece,* they fell eftsoones into a corruption of manners, contrary to all their former discipline, institution, and accustomed manner of living: their auncient lawes and customes established for creating of Magistrates, they mightely abused; selling their voices of election openly in the market place for mony: in like manner did they abuse al other their auncient lawes and customes, namely the lawes and customes, which devided the common-weale and power thereof into the handes of the people and Senators, so as there could not be a reformation of that estate, without a mutation made of those auncient lawes and customes, then growne by the iniquitie of those times out of use.[3] *Sol:* But what neede wee search forraine examples? when *Salamina* doth afforde sundry proofes thereof, where we may beholde many auncient customes and privileges, granted (no doubt) at the first, for the advancement of publike services, but now turned by a generall corruption in the subject, to the ruine of themselves and the lande of *Salamina;* which must of necessitie bee altered and chaunged, before any thorough reformation may there be established: all which may appeare unto such as shall reade the Act of Absentes,[4] which is lefte unto us as a register of the fall and declynation of the state of *Salamina;* wherein it is manifest, that the Lords of the several counties, of *Carthelagh,* and *Wexforde,*[5] being places privi-

---

[2] *Discursus*, 101; *Discorsi* 1.18.5: "since similar forms cannot subsist in matter which is composed in a contrary manner" (Walker, 163).

[3] *Discorsi* 1.18.

[4] The original Act of Absentees (1362) aimed at preventing the erosion of the English colony in Ireland through the absenteeism of English lords and settlers. The act cited this as a cause for the advance of the "wild Irishrie" and stipulated the continuous residence of English landowners in Ireland on pain of deprivation of their lands. This act was periodically renewed by Irish parliaments. Beacon cites the 1537 act and uses it as evidence of the decline of English government in Ireland. See *Stat. Ire., Hen. VI–14 Eliz.,* fols. 46–49; Edmund Curtis and R. B. McDowell 1968, 59–61.

[5] Beacon here specifically refers to the 1537 Act of Absentees, and to the loss

ledged, maie keepe and hold all manner pleas within the same, by occasion and under pretence and collour whereof, the kings lawes, writtes, or other processes, be not obeyed, neither anie other lawe or justice there used or administred, for the quieting and good ordering of [C3] the subject: so as in defaulte thereof, the kings enemies have them in servage; al murders, robberies, theftes, treasons, and other offences, remaine unpunished; the kings wardes, reliefes, escheates, and all other his profits and revennewes are there withdrawne; and the service, strength, and assistaunce of the saide subject, is greatly minished; all which more at large shall appeare to such as shall peruse the saide statute: so as we may conclude, that without a mutation, made of these auncient customes and priviledges now growne out of use, and declyned from their first institution by a generall corruption in the subject, the state of *Salamina* may never be perfitly and thoroughly reformed. For as the state of *Rome*, in manner as afore declined, coulde not by the lawes, *sumptuarii ambitus*,[6] neither by any other new lawe be sustayned and underpropped, without a thorough alteration made of all other the auncient lawes and customes thereof; so may we not expect in these daies a thorough reformation of *Salamina*, by the lawes of *Captainshippe*, the lawes against *Coiney* and *Liverie*, the lawes against taking of pledges, the lawes against wilfull murder, or any other new lawe whatsoever made for the reformation of *Salamina*, without a thorough alteration made of the auncient customes and priviledges thereof, all which we there sometimes imployed in that service, were daily taught, rather by experience then by any learned or deepe discourse, that may be made therof. In like manner if the custome of *Captainshippe*, the custome of *Coiney* and *Livery*,[7] and the custome of taking of pledges, the custome of *Tanis-*

---

of the counties of Carlow and Wexford to the "wild Irishrie," and places the responsibility for the loss of these areas on their absentee lords Thomas Howard the Duke of Norfolk, and George Talbot the Earl of Waterford and Salop (Shrewsbury from 1442), and on the "privileges" and "Liberties" which had been granted to them in the past. The statute returned these lands to the crown. Beacon concludes that Ireland cannot be regained unless the laws are reformed.

[6] *Discursus*, 98; *Discorsi* 1.18; "the sumputary law, a law concerning ambition" (Walker, 161).

[7] For the laws against captainship and coyne and livery, see above, *Solon* I, notes 5 and 6.

tery,[8] the custome of protecting and supporting of traitours, had not beene abolished by lawes, then all newe lawes whatsoever would have beene founde unprofitable for the reformation of *Salamina:* for in such cases it is saide by learned writers, that *leges novæ minus prodesse queant ad tollenda vitia quæ regnant.*[9] Now sith it is evident, that a thorough reformation may not bee made without a mutation of auncient laws & customes, which are found evill in themselves, or els by mutation and chaunge of times have now lost their first vigor and force, it behoveth that we doe understand, what order and rule herein is to be observed, for the more ready effecting thereof.

[C3v]   C A P. 3.

Of the reformation of auncient lawes and customes, and
what things therein chiefly are to be
considered.

E PI: In all mutations made of auncient lawes and customes, three matters especially fall into deliberation: first the meanes; secondly the forme and maner; lastly the subject and matter. The meanes are in number five: the first is authority; the goodwill and consents of the people, the seconde; the thirde perswasions; a sufficient power and force, is the fourth; the fifth and the last is a magistrate, of rare and excellent vertues, which may suppresse the envie and malice of such, as shall oppose themselves against this intended reformation, made by the mutation of auncient lawes and customes.

---

[8] The English term "Tanistery" is derived from the Gaelic "Tánaiste" or "the expected one," referring to the successor designate of a Gaelic lord. Spenser says the "tanaiste" was nominated at the time of the election of a new chief, as a man "next of the blood" to the chief, "who shall next succeed him in the said captainry if he live thereunto." On his inauguration the lord swore to preserve the ancient customs and to deliver up the succession peaceably to the tanaiste. This system was attacked by English commentators in the sixteenth century because in contrast to primogeniture, it opened the succession to a four-generation group (called the "derbfine"), and, despite the designation of the successor, frequently led to conflict on the death of the lord. See Kenneth Nichols 1972, 25–30; Katherine Simms 1987, 54–59, for the reference and quotation from Spenser.

[9] *Discursus*, 98; *Discorsi* 1.18: "new laws can be of less use in destroying the vices which reign" (trans. Carroll).

Sol: But what authority is required for the better effecting of a reformation? For this as the first matter, you have well observed to be
requisit herein. *Epi:* All authority herein graunted is after two sortes:
the one absolute; the other limited by time, and other circumstances.
This authoritie absolute, was given sometime into your handes by the
Athenians; for after such time as they had well tasted of the lawe and
ordinance, called Σεισάχθεια, they forthwith did choose you their
generall reformer of the lawe, and of the whole state of the common-
weale, without limiting this power then granted unto you, but referred all matters indifferentlye unto your will, as the offices of state,
common assemblies, voices in election, judgments in justice, and the
body of the Senate. Finally, they gave unto you all power and authority, to cease[10] and taxe anie of them, to appoint the number, and
what time the cease should continue, and to keepe, confirme, and dis-
anull at your pleasure, anie of the auncient laws and customes, then
in being.[11] But this authority absolute, without anie limitation of the
power it selfe, or of the time and continuance thereof, hath sometimes
turned to the great prejudice and danger of such as formerly have
graunted the same: for the *Romaines* af-[C4]ter they had elected their
Decemviri, for the making of a thorough and absolute reformation of
the common-weale of *Rome,* they forthwith gave into their handes the
sole and absolute power of *Rome,* so as all other authorities and
jurisdictions either of Consull, Senate, or Tribunes, ceasing, they
wholy and only governed *Rome,* without any provocation or appeale
to bee made to any other. Thus when no Magistrate remained, which
might observe the actions of such as were founde ambitious, easily
did *Appius Claudius,*[12] fall into the thoughtes of the principality of
Rome; he doeth strengthen himselfe with friendes, & clyents, and daily
increaseth his wealth, and nowe of a Citizen is become a fearefull
enemy to the state of *Rome;* in such sorte, as they may neither endure

---

[10] "Cease" or cess was the common Irish term for a range of government
exactions (purveyance, cartage, and cesses of laborers) levied to provide royal
officials, and, in particular, the Lord Deputy and his retinue, with food, transpor-
tation, and laborers for building works. The regularity of its exaction due to the
endemic warfare of the second half of the sixteenth century produced widespread
dissent among the Old English of the Pale, see Brady 1986.

[11] North, *Plutarch's Lives,* vol. 1, "Life of Solon," 234.

[12] *Discorsi* 1.40.

his pride and insolencie, neither may they safely suppresse the same without their common perill and daunger. Therefore more wiselie did the *Lacedemonians* give great authority to their kinges; and likewise did the *Venetians* to their Dukes, but yet with certaine limits and bondes, not lawfull for them to exceede; and farther did appoint certaine watchmen, as daily beholders and observers of all their actions and doings.[13] *Sol:* But what limitation of time, in granting this absolute authority, may breede safety unto him that giveth the same? This is the seconde and last matter, nowe remembred by you, and worthie of consultation. *Epi:* The provinciall governement over the *Gaules,* with an absolute power given into the handes of *Cæsar;* for the better reformation thereof, was so long proroged and continued, as at the last with the sword of the *Romaines,* and the money of the *Gaules,* he became terrible, as well to the *Gaules,* as to the *Romaines,* & returned not a Citizen now of *Rome,* but as a fearefull enemie, and conquerour, as well of the Citie, as of all the other territories and dominions thereof. And was not also the provinciall governement of *Spaine,* sometimes given into the handes of *Pompey* with an absolute authority for the reformation thereof, so long proroged and continued, as with one stampe of his foote he was able, (as himselfe reported) to fill the Citie of *Rome* with weapons, and armed men? And did not *Appius Claudius* by proroging his authority but for one yeare, become fearefull to the Citie of *Rome?* And did not the *Romaines* by [C4v] making a Dictator perpetuall, loose the libertye of their Citie?[14] and doeth authority thus easily corrupt the maners of good subjectes? and is the age also wherein we live free from such corruption? Nay, more then that, is there not an enemie on foote, that laboureth the corruption of the whole? Then what authoritie here may be limited so straight, as in this time may not be thought too large? what time may be so shorte, which may not be deemed too long? Therefore let every good and faithfull councellour unto the state, with *Cato* resist here the

---

[13] Sparta and Venice compared to Rome: *Discorsi* 1.6.

[14] Caesar's provincial government over the Gauls: North, *Plutarch's Lives,* vol. 5, "Life of Julius Caesar," 284–85; 290–99. Provincial government of Spain sometimes given to Pompey: vol. 5, "Life of Pompey," 122, 127. Appius Claudius proroging authority for one year: *Discorsi* 1.40; Romans making Caesar dictator perpetuall: vol. 5, "Life of Julius Caesar," 333.

proroging of *Cæsar* his governement, least too late with *Pompey* they acknowledge their errour:[15] it shall not suffice here to graunt but one yeare more unto *Appius Claudius;* neither is it sufficient that *Cæsar* is holden in disgrace with the Citie of *Rome;* neither may we here safely beleeve all which shall saie unto *Pompey, Cæsar* is hated of the garrisons, and souldiers: for when *Cæsar* commeth with his fortune, he shall then force, as well *Pompey,* as the Citie of *Rome,* to acknowledge their former follies and errours: *Sol.* But nowe unto what person may this authority be safely graunted, is a matter herein, not unworthy of consultation. *Ep:* It is safely graunted unto a man approved to be good and honest, with this caution, that he be not of such power and force, as the state may stand in feare of his greatnes.[16] For the best sometimes have fallen by reason of honours and dignities into a generall corruption of manners, and therefore we receive it as a proverbe, *honores mutant mores.*[17] *Sol.* At no time then is it safely committed into the handes of personages of great might, power, and wealth. *Ep:* You have saide the trueth: for what daunger did arise to the state of *Athens,* by constituting *Garralde FitzGarralde* attained, Liuetenant of *Salamina?*[18] who having at once might, power, and soveraigne commaundement in his handes, did eftsoones conspire, and combine, sundry treasons, and rebellions. *Sol:* The recordes of *Salamina* doth witnes so much as you have saide, for there it is alleadged, that he did conspire with the *French* king and Emperour, for the invading and possessing of *Salamina:* he did also in proper person invade the Countie of *Kylkennie,* there burning, destroying, & murthering the kinges subjectes: he did invade also with *Oneyle,* and [D1] his forces, *O Coner,* and other of the saide Earle his friends, alies, and servants, by his commandement the County of *Uriell;*[19] wherein

---

[15] *Discorsi* 1.33.

[16] *Discorsi* 1.18.

[17] "Honors alter manners," a proverb.

[18] "*Garralde FitzGarralde* attained, Liuetenant of *Salamina*": Gerald Fitzgerald the IXth Earl of Kildare. The failed Kildare rebellion of 1533 ended the Tudor policy of delegating power to the native aristocracy, and initiated the policy of direct rule and the appointment of an English-born Lord Deputy. Kildare died in the Tower in 1534 but not before his son, "Silken" Thomas Lord Offaly, led the Geraldine faction in rebellion against the Tudor reform initiatives of Thomas Cromwell. See Ellis 1976–77; Bradshaw 1977. For a summary see *Tudor Ire.,* 85–129.

[19] Beacon draws his analysis of Kildare's rebellion from the 1537 "Act for the

he was aided, and assisted by *Sir John,* brother unto the saide Earle.[20] The like or greater daunger did growe unto the state of *Athens,* by constituting *Thomas FitzGarralde,* sonne and heire to the saide Earle, Lieutenant of *Salamina:* who succeeding in the place of his father, having the like might, power, & forces lent unto him by his friends, alies, and servantes, and soveraine authoritie given from the king, did eftsoones revile that famous Citie of *Athens,* and his lawfull soveraigne, and moved all rebellions against them; and did therewith also addresse his letters unto the Bishop of *Rome,* & the Emperour,[21] for the invading of *Salamina:* and farther did put to death, and cruelly murthered all those which were resident within the lande of *Salamina,* being borne Citizens of *Athens,* and amongst others did put to death that reverende father and faithfull counceller *John Allin* Archbishoppe of *Deublin,* and primate of *Salamina.*[22] More then this, he constrained with his power and forces, the subjectes of *Athens,* to give unto him an oath of obedience, & forthwith besieged the Castle of *Deublin,* where with his whole armie by the sea coast he incamped, for the better resisting, destroying, and murthering the army of *Athens,* as

---

attainder of the Earle of Kildare and others." Kildare's correspondence with the French King Francis I and the Emperor Charles V, his manipulation of the Geraldine revolt from England, and the resulting destruction in the English Pale are all cited as justification for confiscating Kildare's lands. Specifically mentioned are Kildare's use of Gaelic allies Conn Bacach O'Neill of Tyrone ("Oneyle") and Brian Mac Cathaoir O'Connor of Offaly ("O Coner") to invade County Louth ("Uriel") in the Pale. *Stat. Ire., 10 Hen. VI–14 Eliz.,* fols. 37–42; *Tudor Ire.,* 124–29.

[20] The act of attainder also cites Kildare's brother Sir John Fitzgerald as having accompanied O'Neill in his attack on the loyal Ormond territory of Kilkenny.

[21] Beacon suggests that the Kildare rebellion was actually more dangerous because when Kildare appointed his son Thomas Fitzgerald, Lord Offaly, as his vice deputy, the conflict became an ethnic and religious one. Thomas is accused of trying to involve the Pope ("Bishop of Rome") in a crusade against Henry VIII and to exterminate the English in Ireland. Beacon's amended source is again the act of attainder.

[22] Closely following the text of the act of attainder, Beacon here refers to Thomas Fitzgerald's 27 July 1534 murder of John Allen, Archbishop of Dublin, one of Cromwell's appointees, and the anti-Geraldine Primate of Ireland. The rebellion was eventually crushed between October 1534 and May 1536 by the newly dispatched Lord Deputy William Skeffington. In 1537 Thomas Fitzgerald and five of his uncles were executed for treason, thus ending the Kildare hegemony in Ireland.

they landed. No lesse dangers then these formerly rehearsed, appeared at such times, when as the Duke of *Yorke* pretending himselfe Liuetenant of the saide lande, did with his power, and forces, occupie and possesse all the territories and dominions thereof. [*Statutes of Ire: 35. H.8. ca.3. fol.11.*][23] Therefore of late daies, hath the Counsell of *Athens* most providently committed this soveraine authority unto such, as may not be able with forces and power to usurpe the same. But if unto this authoritie thus given, to effect a reformation, the consentes and good-wils of the people be founde agreeable, no doubt the same shall mightily further that action.

[D1v] C A P. 4.

The good-will and consent of the people is a readie meanes
to effect a reformation.

E PI: You have saide the truth: for where the good-will of the people is first wonne and obtained, there the mutation is made, without difficultie and daunger. All which may lively appeare in the history of *Tarquine*, who having lost as well the good-will of the people, as of the Senate, by changing the auncient lawes & customes of the Citie of *Rome*, was easily expelled that kingdome. *Sol:* It is true that you have said; for he did drawe unto himselfe all the authority, as well of the Senate, as also of the liberty of the people, which sometimes they injoied under their former kinges, and for this cause chiefely, he failed of the good-will of the people, in this his mutation and alteration of thinges. But *Brutus* on the contrary, having wonne the good-wil of the people, for the effecting of a reformation, and expelling of *Tarquine*, did chaunge the state of the common-weale, without anie difficultie, daunger, or injurie sustained by anie other, then the expelling of *Tarquine*. Likewise, when the *Medicei Urbe Florentinorum Anno salutis* M. CCCC. XL. IIII. *pellebantur,*[24] the

---

[23] The 1494 "Act annulling a prescription which traitors and rebels claimed within this land" (*Stat. Ire., 10 Hen. VI–14 Eliz.* fol. 25) is mistakenly referred to as 35. Hen. VIII ca.3.

[24] *Discursus,* 476 [*Discursus:* "pellerentur," *Solon:* "pellebantur"] *Discorsi* 3.7: "It was also the case with the government of the Medici in Florence, which when

chaunge was made without daunger and difficultie, for as much as the same was effected by the good-will and consentes of the people. Sith therefore the consente of the people, doth give so great further-aunce unto this action of reformation, it seemeth a matter verie neces-sarie, that everie Magistrate shoulde retaine the arte, skill, and knowl-edge, of perswading and inducing the multitude, as you have in the first chapter of this booke well remembred.

[D2]   # CAP. 5.

The force of perswasions, and how necessarie the same
is to effect a reformation.

EPIMEN: So it is indeede, for the good-will and consente of the people, doeth promise no small security unto the Magistrate which intendeth this action of reformation: and therefore not without cause, *Pythagoras* was of all sortes of persons greatlie hon-oured, for his singular arte and knoweledge in winning the affections of the multitude, and in perswading, and disswading the people, all which *Plutarch* witnesseth after this manner,

Pythagoras *which lov'd to dwell,*
   In highest dignitie:
And had a heart to glorie bent,
   And past in pollicie:
Much like a man which sought,
   By charming to inchaunt:
Did use this arte to winne mens mindes,
   Which unto him did haunt.
His grave and pleasant tongue,
   In sugred speech did flowe,
Whereby he drewe most mindes of men,
   To bent of his owne bowe.[25]

---

it fell in 1494 [for which 1444 is an error], harmed nobody but the Medici themselves" (Walker, 425–26).

[25] North, *Plutarch's Lives*, vol. 1, "Life of Numa," 175.

Though *Lycurgus* was the eleventh which descended from the right line of *Hercules*, though a man of great authoritie, of great force, of long continuance a king, yet indevoring a reformation of many disorders, which did chiefely arise in that estate, by the inequallitie of landes and possessions, therein (as *Plutarch* witnesseth) he used more persuasions, then force: a good witnesse thereof was the losse of his eie.[26] You *Solon* also altered and [D2v] reformed that in the common-wealth of *Athens*, which you thought by reason you shoulde perswade your citizens unto, or els by force you ought to compell them to accept. *Epi:* The *Romaines* therefore well understanding the force of persuasions, in all actions of reformation, did institute the holy order of the *Fæciales*,[27] who retayning the art of perswading, and disswading the people, did much further the common-weale of *Rome;* for they went many times in person to those that did the *Romaines* injurie, and sought to perswade them with good reason to keepe promise with the *Romaines,* and to offer them no wrong: they did also perswade the people, to deliver *Fabius Ambustus*,[28] unto the *Gaules,* as one that had violated the lawes of armes, and farther proved by manie reasons, that a present reformation made of that disorder and injustice, woulde deliver *Rome* from many calamities, then like to insue by the power of the *Gaules.* By this art and skill of persuading, did *Camillus* appease the great sedition and mutinye, raysed sometimes by the people of *Rome* against the Senators, for that they had not their full minde and libertie, to inhabite the citie of *Vies.*[29] By this art and skil, you *Solon* have now of late induced the *Athenians* to make warres with the *Megarians* for the possessing of *Salamina,* contrarie to their former liking, publike lawes, and proclamations made in that behalfe: and the like honour did you sometimes winne by your oration, made in the defence of the temple of *Apollo,* in the citie of *Delphos,* declaring, that it was not meete to bee suffred, that the *Cyrrhæians* should at their pleasure abuse the sanctuarie of the oracle; by force of which

---

[26] Ibid., vol. 1, "Life of Solon," 233–34.
[27] Faeciales, or fetiales, a college of priests whose duties were to represent the state in declaring war, making peace, and entering into treaties. See North, *Plutarch's Lives*, vol. 1, "Life of Numa," 182–83; vol. 1, "Life of Camillus," 367.
[28] Fabius Ambustus: Ibid., vol. 1, "Life of Camillus," 367.
[29] Ibid., vol. 1, "Life of Camillus," 355, 388, 400.

persuasions, the councell of *Amphictions* was thoroughly mooved, so that they sought a present reformation thereof.[30] By this your art and skill, you also perswaded those which in *Athens* they sometimes called the abjectes and excommunicates, to be judged, whereby you did quench and appease two mighty factions, the one supported by the issues of the rebels, that rose with *Cylon*, and the other by the ofspring of *Megacles*.[31] *Sol:* I acknowledge this your friendly reporte, not as a testimonie of anie art or skill, but of the office and duetie which I beare unto the citie of *Athens*. But after this manner sometimes a no-[D3]table mutinye and sedition raysed by the citizens of *Salamina*, against the Justices of assizes and jayle deliverie, in my presence was happely appeased.[32] But nowe sith the necessitie of the art and skill of perswading is sufficiently made knowne unto us, there remaineth, that you describe unto us the art itselfe, with the partes and members thereof.

CAP. 6.

The art and skill of perswading, worthely knowne and observed
of all publike Magistrates.

EPI: The art and skill of perswading, consisteth in the knowledge of two matters especially: first we must know howe to commende the matter, or person of such as we intende to perswade; then how to moove, winne, and dispose the affections of the people.[33] For the first, the Poet saith truly, that he singeth most sweetely, that singeth my praise and commendation. *Sol:* This which you have saide, did manifestly appeare after the battaile of *Xerxes* fought with the *Græcian* army, for then all the *Græcian* Captaines being in the straight of *Peloponnesus*, did sweare upon the altar of

---

[30] Ibid., vol. 1, "Life of Solon," 224.

[31] Ibid., vol. 1, "Life of Solon," 225.

[32] Based on his experiences as the Queen's Attorney in Munster (1586–91), Beacon refers to the difficulties of implementing the regular mechanisms of common law in Ireland.

[33] Compare Sir Thomas Wilson, *The Arte of Rhetorique* (1553), fols. 3v–4r, 13r, 72v–73r.

their sacrifices, that they would give their voices after their consciences to those they thought had best deserved it, where every one gave himselfe the first place for worthines, and the seconde unto *Themistocles.*[34] After this manner, did *Publicola* winne the good-will of *Appius Claudius,* a man of great strength and reputation among the *Sabines,* in giving honour unto him, by the way of an embassage, whereby he gave *Claudius* to understande, that he knew him right well to be a just man, and hated without cause of his citizens; and therefore if he had any desire to provide for his safetie, and to repaire to *Rome,* leaving them which causelesse wished him so much evill, they would publikely and privatly receive him with due honour; by which meanes, *Publicola* did not onely winne *Appius Claudius* with those of his faction, which were great and manie in number, but also staied and turned the warres from the [D3v] *Romaines,* then intended by the *Latynes* and *Sabines.*[35] *Sol:* There remaineth now, that you disclose unto us the knowledge, howe to winne, move, and dispose the affections of the people, as the second part and member, of the art and skill of perswading.

CAP. 7.

The skill and knowledge how to winne, moove, and dispose the
affections of the people.

EPI: Herein three matters especially are founde worthy of consideration: first the affections what they be; secondarilie the subject and matter, wherewith they usually are mooved, and carried awaie, as with the violence of some tempest; thirdly the waies how to winne, moove, and perswade the people, according to the example of the worthiest and wisest in times past. The affections which be the first, are in number these; love, hatred, hope, feare, dispaire, and such like; the matter and subject which is the second, is parentage, consanguinity, friendes, goods, possessions, landes, the custome and manner of living, honours, libertie and life; the presence

---

[34] See North, *Plutarch's Lives,* vol. 1, "Life of Themistocles," 321, 323.
[35] Ibid., vol. 1, "Life of Publicola," 289–91.

whereof wee love and imbrace, and with their absence wee are soone carried away unto wrath, hatred, revenge, hope, feare, and dispaire: therefore from hence as from a fountaine, have the wise governours in former ages, drawne all the force of persuading; by the same have they induced the people to imbrace matters profitable to the common-weale, even against their wils. And how mightely these transitory thinges have alwaies appeared in the eie of the multitude, it may appeare by the aunswere given from the *Athenians* unto *Themistocles*, whereas he perswaded the people to leave their citie, goods, posses-sions, and landes, and to get them to the sea for the better eschewing of the Barbarian forces, which then were so mighty, as the same might not well be withstoode by the proper forces of the *Athenians:* In vaine (saith the people unto *Themistocles*) doe we then seeke the pres-ervation of our lives, when wee shall forsake the [D4]ᵃ graves of our fathers and auncetours. Such was the love they bare unto those transi-tory thinges: and therefore one amongest the rest, spake in choler unto *Themistocles* after this manner; *Themistocles,* for a man that hath neither citie nor house, it is an evill part to will others that have, to forsake all; but *Themistocles* turning to him, replied, we have willingly forsaken houses and walles (saith he) cowardly beast that thou art, because wee will not become slaves, for feare to loose thinges that have neither soule nor life.[36] *Sol:* Now you are to give us to under-stand, of the sundry waies and meanes, how to winne, moove, and dispose the affections of the people, which is the thirde and last matter by you remembred, worthy of every publike magistrate, which shall indevour the knowledge and art of perswading.

CAP. 8.

Perswasions are after two sortes; the waies, and meanes, how to
perswade, and induce the multitude; the art and
skill required in all perswasions ordinary.

EPI: The waies and meanes how to winne, moove, and dispose the affections of the people, are usuallie after two sortes: the one ordinary; the other extraordinary. The ordinary waies and meanes, are in number three: First you shall wisely observe the affec-

---

[36] Ibid., vol. 1, "Life of Themistocles," 308, 316.

tions of such persons, as you intende to perswade; secondarilie, you shall wiselie acquit, and deliver, as well the matter, as the person of him that perswadeth, from all suspition of fraude and guile; lastly you shall draw the people unto a particular consideration of the matter you intende to perswade. We must diligently observe their affections; for so *Phanias Lesbian* writeth, that the mighty and daungerous faction sometimes entertained betwixt the rich and the poorer sort of the citie of *Athens*, was by you *Solon* easelie pacified, in that you diligently observed the affections of either, and did secretly promise the poore to devide the landes, wherewith they remained [D4v] highly pleased, to the rich you promised the confirmation of their contracts, which was the matter they chiefely desired. Also you did not let to feede their humours and affections with the dailie publishing of this sentence, equality doth breede no strife; the which did please as well the rich and wealthie, as the poore and needy sorte; for the one conceived of this worde equality, that you woulde measure all thinges according to the quality of the men, and the other tooke^b for their purpose, that you would measure things by the number, and by the poule onely; thus both being pleased with you, for that you well observed their humours and affections, they gave into your handes soveraine authoritie for the ending of all quarrels, whereby that mighty faction was happely appeased, to the generall good of *Athens*.[37] You also well observed the affections of the people, when as you clothed things bitter and unpleasant, with pleasing names; calling taxes, contributions; garrisons, gardes; prisons, houses; and such like: by the which pollicie, you made even things odious, pleasing and acceptable to the people, and easily thereby perswaded the embracing thereof.[38] In like manner *Themistocles* indevouring like a wise generall to augment his strengthes by the aide of the *Ionians*, in his warres against the *Persians*, did wisely observe the affections as well of the *Ionians*, as of the *Persians* then his enemies: for passing by some places, where he knewe the enemie must of necessity fall uppon that coast for harborough, hee did ingrave certaine wordes spoken unto the *Ionians*, in great letters in stone, which he founde there by

---

[37] Ibid., vol. 1, "Life of Solon," 229.
[38] Ibid., vol. 1, "Life of Solon," 231–32.

chaunce, or otherwise brought thither for that purpose; these were the wordes, that the *Ionians* should take the *Græcians* part, being their first founders and auncetours, and such as sought for their liberty; or at the least they shoulde trouble the army of the Barbarous people, and doe them all the mischiefe they coulde, when the *Græcians* shoulde come to fight with them: by these wordes thus ingraven, and dispersed in fitte places, where the enemy was likely to harborough, he hoped either to induce the *Ionians* to take their part, or at the least, that therby he should make the Barbarous people, jelous and mistrustfull of them.[39]

[E1]   CAP. 9.

How that the Magistrate which intendeth to perswade the
multitude, must wisely acquite himselfe of all
suspicion of fraude.

SOL: Nowe you have sufficientlie discoursed of the first meanes, whereby the multitude doe rest perswaded, the second nowe remaineth, namely, the knowledge howe to deliver the matter and person of him that perswadeth, from all suspition of fraude and guile; for then all perswasions move mightily, and make a deepe impression in the heartes of the people, when like unto cleare waters, they descende from the pure fountaine of integrity. Therefore when *Alcibiades* perswaded the people of *Athens* to invade and occupie the empire of *Sicilia*, wel hoping that the people woulde assigne him general of that armie, *Niceas* a man of rare and excellent virtues, rather regarding the publicke good then his privat profit, disswaded the contrarie; and to the ende the people shoulde be throughly perswaded of his integritie herein, he spake unto them after this manner: in times of peace, the Citie of *Athens* affordeth many Citizens, which shall have place before me, but in times of warre, I nothing doubt but to be the chiefe and first among them; and therefore be you confident in this, that I nowe disswade the warres, for that it standeth more with the

---

[39] Ibid., vol. 1, "Life of Themistocles," 312.

publicke good, then with my private profitte.[40] In like manner *Numa*, the better to deliver himselfe from the suspicion of fraude, in all matters wherein he laboured to induce and perswade the people, hee observed two matters especially: first he perswaded them, that he did worke the reformation of that common-weale by the meanes and helpe of the Gods, in which action no fraude may receive place, for that they be for the most parte, alwaies accompanied with integrity and sincerity of minde; secondlie hee perswaded nothing unto the people, but that which himselfe performed in person: for *Numa* judging it no light enterprise (saieth *Plutarch*) to plucke downe [E1v] the hautie stomackes of so fierce and warlike a people, did pacifie their fierce courages to fight, with daily sacrifices, prayer, and devotion, wherein he ever celebrated himselfe in person.[41] *Epi:*^c In like manner, when you *Solon* were to publish your lawe called Σεισάχθεια, the better to perswade the people of your integrity herein, you were the first that followed your owne proclamation, and clearely released your debters of fifteene talentes then due unto yourselfe. *Sol:* So I did, though it stoode with my losse and hinderance. But nowe there remaineth the thirde and last meanes, wherewith the multitude is mightely induced and perswaded, formerly by you remembred, worthy of consultation, namely, that we drawe the people unto a particular consideration of such matters as we intende to perswade.

CAP. 10.

The magistrate which intendeth to perswade the multitude, must
draw them unto a particular consideration of such
matters as he endevoureth to perswade.

E PI: You have remembred that which I could not well forget, the same being alwaies founde the most assured way to induce the people: for in consulting and disputing of matters in generall, they greatly erre, judging all thinges to proceede from other

---

[40] Ibid., vol. 4, "Life of Nicias," 266. See *Discorsi* 1.53.7.
[41] See North, *Plutarch's Lives*, vol. 1, "Life of Numa," 174.

causes, then from the true causes thereof. Therfore wisely *Camillus*, when as he indevoured to perswade the people of *Rome*, from the inhabiting of the citie of *Vies*, then for the same cause being fallen into a mutinie, he descended unto particulars with the multitude, and pointed with his finger unto the graves of their fathers, and auncetours, saying, will you needes inhabite the citie of *Vies*? And will you forthwith forsake the graves of your fathers and auncetours? And will you now leave the holy temples dedicated to the Gods, and sanctified by *Numa* and *Romulus*? And wil you suffer the holy fire now newly kindled, now once againe to bee put out? And finallie, will you leave this your naturall citie (pointing with his finger unto [E2] the citie of *Rome*) to be inhabited by straungers in time to come, or els to be a common pasture for wilde beasts to feede on? By which manner of perswasion he eftsoones appeased the mutinye, and quenched their ardent desire for the inhabitinge of *Vies*.[42] After this manner, did *Pacuvius* proceede in pacifiyng and subduing the peoples affections from killing their Senatours; which matter by them was fully determined, untill such time, as he conventing the people and Senatours, as for the hearing and determining of some publike and waighty cause, did proceede with them after this manner: now my friends and Citizens (saith he) that which you have even with an ardent desire and affection long wished, namelie the punishment and correction of this detestable and wicked Senate, the same hath fortune now given into your powre and handes, freely to dispose of them at your pleasure, being nowe altogether naked, and closed in on everie side with walles, where, without tumult of the Citie, and perill of your persons, you may freely dispose of them; but least you shoulde preferre the desire of private revenge, before the common safety of al here gathered together, it behooveth before you give sentence of these Senatours, whom you doe mortallie hate, that you proceede first to the choice of others; for of force you must either have Senatours, which alwaies have bene the most wise and fit councellors of free estates; or otherwise you must of necessitie fall into the hands of a Lorde or King, which free estates have ever hated; proceede therefore to the election of new, and make choice of better men, which may supply

---

[42] Ibid., vol. 1, "Life of Camillus," 388.

their places: this matter appearing unto the people doubtfull, did hold them long in silence, but at the last one among the rest beeing nominated, their clamour and noyse farre exceeded their former silence, some affirming they knewe him not, some accusing his person, others despising his base art and science; and much more in the choice of the second, and third, this dissension was increased, they being more base and obscure, then the first: then beholdinge the grounde, with shamefastnes they confessed their former errour, sayinge, they did chuse rather to tollerate an old evill, then a new, which might farre exceede the olde.[43] In like manner the people of *Rome*, con-[E2v]sulting at large, founde that they sustained in all warres the greatest force of the enemie, they found themselves also to be called to all labours and workes, whereby the common-wealth was to be preserved or augmented, and so forthwith they judged themselves as worthy of the office and dignity of the Tribuneship, and Consulship, as any Patrician whatsoever: and thereuppon contended, that the Tribunes should be equally elected, as wel of the one as of the other sorte; the which beeing unto them graunted, and descending to make election, could finde none in particular worthy of that honour, or at the least so worthy as the Patricians and nobles were; then forthwith they did acknowledge their former errour, and made choice of the Patricians only. After this manner, the people generallie consulting of the delaies and cunctation,[44] which *Fabius* used in repelling the forces of *Hannibal*, forthwith they condemned him to be a cowarde and faint harted; but afterward they waighing that their councell by the severall events and overthrowes they received by the rash and over-hasty proceeding of *Varro* the Consull, and of *Marcus Senteinius*, with others, they did soone after adjudge the wisedome of *Fabius* to be some rare and divine influence received from the Gods.[45] In like sort the people of *Rome*, after such time as *Brutus* and *Cassius* had fully executed the conspiracie then intended against the person of *Cæsar*, generally consulting of that action, remained for a time, as indifferent beholders thereof, neither accusing, neither yet making

---

[43] See Livy 22.3; *Discorsi* 1.47.3.
[44] cunctation: the action of delaying.
[45] Fabius Maximus and Hannibal, Marcus Centenius: *Discorsi* 1.53.

allowance thereof; but no sooner did *Cæsar* his friendes shew forth his testament, his severall legacies unto the people, his manie and cruell woundes, and those everywhere freshly bleeding and increasing like a running streame, the people as possessed with some furie or frencie, everywhere in the marketplace, everywhere in the corners of the streete, in privat houses, in the fieldes, and in the woodes also, cruelly murdred all such, as were partakers with *Brutus* in that action.[46] After this manner, the auncient Tirantes of *Athens*, contending sometimes to perswade the people to labour, and especially to til and ploughe the grounde, thereby to render them more obedient unto their governement, did give out a certaine fable; they [E3] tell of the Goddesse *Pallas*, that shee contending with *Neptune* about the patronage of the countrie of *Athens*, brought foorth and shewed to the Judges the Olive tree, by meanes whereof she obtained the preheminence: by which particular demonstration made, the people were mightily induced to labour and till the land.[47] After this manner the people of *Rome*, generallie consulting of the division of landes gained by conquest, did fall into mutinies and seditions against the Senators; then wisely the Senators deducted forthwith certaine colonies out of the confines of *Italie*, whereby eftsoones the multitude were given to understande, of the particular charge, travell, and other sundry inconveniences, that did arise by possessing of lands gained by conquest, wherewith all mutinies were appeased.[48] Thus the magistrate that intendeth to perswade the people, must not generally consult of matters, but must descende unto particulars with them; and therefore that oratour shall most readilie perswade, which shall draw his argumentes and the force of his perswasion, *ab effectibus, ab exemplis,*[49] or such like: and these be the ordinarie perswasions. *Sol:* There remaineth nowe the other sorte,[d] tearmed by you perswasions extraordinary.[e]

---

[46] *Discorsi* 3.6.32.

[47] North, *Plutarch's Lives*, vol. 1, "Life of Themistocles," 326.

[48] Deducting colonies to appease sedition in Rome: Ibid., vol. 6, "Tiberius and Caius Gracchi," 97, 101–2.

[49] To argue "from effects, from examples" is a commonplace of classical rhetoric. See: Cicero, *Topica* 18.71; Quintilian, *Institutio oratoria* 6.3.66; 7.3.29.

CAP. 11.

*Perswasions extraordinary, and when or at what time
they be requisite and necessarie.*

EPI: Such were they which *Themistocles* sometimes used, for (saith *Plutarch*) when all other perswasions failed, and coulde not worke that publicke good which he then intended, hee did threaten the *Athenians* with signes from heaven, and with Oracles, and aunsweres; and when as he coulde not perswade the Citizens of *Athens*, no not for the safegarde of their lives, to departe the Citie at the comming of *Xerxes*, whose forces they were not able to withstande, hee pollitiquely caused a brute to be spread abroade among the people, that the Goddesse *Minerva*, the protector and defender of the Citie of *Athens*, had [E3v] forsaken the Citie, pointing them the waie unto the sea; and againe, he wonne them with a prophesie, which commaunded them to save themselves in walles of woode, saying, that the walles of woode, did signifie nothing else but ships; and for this cause *Apollo* in his Oracle, called *Salamina* divine, not miserable and unfortunate, because it shoulde give the name of a most happie victorie, which the *Græcians* shoulde gette there; by which extraordinarie perswasions, hee did induce them at the last to leave the Citie of *Athens*, and to betake themselves to the sea: by occasion whereof, they did not onely deliver theselves from the handes of their enemies, but became at the last conquerours, and victours over them.[50] In like manner, when all ordinarie meanes of perswading failed to effect the reformation sometimes intended by *Numa*, he made his recourse to these extraordinarie helpes and meanes, laying before the peoples eies a terrour and feare of their Gods, bearing them in hande, that they had seene straunge visions, or that he had heard voices, by which their Gods did threaten them with some great troubles and plagues: whereby hee did pull downe and humble their hearts (as *Plutarch* witnesseth) and made thereby a thorough chaunge and reformation, aswell of the common-weale, as of the manners of

---

[50] See North, *Plutarch's Lives*, vol. 1, "Life of Themistocles," 313.

the people.[51] Therefore *Plutarch* not without judgment affirmeth, that the multitude in matters waightie, and difficult, rest satisfied and perswaded, rather by extraordinarie, then by ordinary meanes: all which he doeth lively manifest, whereas he induceth the multitude exclaiming uppon *Themistocles,* for not sacrificing the three young prisoners, in so much as[f] *Themistocles* forced by their rage and clamour, did sacrifice at the last the three prisoners; wherewith the people remained fully perswaded, that the victorie shoulde be given unto them over their enemies.[52] Againe, sometimes it fareth with the multitude, as with the sicke patient, which being overcome with the greatnesse of his malady, is therby become so impatient, as he refuseth all wholesome medicines, which may breed his health and safety; the which malady sometimes possessed the people of *Athens,* when as they rejected your counsell for the withstanding of the tyranny of *Pisistratus,* ha-[E4]ving then newly with his forces entered the castle, and forte of *Athens,* wherewith the people stoode so amazed, as they shewed themselves more willing to suffer that evill, then able to prevent the same by your counsell.[53] *Sol:* This happeneth oftentimes, when the people with the suddennes or waightines of the matter, are found dulled, mazed, and oppressed, and thereby as with some great malady remaine overcome; or otherwise, when they finde themselves formerly deluded, by the like matter, or by the same persons, & dare not, or wil not nowe give confidence, though for the present he perswadeth nothing, but that which is expedient & profitable for them: the which matters, the people of *Rome* objected sometimes against the Senators, when by the feare of forraine warres, they went about to frustrate the lawe of division: and in these cases as *Danta* reporteth in his Monarchie, even with open voice, they embrace their ruine, and abhorre their safetie and welfare. But now let us proceede unto the fourth way and means, namely, sufficient forces which in such cases are to bee prepared, whereby the Magistrate with greater safety and assurance may effect a reformation.[54]

---

[51] Ibid., vol. 1, "Life of Numa," 175.

[52] Ibid., vol. 1, "Life of Themistocles," 319.

[53] Ibid., vol. 1, "Life of Solon," 256–57.

[54] Beacon quotes *Discorsi* 1.53.2, where Machiavelli mistakenly cites Dante's *Monarchia* rather than his *Convivio* as source (see Walker, 2:83).

CAP. 12.

Howe strength, power, and forces, are necessarie for
the better effecting of a reformation, and how in
good time, the same ought to
be applied.

E PI: In the reformation of *Athens*, you *Solon* found the necessity
of forces, when neither the good-wils and consents of the
people, neither the absolute auctoritie which they gave into
your handes, neither yet the art and skill of perswading which then
in the highest manner you retained, was found sufficient to suppresse
the ambition of *Pisistratus*, or to confirme the reformation which you
had newly established, for that you wanted sufficient power and
forces, for the better effecting thereof.[55] Therefore this magistrate
which shall intende this action of re-[E4v]formation, must with *Publi-*
cola have sufficient powre to execute his vertues and well disposed
minde: for by this meanes especially did hee alter, chaunge, and
reforme a mighty kingdome, which had continued a long time, and
was thoroughly established.[56] *Sol:* For this cause chiefely, I must confesse, that I was altogither unprovident in taking uppon me the function and office of a king, to decide all controversies and broyles, at
the instance of my friendes and citizens, and yet refused the kingly
name and powre, the which then was offred unto mee, and without
the which I founde by experience, that I coulde never safely execute
that which seemed to me then profitable for the beter reformation of
the commonweale of *Athens*. *Epi:* So it appeared; for soone after you
well understoode your former errour, the which you did sometimes
liberally confesse, saying after this manner, that with the authoritie
and power then committed into your handes, a man possiblie

Could not controll
   the peoples mindes,
Nor still their braines
   that wrought like windes.[57]

---

[55] Pisistratus' ambition: North, *Plutarch's Lives*, vol. 1, "Life of Solon," 257.
[56] Ibid., vol. 1, "Life of Publicola," 298.
[57] Ibid., vol. 1, "Life of Solon," 234.

Sol: You have saide the truth: and for the same cause also at another time, I coulde not appease the sedition which did sometimes arise in *Athens* by reason of the inequality of landes and possessions after the example of *Lycurgus,* by making an equall division thereof, for that I had not then the power, forces, and authority of *Lycurgus.* Howbeit I performed that which possiblie I might with the small power and forces then given into my handes by the Citizens of *Athens.*[58] *Epi:* Surely this occasion of reformation is full of difficulties, as you have saide, and manie will still be founde, which shalbe discontented therewith; the which hath beene espied by men of wisedome, and such as have beene experienced in such cases, and sometimes your-selfe not without just cause did acknowledge in these verses follow-ing. [F1]

> *Full* harde *it is all mindes*
>   *content to have,*
> *and speciallie*[g] *in matters*
>   *harde and grave.*[59]

Many and unjust are the accusations and attemptes of the multitude, against such as have authority and commaundement over them; great and many be they in number, especially in common-weales corrupted in manners, which doe labour and travel so with envy against all excellent men, as that they rather wish their countries destruction, then by them a prosperous reformation thereof; by the which occa-sions, the faith and services of men, are oftentimes sinisterly inter-preted, sometimes by opinion, sometimes by malice, as well to the overthrowe of great and profitable actions, as also of worthie and faithfull servitors. *Sol:* Therefore *Moyses,* before he coulde establish the lawes, which God unto him had delivered, and commaunded, founde it necessarie, with forces to remove such, as being pricked forwarde with envie, did oppose themselves against his intended reformation. And *Hieronymus Savanarole* wanting sufficient forces, was soone oppressed by the envie of others, and fayled of his intended reforma-tion, as it may appeare by his sermons, *Contra sapientes huius*

---

[58] Ibid., vol. 1, "Life of Solon," 233–34.
[59] Ibid., vol. 1, "Life of Solon," 249.

mundi.[60] *Ep:* Neither is it sufficient in these cases to have forces, but as necessarie it is to make use thereof, and in due time to applie the same to the better furtheraunce of this action of reformation: whereof *Lycurgus* fayling, did establish his reformation with the losse of his eie, and with no small daunger unto his person, for that he contended rather with perswasions then with forces, to establish a reformation of auncient lawes and customes, and of the landes and possessions of the Citizens. In like manner *Peter Soderin,* having sufficient forces that might well have overcome the envy and malice of such as were founde to oppose themselves against him, did not in time applie the same, and make use thereof, but rather contended with benefites and with a just and honest course of life, to overcome the envie and [F1v]^h malice of such as withstoode his reformation; whereby in a short time, he did not onely perish and undoe himselfe, but also did over-throwe his country and regiment; forgetting that which now is everie where in experience, that the malice of the envious man, may neither with offices nor benefites be pleased and reconciled.[61] *Sol:* If the necessity of forces be great to effect a reformation, (as it plainely appeareth by that which hath bene saide) in such common-weals especially where the manners of the people are found corrupted, then much greater is the necessity thereof, when reformation is to be made of a common-weale, gained by the sword and conquest, as also cor-rupted in manners; for that the people having here sustained many injuries by force and violence, whereunto the conquerour is drawne oftentimes by their disobedience, maie not at anie time after with newe benefites, offices, and rewardes, be reconciled and pacified: neither shall we finde here profitable lawes, or any sufficient meanes to effect a reformation, without sufficient forces, to repell all daun-gers, and difficulties:[62] all which *Salamina* may well witnes unto the worlde; for when as the governour there, did contende to suppresse by publike proclamation thorough out the whole province of *Moun-ster,* that detestable custome of *Coiney* and *Livery,* and other extor-tions, which had then consumed the marrowe and fatnesse of that

[60] *Discursus,* 564–65; *Discorsi* 3.30.4: "against the wise of the world" (Walker, 486).

[61] Soderini's errors: *Discorsi* 3.2, 3.

[62] *Discorsi* 3.4.2.

common-weale of *Salamina;* then it was founde not sufficient to have the same established by late lawes, whereunto the whole parliament had agreed and consented; neither was it sufficient, that the same tended to the universall good of the common-weale; but forces herein also were requisite, to suppresse the *Butlers,* and *Garroldines,* which then on every side did arise in the mainteinaunce of that detestable custome of *Coiney* and *Livery:* all which Sir *Warram Sentlenger,* then provinciall governour, can well witnes: by whose care and diligence togither with the aide and assistaunce of the forces and garrisons of *Salamina,* they were soone suppressed.[63] Forces being thus necessarie for the effecting of a reformation, into whose handes the same is to be given, is the fifth and last meanes worthy of consultation.

[F2]   CAP. 13.

Howe a Magistrate of rare and excellent vertues
is required in this action of reformation.

E PI: This action of reformation with sufficient forces, for the better effecting thereof, is to be given into the hands of some man of rare and excellent vertues, by whose constancy and integrity, the envy and malice of the enemy may be quenched. Therefore the *Florentines* did not a litle erre, which in the times of their difficult warres, helde *Antonie Iacomine* above all others in greate estimation, for that onely he had taught the *Florentine* army, as it were with his finger, to fight, conquer, and commaund: yet in milder times,

---

[63] Sir Warham St. Leger was the second son of the former Lord Deputy Sir Anthony St. Leger, and was appointed Lord President of Munster by Sir Henry Sidney in Jan. 1566. The Queen refused to confirm his appointment, however, and in Nov. 1568 Sir John Perrot was appointed to this position. Since St. Leger returned to England in 1569, missing the joint Butler-Geraldine rebellion which followed Sidney's anti-coyne and livery legislation in the parliament of 1569, Beacon errs in placing St. Leger as provincial governor and chief suppressor of the revolt. If Beacon refers to St. Leger's later campaigns in Munster from 1579 to 1594, he inflates the latter's title, since at that time St. Leger only held the military position of Provost Marshal of Munster. See *DNB; Tudor Ire.,* 253, 254, 265.

when as the warres by his industrie were growne easie and placable, they little regarded those his vertues, in such sort, as when three Captaines were propounded to be chosen for the suppressing of the *Pisans*, he was not accepted to be one of that number; from the which errour this mischiefe did arise unto the *Florentines*, that the *Pisans*, which by the industry of *Antonie* might easily have beene reformed, and forced to have obeyed the *Florentines*, made eftsoones head against those unskilful Captaines so strongly, as the *Florentines* were forced dishonourably to purchase their obedience with money.[64] Againe *Phillip* of *Macedonie*, after he had behelde the affaires of the *Athenians* to be given into the handes of *Molosses, Caridemus*, and such other unskilfull Captaines, he conceived a great hope to overcome them.[65] In like manner, the weakenes and facilitie of *Collatinus* the Consull, did much encourage the traitours, in such sorte, as he had never prevailed against the *Tarquines*, nor reformed the state of *Rome*, if the great vertue and severitie of *Brutus* had not governed at that time the helme and sterne; whereby the courage and boldnes of the traitours, raised by the suffrance and lenitie of *Collatinus*, as a tempest was suddenly calmed and pacified.[66] *Sol:* Therefore pro-[F2v]vident were the counsel of *Athens* in committing this action of the reformation of *Salamina*, sometimes into the handes of the L. *Gray*, sometimes into the handes of Sir *William Russell* as unto another *Iacomine*, by whose rare skill and knowledge in militarie discipline, the *Pisans* have and will be forced at the last to obey the *Florentines*.[67] But let us nowe proceede unto the forme and manner of altering of auncient lawes and customes, as the second parte and member of your generall division, worthy of consultation.

---

[64] *Discorsi* 3.16.5.

[65] Phillip of Macedonie, Molosses and Cardemus: North, *Plutarch's Lives*, vol. 5, "Life of Phocion," 364–68.

[66] Collatinus: *Discorsi* 3.5.

[67] *Discorsi* 3.16.5. For Russell, see introduction, p. xxiv.

CAP. 14.

The forme and manner of altering the auncient lawes and customes of common-weales.

EPI: The forme and manner of altering auncient lawes and customes, is usually after two sortes: either *simulac statim;* or otherwise, *sensim paulatimque, antequam ab omnibus id animadvertatur.*[68] After this first manner, you *Solon* reformed the citie of *Athens:* for you did not straight plucke up the mischiefe by the rootes, but by little and little you chaunged their lawes, customes, and manner of living. After this manner, did *Numa* alter and chaunge the accustomed manner of living, and the manners of the citizens of *Rome,* from a warlike liberty to a life peaceable and obedient, and that by little and little (as *Plutarch* witnesseth.)[69] But others led with the opinion and reason of *Plato,* say, that to reforme a mischiefe after this manner, is no other but to cut of one of the *Hydraes* heads, of the which came afterwardes seven in the place: and therefore *Agis* and *Cleomenes* toke upon them to make a chaunge and innovation even at once, and as it were with one constant stroake of the hande, to cut of all the mischiefes of their country, so as wee may conclude, that the formes and maners of reforming of mischiefes in the common-weales, be sundry and diverse, the which proceede sometimes of the diversitie of meanes and occasions, which diverslie doe offer themselves; as also from the diversitie of the subject and matter, which being [F3] diverse in itselfe, requireth a different forme of governement.[70] *Sol:* You have saide the truth; and therefore a wise governour doth governe diverslie according to the meanes and occasions offred, taking every thing in his best time wherein hee meanes to deale, the which commendacion was sometime given not undeservedly unto *Publi-*

---

[68] *Discursus,* 98; *Discorsi* 1.18.5: "Now defective institutions must either be renovated all at once as soon as the decline from goodness is noticed, or little by little before they become known to everybody" (Walker, 163).

[69] North, *Plutarch's Lives,* vol. 1, "Life of Numa," 174.

[70] Agis and Cleomenes: *Discorsi* 1.9.5; Plato's judgment of reformation little by little: *Republic* 426e, cited in North, *Plutarch's Lives,* vol. 6, "Comparison of Tiberius and Caius Gracchi with Agis and Cleomenes," 115.

cola.[71] *Epi:* You *Solon* did sometimes reforme the citie of *Athens*, not as you might have done, neither yet as the necessitie of that common-weale required, as well in respect that the first institution thereof was meere popular, corrupt, and not durable, as also for that it was declined by many and infinite disorders, so as it could not for these causes rehearsed have long continuance, without making a thorough reformation of auncient lawes, customes, and governement, and with-out pulling up the mischiefes even by the rootes; the which with that small powre and meanes then left unto you, you durst not attempt, least by turning upside-downe the whole governement, you might afterwards have never beene able to settle and establish the same againe: for these defectes chiefely in that reformation, it hath beene observed even of the wisest, that you *Solon* have already seene the overthrowe of your common-weale of *Athens*, and the tiranny of *Pisis-tratus.*[72] *Sol:* Yes verily, I did well foresee the same, but yet having neither meanes nor power to resist so hard destinies, I was forced to sustaine the person, rather of a sorrowfull beholder, then a reformer of so great calamities: but more happie and fortunate was *Lycurgus, Publicola,* and *Cleomenes,* and such others, though nothing superiours to my selfe in that care and love which every citizen beareth unto his Countrie, for that they had sufficient power and meanes left unto them (as *Plutarch* witnesseth) to execute their vertuous desire, where-by they made a thorough chaunge and reformation of their common-weales, by cutting up all mischiefes by the rootes, by reason whereof the state of their common-weales continued long, happy, and pros-perous.[73] *Sol:* But what difficulty ariseth from the diversitie of the subject and matter?

---

[71] Ibid., vol. 1, "Life of Publicola," 289–91.

[72] Criticism of Solon, and of purely popular governement: Ibid., vol. 1, "Comparison of Solon with Publicola," 297.

[73] Ibid., vol. 1, "Life of Lycurgus," 113; vol. 1, "Life of Publicola," 298; vol. 6, "Agis and Cleomenes," 34.

C A P. 15.

The consideration of the subject and matter of all reformations,
and howe the same is divers in itselfe, and con-
sequently requireth a different forme
of governement.

E PI: The matter and subject of all reformations is diverse in
itselfe, and therefore admitteth the sundry formes of reformation aforesaid: for sometimes the matter or subject which is to
be reformed, is a mischiefe or evill by long continuance inveterate,
and growne to the height of his strength and perfection, and there the
same shalbe more wisely sometimes indured, then hastily rooted out,
to the overthrow of the common-wealth: the which caution if *Tiberius*
Gracchus had sometimes well observed, the citie of *Rome* had not so
hastily declined, and fallen to her last ruine and destruction. *Sol:* But
Plutarch led with a contrarie opinion, commended the law *Agraria*, as
the worthiest act that ever *Tiberius* performed.[74] *Epi:* Therein he
erred much: for this law was not unworthy onely of a wise citizen in
those times, and in that manner as he then preferred the same, but
farther was the overthrow of the common-weale. *Sol:* It seemeth also
requisite, that so often as the subject or matter of this reformation
commeth in question, that we make a difference in the manner of
reforming of a free and popular estate, from the Monarchy; for in this
one, we shal wisely make a thorough alteration and change, without
leaving any resemblaunce or shadow thereof; but in the other, we are
to chaunge the substaunce, leaving in the place onely a shadowe and
resemblance of that which is chaunged, for the better contentment of
the people; for they discerne all things by the outward sence, and not
by the sounde discourse of reason, judging thinges to be such as they
seeme to be in outwarde appearance. This order did the *Romaines*
sometimes observe in instituting of there popular governement, and
in reforming of auncient lawes and customes, after they had expelled
their kings; for they [F4] altered the substaunce, and left in place

---

[74] Praise of Tiberius Gracchus by Plutarch: Ibid., vol. 6, "Tiberius and Caius
Gracchi," 74–81.

thereof onely a shadow and resemblaunce of the thinges altered; for in place of their kings they produced two Consuls, *sed unum tantum faces habere voluerant, & quidem totidem numero quot reges usurpare solerent:* and whereas their kings in person did perfourme certaine publicke sacrifices, *regem sacrificulum creant qui hisce sacris præesset, ut nequaquam apud eos regum desiderium esset.*[75] Thus by retayning the shadowe onely of auncient lawes and customes, the people remaine thereby perswaded, that nothing of the substaunce thereof is taken away or diminished: in like manner, they carefully observed this rule of pollicie in the creation and election of Magistrates and officers, for although they assigned unto them newe offices & functions, yet they did wisely holde the auncient names, stile, and number with their former magistrates, that the people might deeme thereby nothing to be altered and chaunged.

CAP. 16.

Of the right institution and reformation of a monarchie.

BUT otherwise wee are to institute and reforme a Monarchy, by making there a thorough alteracion and chaunge of auncient lawes, customes, and governement, yea and of the honours, titles, and dignities also, not leaving any shadow or resemblaunce in place thereof. For after this manner did king *David* establish an universall reformation. In like manner *Lysander,* did pull downe the pride of the citie of *Athens,* and tooke from them the libertie of a popular governement, whereby in former times it was ruled and governed, and established there sharpe and severe magistrates. But some others carried with a contrarie disposition of minde, have not attempted a thorough and generall reformation of the common-wealth, but reserved onely

---

[75] *Discursus,* 120, *Discorsi* 1.25: "when in place of a king they appointed two consuls, they decided that the latter should not have more than twelve lictors, so as not to exceed the number which had ministered to the kings ... and they did not wish the absence of the kings to arouse in the people a desire for anything pertaining to the past, they appointed a 'master of ceremonies' whom they called the 'sacrificial king' and put him under the high priest" (Walker, 175–76).

unto themselves a principalitie and commaundement, the which forme of governement was observed by *Sylla;* for when he had taken the citie of *Athens,* after the citizens had made fierce warres with him, yet hee [F4v] lefte it free unto them, enjoying their owne laws.[76] The same counsell did other of the *Romaines* followe, as it appeareth by the wordes of *Camillus* used unto the Senate after he had conquered the *Latines: Dii immortales ita vos potentes huius consilii fecerunt, ut sit Latium an non sit, in vestra manu posuerint, si vultis crudelius consulere in deditos victosque; sed si vultis exemplo maiorum augere rem Romanam victos in civitatem accipiendo, materia crescendi per summam gloriam suppetit.*[77] It seemeth therefore by the wordes of *Camillus,* that the *Romaines* made not at al times a thorough and universal reformation of common-weales which they gained by conquest, but embracing rather the counsell of *Sylla,* reserved onely a principalitie[j] and commaundement; for by this meanes, they did easily nourish the ambition which they had in conquering: for such as have a purpose to performe great actes, and to winne fame and glorie, having a mighty power to effect the same, they maie safely follow the steppes of *Sylla,* and other of the *Romaines,* they may say with *Camillus,* let us *exemplo maiorum augere rem Romanam victos in civitatem accipiendo, materia crescendi per summam gloriam suppetit:*[78] but such as shall contend to make continuance of their conquest, being not of great forces and power, should imitate *Lysander,* and make a thorough and absolute reformation of the whole common-weale. For *Plutarch* erred not, when he saide that *Sylla* did performe the greater actes, but *Lysander* committed the fewer faultes, and did possesse with greater securitie that which he conquered.[79] *Phillip* of *Macedonie,* followed the steppes of

---

[76] North, *Plutarch's Lives,* vol. 4, "Comparison of Sylla with Lysander," 120.

[77] *Discursus,* 366; *Discorsi* 2.23.2–4: "The immortal gods have vouchsafed to you the power to decide whether Latium is to be or not to be. Its future lies in your hands. In so far as the Latins are concerned, it rests with you to make a peace which shall be perpetual, either by punishing them cruelly or by pardoning them. Do you think it advisable to be brutal towards those who have surrendered and been conquered? If so you wipe out the whole of Latium. Do you want, after the manner of your forefathers, to augment the Roman state by admitting the conquered to citizenship? The material whereby to increase it to its great glorification lies ready to hand" (Walker, 348).

[78] See above, *Solon* II, note 77.

[79] North, *Plutarch's Lives,* vol. 4, "Comparison of Sylla with Lysander," 120.

Lysander, whereby, possessing at the first but a small kingdome, he became in a shorte time a mighty commaunder of all *Greece. Solo:* The Gaules in like manner following the steppes of *Lysander*, did securely possesse for a long time the partes of *Italie*, called *Longobardia:* some others have beene found neither to imitate *Sylla*, nor *Lysander*, but have helde a meane course betwixt both, in establishing their governement. Such were the *Florentines*, which in suppressing the rebellion of the *Aretines*, did remove some of their principall commaunders from their place and offices, others they bannished, manie they condemned, but they did not resume into their handes the landes, which might have afforded sufficient [G1] maintenaunce unto their citizens, neither did they destroy the principall citie, but preserved the same; whereby they lost the opportunitie of confirming their empire and governement, and of augmenting their common-weale. This meane course hath never as yet beene founde happy and prosperous: For not throughly conquering our enemy, neither by sworde, neither yet by our bountie and liberalitie, we may not long holde them, either as subjects or friendes.[80] Therefore such as shall contend to be prosperous, and make continuance of their state, and governement, must with the *Romaines*, so suppresse and sharpely punish the *Latines*, as at no time they be able to rebell, or with bounty and goodnes so winne the affections of the privernates, as at no time they should be willing to rebell.[81] *Epi:*[k] The meane course in times past hath beene holden for the governement of *Salamina* by a long space; In which times they were never founde happy and prosperous in their governement. *Sol:*[l] Now sith we have discoursed at large, of the reformation of auncient lawes and customes, and of the helps meanes and other rules therein to bee observed, as the first and principall matter in all reformations absolute and universall to be respected, there remaineth now a reformation of manners in the people, as a second matter worthily considered.

---

[80] Florence and the middle course: *Discorsi* 2.23.3.

[81] Rome and the Privernates: *Discorsi* 2.23.4. Machiavelli relates how the rebel Privernates, citizens of the Latin town of Privernum, were subdued by the Romans and liberally granted citizenship as a means of preventing further disturbances.

CAP. 17.

Of the reformation of manners, and how that this universal and
absolute reformation maie not be effected without
the same, and how that the corruption of
manners may be discerned by
his fruites and effectes.

PI: The reformation of manners, doth mightily advance all common-weales, and doth render them prosperous, and fortunate, of long continuance. *Sol:* Therefore not without cause did the *Romanes,* constitute Judges, and Censors of the manners of the people, which did carefully from time to time, execute all the lawes, *De morum censura.*[82] Neither was the place [G1v] of the Censores holden to be sacred, without due consideration of the common-wealth: Neither were they without cause above all other officers honoured in that common-wealth, in such sort, as they did depose, and displace, sometimes the Consuls, sometimes their Dictator, at their pleasure; for no doubt, what by the reformation made by the industry of their Censors, and by their skill and knowledge in militarie discipline, they quietly governed at home, and fortunately conquered abroad in all partes of the world.[83] Therefore since the reformation of manners, is a matter of so great importaunce unto estates and common-weales, it shall bee convenient, that you doe describe at large unto us what you intende thereby. *Epi:* We intende nothing els by a corruption of manners, but a departure from the feare and reverence of God, from the honour and obedience due unto Princes governours and Magistrates, from the love which wee owe unto our Country, and generally a declining from a just care and regarde of publike affaires, and all heroicall vertues, unto pleasures, wantonnesse, vices, and other such private respectes and regardes. *Sol:* You have exactly described the same; for as the fatnesse and goodnesse of the earth, is easily discerned by the large profit and benefite it yeeldeth to the labouring hande; and the goodnesse of the tree by his pleasaunt

---

[82] *Discursus,* 423; *Discorsi* 3.1: "the censorship" (Walker, 387).
[83] Institution of the censors: *Discursus,* 201–5; *Discorsi* 1.49.1–5.

fruite; so the corruption of manners in the people, by his infinite evils, miseries, common calamities, ruines, and destructiones of states, which everywhere it begetteth and bringeth forth, as by his several fruites and effectes may be discerned. For it breedeth in men a base opinion and estimation of vertues, and a contempt of magistrates, it offreth in open market the sale of offices, the voices of election, yea even Justice itselfe, it enableth *Cæsar* with the money of the *Gaules* to purchase not onely favour, and offices, but even the libertie of *Rome*. From this fountaine springeth ambition, desire of revenge, mutinies, sedition, treason, and rebellion, finallie it leaveth no place, no not the Senate house of *Rome*, nor the pulpit for orations, nor the image of *Pompey*, no not the open & publicke market places undefiled and free from bloud, no not the pallace of princes, *Ubi*[m] *Galba & Pertinaci accidit*, both which [G2] most vertuous kings were killed by their subjectes; the which mischiefe did arise unto them, chiefely for that the manners of their subjectes and souldiers were corrupted by the malice and evill governement of their predecessors, so as generally it may be reputed the mother, and nourse of al common calamities.[84] *Epi:* That detestable custome, and more detestable confirmation thereof, for receiving and supporting of traitours, rebels, and evil disposed persons, comming and arriving into the lande, did first occasion so generall a corruption of manners in *Salamina*, as more at large the same may appeare in the act of repeale thereof made by king H. the 7. [*Anno. 10. H.7*][85] *Sol:*[n] Sith then this generall corruption of manners doth draw with it so many publicke miseries and calamities, as are before remembred, we can not, except men be altogither voide of humanity and reason, but abhorre even the remembraunce of these lamentable times, and be forthwith kindled with a desire of reformation.

---

[84] *Discursus*, 59; *Discorsi* 1.10.6: "Where Galba and Pertinax were killed" (Walker, 136).

[85] Earlier (see above, *Solon* II, note 23) Beacon cites "An act annulling a prescription which traitors and rebels claimed within this land" as necessitated by the abuses of Richard III. The act abolished the custom of "protecting" and supporting rebels.

CAP. 18.

*The severall occasions which breede in the heartes of the people
or nation, a generall corruption of manners.*

EPI: That we may the better effect this reformation of manners,
it behooveth us to understande the severall occasions which
doe nourish the same, and lastly the sundry waies & meanes
which may be found for the better reformation thereof. *Sol:* First let us
understand the occasions as you have saide. *Epi:* Sometimes we
remaine corrupted in manners by ease, wealth and security, with the
Romaines after their severall conquestes of *Asia, Africa,* and the greatest partes of *Greece,* and with the invincible army of *Hanniball,* by the
pleasures of *Capua;* sometimes by bitter adversities, with the *Athenians*
we become haters & despisers of vertue, and we make unto ourselves
that hatefull lawe of *Ostracismus,*[86] whereby we banish and put to
death men of rare and excellent vertues, with the *Hectomarii* and
Hiereling; some-[G2v]times we mutine, and rise in armes against the
rich, and other times with the poorer sort of the oppressed faction of
Marius, we compasse the Senate house, and demaunde the delivery of
Cæsar; sometimes by the malice and practises of forreine enemies with
the *Ile* of *Euboea* and the other partes of *Greece,* by corruption of *Phil-
lippe* of *Macedonie* we depart from our obedience; sometimes by contempt and neglect of religion and the professors thereof with *Samaria*
& the citie of *Ninivie,* we fall into a generall corruption of manners,
lastly either by our lightnesse or incredulitie with the *Vandales,* sometimes in *Africa* of the *Arrian* sects we dismember the body of the
Church by sects and factions, so as either with the Churches of *Greece,
Rome,* and *Ravenna,* we rise in armes one against another, or at the
least the common people amiddest so great variation of sectes and
opinions, finding no ancore or place of rest, that may quiet their
troubled soules and consciences, die and live for the most part in
great anxietie and incredulitie.[87] *Sol:* Nowe you have at large dis-

---

[86] Ostracism: *Discorsi* 1.28.2; Walker, 179; North, *Plutarch's Lives,* vol. 3, "Life
of Aristides," 119–20.

[87] Hectomarii: *Solon* I, note 38; Faction of Marius: *Discorsi* 1.17.2; North,
Plutarch's Lives, vol. 5, "Life of Julius Caesar," 273. Ile of Euboea: Ibid., vol. 5,

cussed the occasions which maie draw the people into a generall corruption of manners, it shall not be impertinent, to intreate of the severall remedies which may be found to resist so great an evill, which worketh the ruine of states and common-weales.

CAP. 19.

The readie waies and meanes to reforme and resist a generall corruption of manners.

EPI: The chiefe and principall remedies are found to be in number three: namely a secret prudence and wisedome; secondarily good lawes well executed; thirdly a succession of severe Magistrates: for no doubt like as the wilde olive and figge tree, by the continuall addressing of a skilfull husbandman, is made at the last kindely, profitable, and fruitfull, and not inferiour to the naturall braunches; so a common-wealth overgrowne with a generall corruption of manners, and thereby become savage, barbarous, and barren, like unto the wilde [G3] olive and figge tree may by the continuall pruning and addressing of a skilfull magistrate, be made obedient, civill, and profitable unto that prince, whom God hath constituted to be the labourer in that vineyarde;[88] the which is to bee effected by the three waies and meanes before remembred: the first whereof is a secret prudence and understanding, wherein two matters principallie are found worthy of consideration: first the subject and matter; secondarily the time; for as the infirmities in our naturall bodies, growing uppon contrarie causes, receive not their cure by one selfesame councell, and medicine, for the which cause we endevour, to cure the frenzie by rest, and by motion the lethargie; so it fareth with the infirmities of a pollitike body; for where the corruption of manners in the multitude groweth by wealth, rest, and securitie, there it receiveth his present cure with the lethargie by motion, dispersing the humours, and finally by sharpe correction and discipline: but otherwise it is

---

"Life of Phocion," 362; Samaria and Niniveh: Jonah 1. Churches of Greece, Rome, Ravenna: Fenton, *Historie of Guicciardin* 4, 235–36.

[88] *Discorsi* 2.3.1.

where the same proceedeth from extreame adversitie for there it
receveth a happy cure, with the frenzie by ease, pacience, and suffer-
ance, for *Contraria subiecta non debent eodem modo tractari:*[89] Wherein
Charles the fift hath lefte unto us an example, when as he stoode
before *Meats* in *Loranie* with his army, which was then so distressed
by extreame sicknesse and famine, as they openly railed on him, especiallie his *Spanish* woulde call him the sonne of a mad woman with
all° the vile wordes they could devise, yet he would not heare them,
but threw crownes amongest them, saying to his nobilitie, harken
these knaves, yet if I call the worst by his name, he will not refuse to
doe anie thing for me though it cost him his life.[90] The like wisedome was shewed in the like matter by *Cato,* and other Senatours of
Rome, at such time as when the poore and needy persons which at
that time had reposed all their hope and confidence in *Cæsar,* had
compassed the Senate house and called aloude for *Cæsar* then accused
before the Senatours, bidding them to let him out, *Cato* then to
acquite the common-weale of the insurrection of the poore and needy
persons, did not severely correct them, but contrariwise perswaded
the Senate to make a francke distribution of corne amongst them for
one moneth the which amounted. to one [G3v] hundreth and fiftie
Myriades made at the common charge of the citizens, by the which
councell he quenched not onely a present great feare, but did in
happy time scatter and disperse abroade the best part of *Cæsars* force
and power, at such time as hee was made Prætor, and that for respect
of his office he was most to be feared.[91] The same councell did *Peri-*
cles sometimes imbrace, when as the people of *Athens* did mutine
against him, for that he would not suffer them to hazarde the battaile
with the *Lacedæmonian* army, then burning and spoiling in all the
partes of their countrie; for he did not then with bitter speeches and
sharpe punishmentes pacifie that mutinie, but contrariewise with a
large distribution which he caused to be made amongst them out of
the common treasure, and division of lands that were gotten by con-

---

[89] See above, *Solon* II, note 2.
[90] Charles V first conquered Metz in 1544 but was forced to raise his second
siege to reconquer Metz at the beginning of January 1553. See Bodin, *De Republica*
5, 5, for a description of the hardships of his army.
[91] North, *Plutarch's Lives,* vol. 5, "Life of Cato Utican," 422.

quest, he did quench that sedition.[92] And it is said, that when *Lucta-tius*, one of the greatest authority at that time in *Rome,* did inveigh against *Cæsar,* in that he had seditiously set uppe the honoures and victories of *Marius* contrarie to their publike lawes and decrees, and urged then a condigne punishment aunswerable to so greate an offence, he spake nothing for the punishment of the people which then gathered themselves together for the aide of *Cæsar,* and the rather for that they being of the faction of *Marius,* had bene long op-pressed and troden under foote by the authoritie of *Sylla.*[93] In like manner, when we shall beholde men of rare vertues and great des-ertes towardes the common-weale, in times of peace and libertie con-temned and despised, with *Narcetus* that rare and excellent captaine, least thereby they fal with him into a generall corruption of manners, and combine with the king of *Lombardy,* for the invading of *Italy,* wee shall wisely with the *Venetians* in such cases, alwaies better the fortune of those which have faithfully served, & never remove them from their former dignity, without giving to them places of higher and greater commaundement, and with *Themistocles* not only speedily revoke the banishment of *Aristides,* and such others of his quality, but also to advaunce them to greater honour then before, fearing least otherwise he take part with the Barbarian nation to the ruine of the state of *Greece.*[94] But herein one caution is wisely observed, that in such cases contending to [G4] remove a corruption of manners, which may otherwise possesse the mindes of rare and excellent personages, by a contempt and disdaine which followeth them, chiefly in times of happinesse, wealth, and securitie, wee doe not endaunger thereby the whole state of the common-wealth, the which wee shall then easilie prevent, if we shal not imploy them in the greatest places of

---

[92] Pericles' land distribution: *Discorsi* 2.10.8; North, *Plutarch's Lives,* vol. 2, "Life of Pericles," 13–14.

[93] North, *Plutarch's Lives,* vol. 5, "Life of Julius Caesar," 272–74.

[94] Narcetus: Machiavelli, *Istorie fiorentine* 1.8. Machiavelli derives from Isidore of Seville *Chronicon* 104, and Paulus Diaconus, *de Gest. Long.* 2.1–5 the legend of how Justinian dismissed the general Narsete (Lat. Narses), who then in revenge collaborated with the King of the Longobards, Alboin, to invade Italy. Beacon also alludes to his own career here, since Narcetus was dismissed by Justin for excessive extortion from the conquered inhabitants of Italy. Themistocles's ban-ishment of Aristides: North, *Plutarch's Lives,* vol. 1, "Life of Themistocles," 315.

commaundement, least contending to acquit themselves with *Claudius Nero*, of all disgraces and injuries wrought by the deceit of *Hasdruball*, they desperately hazarde, and put in adventure the whole state thereby.[95] Neither are wee in such cases with the *Romaines*, to give unto *Camillus* discontented with his banishment the supreame commandement of the City and army; for after slaughter made of all other their captaines by the power of the *Gawles*, they were ledde thereunto rather by necessitie, then by wisedome; neither doe all men banished and disgraced, carry with them that honourable minde of *Camillus*, and that ripenesse of judgement, to preferre the honour and publike good of the common-weale before his private reputation and welfare:[96] But on the contrary, if we shall labour to cure the corruption of manners that groweth by peace, wealth, and securitie, we are in such cases, with *Luctatius* to remove the same by sharpe discipline, whose councell if the Senatours had then followed, many miseries and publike calamities, which the ambition of *Cæsar* soone after wrought against the citie of *Rome*, had beene wisely foreseene and prevented: or otherwise in such cases, if wee shall like unto the wise phisition disperse abroad those pestilent humours according unto the example of *Camillus*, and with him imploye the citizens of *Rome*, now puffed up with the pride and insolency of their new obtained victorie and conquest of *Vies*, and with the rich spoiles thereof, now in mutinie against the Senatours and nobles, now resorting with great tumult about the pulpit for orations, for establishing of laws tending rather to the destruction then to the division of *Rome*, as in the warres against the *Phalerians*, and there besiege the chiefe citie, not so much with a purpose to winne the same, but rather with him to keepe our countrie men busied, least by repayring to *Rome*, they should take occasion to, mutine; [G4v] whereby with the wise phisition we shall desperse abroad those humoures, which may trouble the quiet state at home.[97] Lastly if wee shall wisely take holde of time, whilst she is running her swiftest course with her force and violence, perhaps we may be caried more then with an ordinary expedition unto the height

---

[95] Claudius Nero and Hasdruball: *Discorsi* 2.10.7.

[96] Punishment of Camillus: *Discorsi* 1.29.6.

[97] North, *Plutarch's Lives*, vol. 1, "Life of Camillus," 355.

of our thoughtes and desires; for the times which shall represent unto us the shew and face of publike calamities, as famine, plague, pestilence, povertie, and warres shall mightily advaunce this action of reformation: for so the Senatours of *Rome* by an appearaunce of forraine warres did often pacifie the mutinies and seditions of the citizens of *Rome,* raised for the law of division of lands gained by conquest: and the *Romaines* after the battell of *Cannes* gave due obedience unto Magistrates, and did severely prosecute their lawes against the *Vestall* Nuns, and finally whatsoever the Magistrates did commaunde, the people would most readily obey.[98] The like obedience was sometimes found unto lawes and Magistrates, after the people of *Rome* had received their overthrow by the power of the *Gawles,* in such sort, as the corruption of manners that then reigned in them was soone quenched and reformed. The times also which did produce sundry publike calamities in *Ulster* parcell of the dominions of *Salamina,* did worke there the like effectes, as it appeareth in the statute of Attainder of *Shane Oneile;* where it is saide after many publike calamities sustained by the warres, they cried first for mercy, and then for Justice, in such sort, as the reformation of that country did offer itselfe easie unto the handes of the Magistrates that woulde laie holde thereof, as by expresse wordes of that statute more at large may appeare.[99] Wisely therefore *Plutarch* in comparing the actes of *Fabius* with *Pericles,* saith, that *Pericles* governed the *Athenians* in their chiefest prosperity and wealth, whereby they were corrupted in manners, and rendered insolent, and mutenous, and not easily governed; but *Fabius* then governed *Rome,* when as it was humbled by many adversities, esteeming it a matter of no great difficultie, to rule a citie all ready brought low by adversitie, and which compelled by necessitie is contented to be governed by a wise man.[100] [H1] *Sol:* But sith this matter is at large discoursed, let us proceede unto the other meanes which are lefte unto us for the better resisting of a generall corruption

---

[98] Enforcement of laws against the vestals: Ibid., vol. 2, "Life of Fabius Maximus," 86–87. On the vestals: Ibid., vol. 1, "Life of Numa," 178–82; vol. 1, "Life of Camillus," 372–73.

[99] "the statute of Attainder of *Shane Oneile,*" see *Stat. Ire., 10 Hen. VI–14 Eliz.,* fols. 156–65; and see above, *Solon* I, note 3.

[100] North, *Plutarch's Lives,* vol. 2, "Pericles and Fabius," 101–5.

of manners, and what force, good & profitable lawes may have therein.

CAP. 20.

The necessitie of good and profitable lawes
for the better effecting of a
reformation of manners.

E PI: The *Ægyptians* by a long space prevented this generall corruption of manners, which either peace, wealth, security, or otherwise the fertility of place might breed in the hartes of the subjectes. The like lawes did *Romulus, Numa,* and other governoures which succeeded them, carefully from time to time establish, as neither their long peace and rest which they enjoyed in the governement of *Numa,* neither yet the fruitfulnesse of the soile of that empire, nor the commodities of the sea, neither their daily victories, could by the space of a long time and many ages, corrupt the manners of the people.[101] In like manner the *Germanes* above all others have best continued the integritie of manners in the subject, chiefly for that they have not onely beene most studious of profitable lawes, but also most faithful observers thereof, the which thing above all others hath preserved their people and country, as well from this corruption of manners, as also from the servitude and oppression of others. And where it is said, that *Spaine* hath not fallen so deepely as *Italy,* and *Fraunce,* into a generall corruption of manners, this proceedeth not from the goodnesse of their nature, but from the strict observation of the auncient lawes and customes of that kingdome.[102] *Sol:* I have viewed the lawes of *Salamina,* and I finde them no lesse profitable then the lawes either of the *Ægyptians, Romanes, Germanes,* or others whatsoever, for the reformation of manners, so as there remaineth nothing, but that with the *Germanes* wee be faithfull observers of our lawes: for so it may appeare [H1v] by expresse wordes contained in the statute made against marying and fostering, where it is related after this manner: [*Act 28. H.8 c.33. fo.1.*][103]

---

[101] *Discorsi* 1.1.11.

[102] Corruption in Germany, Spain, France, and Italy: *Discorsi* 1.55.2–3.

[103] "An act that none shall foster or marry with or to Irishmen," *Stat. Ire., 10 Hen. VI–14 Eliz.,* fols. 57–58.

Notwithstanding diverse good statutes and actes of parliament made for the reformation of that countrie, wherein is contained, that every of the kings subjectes offending the same, shoulde be a traitor attainted, yet by the default and negligence of the heads and rulers of that lande under the kings highnesse, the saide statutes were not duely put in execution, so as no reformation hath followed the same. In like manner, disorders were sometimes committed in the countries of *Flamminia* and *Emillia,* by the negligence of Magistrates in not executing the lawes, before Pope *Alexander* the sixt had wisely displaced and removed the negligent governoures thereof; before which time, these regions were full of theft, robberies, and rebellions, the which offences did not arise from the nature of the place or people, as some did then suppose, but rather from the malice and negligence of their governoures; for they beeing poore, woulde notwithstanding live richly, and sumptuously; they made lawes, and were the first that offended against the same, and by their example invited others thereunto; neither did they punish any that offended the lawes, untill they increased to great strengthes and numbers, *ac tunc demum* (saith the author of this historie) *non Iusticiæ conservandæ causa, sed prædæ dulcedine permoti, pœnas*[p] *ab omnibus simul gravissimas exigebant; ex qua re hoc sequebatur absurdum, ut expilati assiduis illis mulctis homines ad paupertatem redigerentur, atque hinc impellerentur ad vexandos alios, quibus existimabant se viribus esse superiores, quo quidem modo vitia non emendabantur, sed ad homines instituebantur, dependebantque hæc omnia ex prava eorum regulorum natura.*[104] Lastly, the many and sundry priviledges are found to give impediment unto the execution of profitable lawes, and to nourish a corruption of manners in the subject; as more at large it doth appeare in the act of Absentes, which is lefte unto us as a register of the fall and declination of the state of *Salamina,* wherein it is manifest that the Lordes of the several countries of *Catherlagh*

---

[104] Alexander VI and Romagna: *Discursus,* 559–60; *Discorsi* 3.29: "They then had recourse to punishment, not out of zeal for the laws they had made, but out of cupidity, that they might collect the fines imposed. This gave rise to numerous inconveniences, of which the worst was that it impoverished the people without amending them, and those who were impoverished sought to get the better of their weaker brethren. It was in this way that there arose all the evils mentioned above" (Walker, 483). For "ex qua re hoc sequeborur obsurdum." *Discursus* reads "ex qua re hoc existimarent."

and *Wexforde* being places priviledged, may keepe and holde al manner pleas within the same, under colour whereof the kings lawes, [H2]^q writtes, or other processe bee not obayed, neither any other Justice there administred, for the quieting and good order of the subject, so as in the default thereof, the kings enimies have them in servage, all murders, robberies, theftes, treasons, and other offences remaining there unpunished.[105] *Sol:* But what Magistrate may be found sufficient to establish a reformation of manners? *Epi:* A severe Magistrate is herein required: for that a common-weale mightily corrupted in manners, is squared and reformed onely by the rule and line of Justice which wee call distributive, the which for the inequality thereof, may not without great motions and sharpe remedies reforme the enormities and mischiefes of the common-weale. Lastly where the manners of the people remaine corrupted, there the lawes, *De morum censura*,[106] and all other lawes are found unprofitable, unles by a severe and stout Magistrate they be supported and maintained. For if *Brutus* had not severely proceeded, as well against his owne sonnes, as against all other traitours, he coulde not have reformed the corruptions of *Tarquine,* and of other his confederates.[107] *Sol:* He that shal in these waighty actions of reformation proceede as you have saide with lenitie and softnesse, shall never with *Collatinus* bee able to suppresse a corruption of manners in the subject, but he shall by that course rather imbolden and comforte traitours in their intended purposes;[108] therefore herein the wisedome of *Valerius* was highly commended, who though by nature curteous, and gentle, and thereof surnamed *Publicola,* yet by wisedome now became so severe & sharpe for the reformation & good of his countrie, as he most sharpely and bitterly prosecuted the treasons of *Tarquine.*[109] *Epi:* They which shall

---

[105] The 1537 act of absentees also eliminated the liberty jurisdictions of the absentee lords of these areas in Leinster, see above, *Solon II,* note 4.

[106] *Discursus,* 423; *Discorsi* 3.1.5: "the censorship" (Walker, 387).

[107] Sons of Brutus: *Discorsi* 1.16.10.

[108] "Collatinus softnes perilous": North, *Plutarch's Lives,* vol. 1, "Life of Publicola," 268.

[109] Valerius's severity in prosecuting the Tarquines commended: Ibid., vol. 1, "Life of Publicola," 262–70; vol. 1, "Comparison of Solon with Publicola," 298. In contrast, Machiavelli praises Valerius's gentleness as more effective than Manlius's harshness: *Discorsi* 3.22.5, 9.

live and governe *Sparta*, where the people are in manners corrupted, must with *Cleomenes* sharpely prosecute and punish offendours; but where the manners of the people be not corrupted, there a milde course of governement doth worke his office, and carrieth with it allowance and commendations.[110] For this cause it is said, that the patience of *Peter Soderin* was profitable as well to the common-weale as to himselfe, so long as age and time continued milde and gentle, but after the times were chaunged into an iron age, the [H2v] same then required a greater severitie then could be found in *Peter Soderin*, which by no meanes nor occasions, nor by the change of times, could be ledde from his accustomed patience, by the which he did not onely overthrow himselfe, but did also perish his whole countrie. Therefore very well saith a learned author, for the better reformation of manners corrupted in the people, and for the better reviving of the force of auncient lawes, a severe Magistrate is requisite.[111] *Sol:* But great is the hatred which in such cases followeth the person of a severe Magistrate, and it draweth with it sometimes perill and daunger unto Princes. *Epi:* This question admitteth one other distinction: for an absolute Prince is to imitate the humanity of *Cyrus* described by *Xenophon*, but such as shall governe by way of deputation, are rather to follow the severitie of *Manlius Torquatus*, least otherwise with *Peter Lawredane*, we doe not onely make the *Venetians* jelous, but also disable ourselves by our lenitie and softnes, to performe this difficult action of reformation, wherein severitie is required.[112] To conclude, it must be that grave and severe *Tymasitheus*, that shall reforme the licentious citie of *Lyparensis*, and drawe them from spoiling, praying, and rebelling. Lastly, wee must make a continuall succession of severe Magistrates, as before I have remembred. For *Epaminondas* with a just severitie may reforme a corruption of manners in the *Thebanes*, but if he once fortune to dye, the *Thebanes*

---

[110] *Discorsi* 1.9.5, relates how Agis, King of Sparta, was killed by the ephors. His successor Cleomenes realized that to maintain power he had to set himself up as sole authority and so had the ephors killed.

[111] Piero Soderini's errors, i.e., his "inability to emulate Brutus": *Discorsi* 3.3.2–3. For the need for a severe magistrate, see *Discorsi* 3.1.5.

[112] Machiavelli citing Xenophon on Cyrus: *Discorsi* 3.22.6; Manlius Torquatus: *Discorsi* 3.22.1–5; Peter Lawredane and the Venetians: *Discorsi* 3.22.11.

shall eftsoones returne to their former corruptions.[113] *Sol:* Nowe sith you have at large discussed of the two partes and members of this universall and absolute reformation, namely the reformation of auncient lawes, customes, and lastly the corruption of maners in the people, there remaineth nowe a newe and better institution then before prescribed, as the third and last member of your generall division. *Epi:* I will proceede then unto the institution itselfe, wherein foure matters are found worthie of consideration: first, the soveraintie and commaundement; secondly, the forme of governement; thirdly, the forme and manner of the institution itselfe: lastly, the severall endes and scopes of this institution.[r] For the first, which is the soverainty and commaundement, the same is given sometimes into the hands of one, [H3] sometimes in the handes of fewe, and sometimes into the handes of all in generall. This one is termed a *Democratia,* or a popular estate; the other an *Aristocratia;* the last a Monarchie. Thus be common-weales properly distinguished by the soveraintie and commaundement, and not by the diversity which sometimes appeareth in the forme and governement thereof: for all institutions are made after the one of these kindes, and all other are but corruptions of these estates, and no proper or distinct common-weales.[114] *Sol:* But which institution is to be preferred above others? *Epi:* The institution no doubt of the Monarchie, is the most firme and durable, and freest from al dissention, mutinies, and sedition. And the wise men of *Rome* were not deceived, when beholding the market place filled with bowes, slings, and swordes, and the pulpit for orations sprinckled with bloud, they said, there remaineth nowe no other way to give helpe and remedie to these troubles of our common-weale, but the authority of one man onely, that may commaunde us all. And as this estate is freest from trouble, as you have saide, so is it of all others most honourable and glorious, and even the very lively image of God and nature, as *Artibanus* did sometimes faithfully deliver unto *Themistocles.*[115] The next manner of institution in account, seemeth to be

---

[113] Timesitheus, Lipari: Livy 5.28; North, *Plutarch's Lives,* vol. 1, "Life of Camillus," 358; Epaminondas: *Discorsi* 1.17.5.

[114] See *Discorsi* 1.2; Aristotle, *Politics* 2.6, 3.6; *Nichomachean Ethics,* 8.10.

[115] Themistocles & Artibanus: North, *Plutarch's Lives,* vol. 1, "Life of Themistocles," 336–37.

the *Aristocratia*, for that it acquiteth itselfe best of al other common-weals, from corruption & errours in their censures and judgements: for as the large and running waters, are not so easily corrupted, as the standing poole; so many wittes, and mindes, are not so easily deluded and corrupted, as one. But worst of all others doeth this common-weale acquite itselfe of envie, dissention, and emulation amongest themselves, which like unto a mothe or worme, gnaweth asunderᵉ the heart and intralles of that common-weale, and at the last confoundeth and destroieth the same. But yet the popular estate is of all others least permanent, especially where the common-weale is mere popular, aswell in regard of the soveraintie and commaundement, as of the forme & manner of governement; wherof the common-weale of *Athens* maie be unto us an example, which was instituted by you *Solon*, and after in the same age confounded by *Pisistratus. Solo:* [H3v] So it was: for wanting sufficient power and forces, I was forced to make such lawes for the instituting of that common-weale, as they were willing to receive, and not such as I was willing to give: for I must confesse, that popular institution, which is equallie tempered, and compounded of the three sortes and formes of governement, after the maner and institution of *Rome,* to be more firme and durable; and this forme of governement also doeth give a perfection and continu-ance to all other estates before remembred.[116] Therefore *Romulus* after the death of *Remus,* and *Tatius Sabinus,* did ayme at that forme of government in the institution of the common-weale of *Rome;* for he reserved unto himselfe the sole and kingly auctority over the armie onely, and to convent the Senators for the affaires publicke, the which forme of governement, in his person was kinglike, and after the forme of a Monarchie; but in the person of the Senators, who had auctoritie to consulte, and publikely to perswade and disswade the attempts for wars, and to discusse all other civill causes, as the state of that com-mon-weale required, the forme of an *Aristocratia,* was rightly by him observed; and in the other partes of his governement, as in framing of his lawes and such like, he rather affected a popular liberty, then a Monarchie.[117] *Epi:* After this manner the king of *France* hath

---

[116] Praise for Rome's mixed constitution: *Discorsi* 1.2.17–18.
[117] Tatius Sabinus & Remus, killed by Romulus: *Discorsi* 1.9.1–4.

reserved unto himselfe a kingly name, stile, honors,ᵗ authority, and
commandement over the Senate, and to assemble them for the affaires
publicke, and a sole absolute and royall authority over the armie for
making or finishing the warres, lastly an authority for the levieng and
receiving of the revenews belonging to the crowne, but the execution
of lawes he leaveth to the Senate, and Judges, who governe by such
lawes as respect a popular liberty and free estate, in the making of
which lawes, the people have also their voices, like as in popular
estates, where the people holde the soverainty and commaundement;
so as by this forme of governement as well to the king, and the
nobles, as also to the people, such power is graunted, with so just and
equall proportion, as either the dignitie of the one, or the liberty of
the other may justly require; in the well tempering wherof, all the
skill, arte, and pollicie of governement is wholy contained, and he
that [H4] shall holde the best and most just temperature herein,
commeth nearest to the perfection of nature; who by how much more
equally shee doth temper the foure humours and elements in our
naturall bodies, by so much we receive a more perfit strength, & a
longer being & continuance.¹¹⁸ *Sol:* This is the best forme of instituting of common-weales, the which you have now described; but in this
institution some are founde to ayme at peace, some at honour, as the
butte and scope of all their actions; so as their ende and scope being
divers, it seemeth they may not imbrace one forme of institution. *Epi:*
You say well: for they which shall aime at a common-weale peaceable
& permanent, it behoveth them to seclude strangers, not to traine
their people and subjectes in militarie discipline, according to the
example of the *Lacedæmonians,* and to possesse a place or fort, as well
by nature and the situation thereof, as by art rendred invincible,
according to the example of the *Venetians.*¹¹⁹ But such as shal ayme
at honour and glory, as the butte & scope of their institution, must
entertaine straungers, they must indevour to render the common-
wealth populous, they must daily traine and exercise the people in
military discipline, and they shal wisely deliver the feble, and weake,
from the hands of the oppressour, they must entertaine many associ-

---

¹¹⁸ Praise for France: *Discorsi* 1.16.9.
¹¹⁹ Example of the Spartans and Venetians: *Discursus,* 36–38; *Discorsi,* 1.6.2–7.

ates & friends, by the which pollicies they shall render themselves
everywhere invincible according to the example of the *Romanes*. *Sol:*
But what manner of institution is most permanent and to be preferred? *Epi:* Neither the one nor the other may be founde so happy
and permanent, but at the last, with the apple in his ful ripenes, they
fall with their owne weight and poyse to the ground; the one by
discord and mutinies of the soldiours, for that their citizens are
rendred bold by the continual use and trayning in military discipline;
the other by effeminacie, ease, rest, and security, hasteneth in like
maner unto mutinies and discords, as to his last ruine; so as either by
a fatall destinie (as it were) imbraceth there owne confusion: but not
after one manner; for the one like unto a flowre, or the pride of
youth, in the height of his glory, vanisheth, away, and leaveth the
image of true glory, as a lively picture, to invest a perpetuall memory
of a worthy and excellent Institution. But the common-weale [H4v]
which in his first Institution aymeth only at peace and permanency,
with effeminacy, discorde, and mutinies, bredde by long ease, rest,
and security, embraceth with the other his final & last destruction, but
leaveth not the like memory of his Institution. *Sol:* It seemeth then by
that which you have said, that the institution of that common-weale,
which aymeth at vertue, honour, and glorie, is to be preferred before
the other, & of princes much more to be desired. But may not one
selfesame common-weale, ayme at the one and the other? *Ep:* No
verily: for as the tree which hath but a slender roote, may not long
support waighty and mighty braunches, against the furie and violence
of the winde and tempest; so common-weales which ayme at peace,
having but a slender roote, and foundation, laide for the supporting
thereof, as before I have remembred, may not be long victorious, and
hold themselves upright in actions of great importance: and if they
fortune to be so with the *Venetians*, which have much regarded this
manner of institution, they shal no sooner winne, but eftsoones for
want of proper forces to defende, they shall loose the same againe: so
as for free estates and common-weales, this manner of institution
seemeth not to be the best, but for servile common-weales, and such
as have lived alwaies subject to others, as *Pisa* sometimes to the *Florentines*, *Cremona* to the *Venetians*, and *Salamina* to *Athens*, it may be
holden for the safest: for by this maner of Institution, they shall more
easily retaine the subjectes in their obedience and subjection.

THE THIRD BOOKE OF
Solon his follie.

CAP. I.

A defcription of this worde Declination, with the feverall
fignes and tokens thereof, whereof fome are tear-
med ordinary, others extraordinary.

 OL: You have made a perfect anatomye of this
worde Reformation, and not onely with the cun-
ning Painter you have defcribed the outwarde
fhews and lineaments, but with the wife Phifition
you have well knowen, and laid open the inward
partes therof: but now difclofe vnto vs, the fecrets
which lie hidden vnder the words fubfequent, and contained in
the firft and generall defcription, namely of a declined common-
weale, *Ep:* Thefe words offer fundry matters worthy of confidera-
tion. *Sol:* What be they? *Epi:* Firft, the defcription of this word
Declination; fecondly, the fignes and tokens; thirdly, the times;
fourthly the partes and members; fiftly, the caufes and occafions;
and laftly, the meanes to refift the fame. *Sol:* Make the firft ftep
vnto the defcription thereof, which is the firft matter herein to be
confidered. *Epi:* A Declination of a body politicke, is nothing els
but a fall and departure from his firft inftitution, and perfection, fo
as we may rightly tearme it the fubiect and matter of this our reformation. *So:* You have aptly defcribed the fame: therefore make
your progreffion vnto the fecond matter, and declare vnto vs the
fignes and tokens, which with *Ionas* as forerunners and meffen-
gers, giveth the City of *Ninivie* to vnderftand of their declination,
and deftruction. *Epi:* The death of noble and worthy perfona-
ges, doeth threaten a declination of the welfare and happines of

I

eftates,

THE THIRD BOOKE OF
Solon his follie.

CAP. 1.

A description of this worde Declination, with the severall
signes and tokens thereof, whereof some are
tearmed ordinary, others extraordinary.

 *OL:* You have made a perfect anatomye of this worde Reformation, and not onely with the cunning Painter you have described the outwarde shews and lineaments, but with the wise Phisition you have well knowen, and laid open the inward partes therof: but now disclose unto us, the secrets which lie hidden under the words subsequent, and contained in the first and generall description, namely of a declined common-weale. *Ep:* These words offer sundry matters worthy of consideration. *Sol:* What be they? *Epi:* First, the description of this word Declination; secondly, the signes and tokens; thirdly, the times; fourthly,[a] the partes and members; fiftly, the causes and occasions; and lastly, the meanes to resist the same. *Sol:* Make the first step unto the description thereof, which is the first matter herein to be considered. *Epi:* A Declination of a body polliticke, is nothing els but a fall and departure from his first institution, and perfection, so as we may rightly tearme it the subject and matter of this our reformation. *So:* You have aptly described the same: therefore make your progression unto the second matter, and declare unto us the signes and tokens, which with *Jonas* as forerunners and messengers, giveth the City of *Ninivie* to understand of their declination, and destruction.[1] *Epi:* The death of noble and worthy personages, doeth threaten a declination of the welfare and happines of [I1v] estates, and common-weales. For the first token (saith *Plutarke,*) that threatned some great mischiefe to the common-wealth of

---

[1] Jonah 1.

Rome, was the death of *Iulius* one of the Censores: for the *Romanes,* saith he, doe greatly reverence the office of a Censor, and esteeme it as a sacred place.[2] *Sol.* And hath not the cittie of *Rome,* of late yeares beene deprived of grave and worthy Censores, by untimely death, not inferiour to *Iulius?* *Epi:* Yes verily: and for this cause we are greatly to feare that chaunging our auncient Consuls for new *Decemviri* with the citie of *Rome,* wee perish and fall in actions of great importaunce and difficulty: and therefore with that faithfull and worthy citizen *Camillus,* I pray dailie uppon my knees, that this bitter calamitie unto us now threatned, if the same may not be turned from us, doe light upon myselfe, and such other private citizens of *Rome,* that have deserved the same, so as the citie with her noble armie and forces may be preserved.[3] *Sol:* Passe this over with this comfort, that the new *Decemviri* retaine in them the great vertue and worthines even of the auncient Consuls; and proceede unto signes of declination. *Epi:* There may not be greater signes founde of common calamities ensuing, then an universall securitie, which sometimes possesseth the mindes and heartes of the subjectes. The which was founde in the *Romanes,* at such time as they sustained the great overthrow by the power of the *Gawles;* for then all sortes of persons in the citie were founde to be possessed with a generall securitie, in so much[b] that they neglected all religion, they contemned the holy order of the *Fæcials,* and made no account of their propounded religion, and lastly they were founde so secure, as they neglected all their former discipline of warres, yea they jested and made themselves merry with *Marcus Cedicius,* which gave them warning thereof.[4] In like manner a generall security did possesse the *Philistians,* when as *Jonathan* said to the young man that bare his armoure, come, and let us go over unto the garrison of these uncircumcised, for it is not hard for the Lord to save with many or with few, so as they both shewed themselves to the *Philistians;* but they as men secure, scorned *Jonathan,* and said, see the *Hebrewes* come out of the holes wherein they have hid themselves for a [I2] long

---

[2] The death of Julius the Censor was seen as a sign of the coming war with the Gauls: North, *Plutarch's Lives,* vol. 1, "Life of Camillus," 363.

[3] Fear of Decemviri: *Discorsi* 1.40.6.

[4] Fetiales: North, *Plutarch's Lives,* vol. 1, "Life of Camillus," 367; Marcus Cedicius: Ibid., 364.

time, but *Jonathan* eftsoones put them to the sworde.[5] But for that the
histories and reportes of ages past, doe afforde infinite proofes and
examples hereof, let us proceede readily unto other signes and tokens
of declinations. *Sol:* Before a generall declination, the people are found
possessed with a generall feare; for before the overthrow given by
Samuel unto the *Philistians,* the people were holden with a mighty
feare of their future fortunes, and of the event of those warres, inso-
much as it is saide, there was a feare in the hoast, and in the fielde,
and amonge all the people, the garrison also and they that went out
to spoile were afraide themselves, and the earth trembled, for it was
striken with feare by the Lord.[6] And after this manner *Christe* pro-
phecieyng of the destruction of *Jerusalem,* unto such as asked what
signes shal there be when these thinges shall come to passe, he saide,
there shall be trouble upon earth, and amonge nations perplexity, &
mens heartes shall faile them for feare, and for looking after those
things which shall come on the worlde.[7] *Epi:* After such time as
Camillus was unjustly condemned and banished, there was not a
Romane of any understanding, but believed certainely, that some great
punishment would follow them incontinently, and that the wronge
and injurie which they had done him, would be quicklie requited
with some sharpe and terrible revenge, not onlie unpleasaunt to
thinke uppon, but farther most notable to be spoken of thorough the
world: then fell out so sodainely upon the same, such mischiefes towardes the citie of *Rome,* as it was doubted to bee the handy worke of
some God, that woulde not suffer vertue to be unrecompensed with
ingratitude.[8] *Sol:* There remaineth yet a greater signe of declination.
Epi: What may the same be? *Sol:* When the common-wealthes shall
generally depart from all the partes and right rules of governement,
the same is a manifest signe of declination. For before the overthrow
of *Rome* by the power of the *Gawles,* there was found all disorder and
confusion, they were not governed by one selfesame commaunder, as
in former times, but their governoures being many, contrary to the

---

[5] 1 Samuel 14.6,11.

[6] Fear of Israelites: 1 Samuel 7.7.

[7] Matthew 24; Luke 13.34; Mark 13.

[8] Banishment of Camillus: North, *Plutarch's Lives,* vol. 1, "Life of Camillus,"
363.

discipline of warres, bredde naught else but confusion. The like disorder did they admit in all the other partes of [I2v] their governement,
as in the historie thereof more at large appeareth, the which did
breede the ruine and destruction of that citie. These bee the ordinary
signes of declination. *Sol:* You seeme hereby to give us to understande
of signes extraordinary. *Epi:* Yea verily. *Sol:* What be they? *Epi:* Great
earthquakes shalbe in divers places, hunger, pestilence, and fearefull
thinges, and great signes shall there be in heaven, there shall be
signes in the sunne, and the moone, and in the starres, the sea and
waters shal roare; this is the time wherein *Jerusalem* shal be troden
under foote of the *Gentiles,* untill the time of the *Gentiles* be fulfilled;
these be the times wherein they shall fall on the edge of the swoorde,
and shalbe ledde captive to all nations; these be the signes whereby
as by the budding of the figge tree, wee knowe summer to bee neare
at hande, so by these we may discerne common calamities a farre of,
as also when they approach neare unto us.[9] *Sol:* Before *Cæsar* was
murdered in the Senate house, there appeared many terrible signes in
the heavens, in the aire, and uppon the earth, which did threaten his
overthrowe and destruction, and many common calamities unto that
citie: in like manner before the sacking, burning, and destroying of
Rome by the *Gaules,* one *Marcus Cedicius* a man of faire condition,
honest, and of good conscience, tolde unto the Tribunes a thing that
was well to be considered of: for he saide that the night before as he
was going on his waie, in the new streete, he harde one call him
alowde, and returning backe to see what it was, he sawe no living
creature, but onely hearde a voice bigger then a mans, which saide
unto him, *Marcus Cedicius,* goe thy way tomorrowe morning to the
Tribunes of the souldiers, and bid them looke quicklie for the
Gaules.[10] *Epi:* Surely God governeth the worlde, and the creatures
uppon earth, mercifullie and lovingly, in sending sometimes *Marcus
Cedicius* unto the citie of *Rome,* yea sometimes *Jonas* unto the citie of
Ninivie, nay that which is more, in making the dumbe creatures, as
well in heaven as in earth, to speake unto us, and foretell us of our

---

[9] Luke 20.24.

[10] "signes that were sayd to be seene before Caesars death": North, *Plutarch's
Lives,* vol. 5, "Julius Caesar," 341. Marcus Cedicius, see above, *Solon* III, note 4.

destruction. *Sol:* To the good they be tokens of his mercie and favour, and to the wicked they threaten his Justice and judgement, so as what the highest hath determined in his se-[I3]cret fore-knowledge, the same shall stande and may not passe. For in vaine shall *Calphurnia* crie out in the night, *Cæsar* is slaine, for hee shall not give credit unto dreames; in vaine shall she perswade him in the day to keepe his house, & not to go abroad, for he shalbe deluded with the hopes and flatteries of *Brutus;* in vaine shall the southsaier forewarne him of his destruction, for he shal not regarde prophecies; in vaine doe his friendes and welwillers set downe in writing the daies, times, and meanes of his destruction, and deliver the same into his handes, for he shall not once reade or regarde it; so the highest hath determined and the same shall stand and may not passe: *Brutus* shall flatter, wounde, and kill him, and he shall fall with the stroke thereof; in vaine shall *Marcus Cedicius* forewarne the Tribunes of the people, that the *Gaules* with their armie are marching towardes *Rome,* for they shall laugh and make themselves merry thereat, and not foresee howe they may resist them; they shal be as men amazed and bewitched, and forget even their ordinarie discipline, and fall into all disorder of governement, their Citie shall be wasted and destroyed; for so the highest hath determined, and the same shall stande and may not passe. *Epi:* To this purpose *Plutarch* writing of the death of *Cæsar,* saieth, that the declinations and destinies are more easily foreseene then avoided.[11]

CAP. 2.

The times wherein common-weales doe usually fall and decline.

S OL: But what may be the times ordained by a secret fore-knowl-edge in the brest of the highest, of the declination of common-weales? *Epi:* The same onely is known to the highest, and to us left uncertaine. *Sol:* But what doth hee not manifest everywhere by his ordinary power and governement of this inferiour worlde, of that

---

[11] North, *Plutarch's Lives,* vol. 5, "Julius Caesar," 340–41.

whereof we may in no sort be ignorant? *Epi:* By his ordinary governement you meane naught els but his power, wherby he giveth to all
things their first being, pro-[I3v]gression, continuance, perfection, and
declination. *Sol:* Thus you make the perfection of all thinges, to be the
ende of his continuance, and the beginning of his declination, and to
be the last shewe of his being, and the first of his declining. *Epi:* I will
shewe you the trueth, even from the mouth of that Prophet *Daniell,* a
mighty king shall stande up, saieth he, that shall rule with great dominion and doe according to his pleasure, and when hee shall stande
uppe, his kingdome shall be broken, and shall be devided towardes
the foure windes of the heavens, and not to his posterity nor according to his dominion, which he ruled, for his kingdome shalbe pluckt
uppe by the rootes, and the same given unto others.[12] *Sol:* By this
example, you seeme to inferre, that kingdomes and principalities,
being at the highest, doe then decline and fall: for so did this mighty
king *Alexander* (whome the Prophet *Daniell* nowe intendeth) sometimes rule great dominions, but even then saieth the Prophet did he
perish, even when he commanded at his pleasure, and lastly, even
when this king (saith the Prophet) did stand uppe, and was at the
highest, even then did he fall with a disease which followed his
drunkennes and superfluitie, or otherwise by the poison which was
given by *Cassander,* even then was his kingdome broken, saith the
Prophet, and pluckt uppe by the rootes, even then was the time
wherein it was devided amongst straungers, namely his twelve
chiefe princes, and not given unto his posterity, then it was wherein
his posterity did murther and destroy one the other, even these were
the times, wherein his kingdome soone after was devided towardes
the foure windes of the heavens: for *Seleucus* had *Siria, Antigonus Asia
Minor, Cassander the kingdome of Macedonia,* and *Ptolomæus Ægypt.*[13]
Ep: You well understande as well the matter, as my meaning, and to
the same purpose, saieth the Prophet *Daniell,* there shall arise a king
so mighty, that he shall doe what him list, he shall exalte and magni-
fie himselfe, against all that is God, but when his glorie shall be

[12] Daniel 11.3–4.
[13] Commentary on Daniel 11.3–4, *Geneva,* 363. See also: North, *Plutarch's Lives,*
vol. 5, "Life of Alexander the Great," 263–65.

everywhere encreased, then the king of the South shall pushe at him, and the king of the North shall come against him, and like a whirle-winde, with chariots, and horsemen, and with manie shippes, shall enter his pleasant [I4] countrie, and have power over all the treasures of golde and silver, and over all the princes things of *Ægypt*, and none shall bee founde that may withstande him, he shall plant the tabernacles of his pallace, betweene the seas and the glorious and holy mountaine, but even then is the time, saieth the Prophet, that he shall come to his ende, and none shall helpe him.[14] *Sol:* These were the *Romanes,* which sometimes raigned upon earth like Gods: but even then eftsoones they perished as men. For when *Augustus* had overcome the *Parthians,* and recovered that which *Antonius* lost, when they were found to raigne quietly from sea to sea, and in *Judea,* then came they to their ende, and none was founde that could helpe them.[15] *Epi:* The same Prophet saieth, the king of the South shall be angry with the king of the North, and shall set forth a great multi-tude, and fight with the king of the North, and the multitude shalbe given into his handes, then the multitude shalbe prowde, and their hartes shalbe lifted uppe, for he shal cast downe thousandes, but he shall not still prevaile, for the king of the North shall come and cast uppe a mount and take the strong Citie, and the armes of the South shall not resist, neither shall there be anie strength to withstand, but he shall come and doe with him what he list, and none shall stande against him.[16] *Sol:* The Prophet intendeth *Philopater* which sometimes governed great dominions, yet coulde he not withstand the power of *Antiochus,* & *Phillip* king of *Macedonie,* which then came against him, neither shal the *Ægyptians* be able to resist *Stopus Antiochus* captaine, for this is the[c] time wherein none shall bee founde that may with-stande them.[17] *Epi:* And in the same place it is saide, that when the king of the North shall take the stronge citie, yea even when the

---

[14] Daniel 11.3–45.

[15] "For Augustus overcame the Parthians, and recovered that which Antonius had lost. The Romaines after this reigned quietly through all countries & from sea to sea, and in Judea: but at length for their crueltie God shal destroy them" (commentary on Daniel 11, *Geneva,* 365).

[16] Daniel 11.11–17.

[17] Commentary on Daniel 11.10–15, *Geneva,* 363.

armes of the king of the South shall not resist him, yea then when
there may not be founde any strength to withstande him, even then
when he hath planted himselfe in the pleasant lande, even then, saith
the Prophet, shall a Prince be founde, which shall cause his shame to
light uppon him, beside that hee shall cause his owne shame to turne
uppon himselfe by retiring towardes the fortes of his owne lande, but
he shall be overthrowne and fall, and be no more founde.[18] *Sol:* Thus
did *Antio-*[I4v]*chus* sometime fall, whom the Prophet heere intendeth,
when as *Attilus* and *Lucius Scipio,* did put him to flight, so as for feare
of the *Romanes,* hee was forced to flie to his holdes and fortes, and
after robbing the temple of *Iupiter Dodonæus,* was slaine by the people
of the country:[19] so as we may inferre by these examples nothing els,
but that common-weales doe participate with the qualitie and nature
of all other creatures, in that first they have their being, their progression, their continuance, their perfection, and lastly their declination;
so as from their being they receive progression, from progression they
receive continuance, from continuance a perfection, from their perfection a declination: for his perfection is naught els, but his ripenesse
which is gathered by continuance, by whose poyse and weight, eftsoones it falleth to the ground and declineth. *Epi:* You well understande the matter. *Sol:* Then let us make our progression unto the
partes and members of every declination.

CAP. 3.

All declinations are in number two, the one ad sanitatem,
the other ad interitum.

E PI: All declinations are after two sortes: the one, *ad sanitatem;*
the other, *ad interitum;* both which declinations did sometimes
appeare in the common-wealth of *Rome:* the one, when as the
Senate and people by contending for honours, gave occasions of most
happy lawes, and more happy restitution of the declined state of that

---

[18] Daniel 11.16–19.

[19] Anticochus: robbing the temple of Jupiter Dodonaeus: Commentary on
Daniel 11.18–19, *Geneva,* 364. See also: Lucius Scipio's defeat of Antiochus, Livy
27.59.

polliticke body. But after declining by peace, rest, and security, unto a corruption of manners, they never could give an ende unto their contentions then raised for profitte and gaine, so as the same may be said to be a final declination, not *ad sanitatem*, but *ad interitum*.[20]

CAP. 4.

The severall occasions and causes of all declinations, and first of occasions malitiously suggested.

SOL: There remaineth nowe that we doe proceede unto the occasions and causes of all declinations, which is the fifte matter remembred by you worthy of consideration. *Epi:* You have well put me in remembrance thereof. For as the declination of our natural bodies ariseth chiefely either from occasions, as rest, labour, heate, colde, hunger, thirst, superfluity, abundance, or from the malice or distemperature of the disease or sickenes itselfe: so the declination of this polliticke bodie groweth partly by occasions, and partly from the malice and corruption of the subject, as from the unnatural distemperature of that body. *Sol:* The truthe of your opinion neither wanteth proofe nor example: for in the declination of the commonweale of *Rome*, in the times and regiment of *Tarquine*, we may behold first a generall distemperature bred in the body of that commonweale by his misgovernment, so as the people and Senatours did expect nothing more then a fitte occasion to execute the same. And if the deflowring of *Lucretia* had not happened, yet noe doubt this distemperature and malice of the subject would have attended other occasions, as they should conveniently have offered themselves. But if this malice and distemperature had not proceeded with the occasion, or if the occasion had not accompanied this distemperature, no doubt *Brutus* and *Collatinus* would have desired the just punishment of this offence, rather at the hands of *Tarquine*, then by the aide &

---

[20] declination, not *ad sanitatem*, but *ad interitum*: not for health but for destruction. Machiavelli explains how discord between the Senate and people promoted Rome's liberty (*Discorsi* 1.4) but also brought about its destruction through the Agrarian laws (1.37.5,8).

helpe of the people.[21] *Ep:* Therefore wisely saith one, *sine occasione frustra virtus, sine virtute frustra occasio sese obtulit.*[22] For in vaine shall occasions profer themselves, where they finde not the malice of the subject ready to rescue and assist them. And in vaine likewise shall the malice of the subject swel and overflow his bounds, when all occasions shall be removed, which are in place of the feete and [K1v] legs[d] that support this distemperature. *So:* To disclose therefore the chiefe & principal occasions, which may further and nourish any way the distemperature of this polliticke body, seemeth a matter not unworthy of deliberation. *Epi:* Nay it is a matter rather which should possesse the highest thoughts of the minde & understanding of Princes and Emperours. *Sol:* Let us proceede to enumber them if we may, and set them downe under the accompt of matters necessarie for the better sustaining and upholding of this polliticke body. *Ep:* Occasions are usually after two sortes: either given; or malitiously sought and suggested. *Sol:* You have saide the truth: for when *Darius* preferred *Daniell* above all the other rulers and governours, because the spirit in him was excellent, they sought an occasion against *Daniell*, concerning the kingdome, but they coulde finde no fault, and therefore it is saide, we may finde no occasion against *Daniell*, except we finde it against him concerning the lawe of God: whereupon the rulers craftely conspired to go unto the king, and after this maner to advance their malice they spake unto him, king *Darius* live for ever: all the rulers of thy kingdome, the officers and governours, the counsellers and dukes have consulted togither to make a decree for the king, and to establish a statute, that whosoever shall aske a petition of any God or man for thirty daies save of thee O king, he shall be cast into the denne of Lions. Nowe O king confirme the decree, and seale the writing that it be not chaunged according to the lawe of the *Medes* and *Persians* which altereth not. This request feeding the ambition of king *Darius*, was eftsoones sealed by him, & he made a law and decree. Then these men assembled and found *Daniell* praying and making supplication unto his God. The which eftsoones they embraced as a fit occasion

---

[21] *Discorsi* 3.5.1.

[22] Telius, 32; *Principe* 6: "without opportunity their prowess would have been extinguished, and without such prowess the opportunity would have come in vain" (Bull, 50). Beacon's translation follows the quotation.

lente for the destroying of *Daniell*, and repayring to the king, saide
unto him after this manner, hast thou not sealed the decree that every
man that shall make request to any God or man within thirty daies
save to thee O king shall be cast into the denne of Lyons? the king
answered and saide, the thing is true according to the lawe of the
Medes, and *Persians,* which altereth not. Then aunswered they and
saide unto the king; this *Daniell* which is of the children of the [K2]
captivity of *Judah,* regardeth not thee O king, nor the decree that thou
hast sealed, but maketh his petition three times a day. But understande O king, that the lawe of the *Medes* and *Persians* is, that no
decree or statute which the king confirmeth, may be altered or broken. Then forthwith by the kings commandement, *Daniell* was cast
into the Lyons denne. This one example may suffice for occasions
malitiously suggested.[23]

CAP. 5.

Of occasions given by misgovernement, and such other meanes.

SOL: Let us now proceed to enumber the occasions given. *Ep:*
Occasion of declining is then given, when the nobility is not respected: for *Cæsar* by holding a light estimation of the Senators
and nobles, as such time as they repayred to give unto him honours,
and by depriving and abusing the Tribunes *Marullus* and *Flavius,* did
give the first occasion, saith *Plutarch,* of his fall & declining: & *Romulus* intreating the Senators and nobles of *Rome,* more severely and rig-
orosly then in former times they were accustomed, was for this cause
by treason murthered.[24] *Sol:* And no lesse occasion is then given of
falling and declining, when either by the iniquity of times, or the proper industry of princes, the nobilitie is in so great measure advanced,
as they become thereby dangerous & feareful unto the state: by the
one occasion *Salamina* hath often & sundry times declined. *Epi:* What
by the iniquitie of times? *Sol:* Yea verily: for upon the division of the

---

[23] Daniel 6.3–9; 11–13; 15–16.

[24] Caesar, Marullus, and Flavius: North, *Plutarch's Lives,* vol. 5, "Life of Julius
Caesar," 339. Murder of Romulus: Ibid., vol. 1, "Life of Romulus," 92.

house of *Lankaster* & *Yorke*, justice there declining, the nobility helde as it were a soveraigne commandement over the commonalty, they call their lands by the name of their cuntries, their tenants by the name of their followers and men, they give laws, and prescribe unto the people their manner of living, they oppresse where they dislike, they reward whom they favour, they perish whom they hate, and finally they make themselves judges and arbitrators of the goods, lands, life, liberty, and of all the fortunes of the subject. The which overgreat power and commandement doth lively appeare in the act made for the taking away of the great authority of Captainship with all exactions: [*Anno uno decimo El. cap.7. fol.168.*] wherein it is declared, that the Lordes of *Salamina* in the [K2v] time of justice declination, under the pretence of defending the people of *Salamina*, & their own possessions, arrogated unto themselves absolute and regale authority within large circuits; by the distribution whereof each man had as much righte as force would give him leave, by meanes whereof they grew unto such greatnesse as they acknowledged no superiour, no obedience unto the counsels of *Athens;* they holde for lawes there owne willes and desires, by their proper authority they gather and assemble the people of the saide pretenced countries, rules, and Captaineships, to treat, conclude, and agree for making of warre, or peace, roades, injuries, granting of ceases,[25] benevolences, finding of men of warre, as horsemen, footemen, galloglasse,[26] kearne, hasbutteres,[27] horses, horseboyes, huntes, studkeepers, officers, and adherentes: and more then this, these Nobles and Lordes did leade as Captaines, the people thus assembled unto the accomplishing of act and actes offensive, and invasive without speciall authority.[28] *Epi:* By

---

[25] As above, *Solon* II, note 10.

[26] The term "galloglasse" or "gallowglass" refers to the ethnically Scottish heavily armed professional foot soldiers which constituted the mainstay of the Gaelic military apparatus.

[27] More than likely "hasbutter" refers to a soldier armed with a "hackbutt," more commonly referred to as a harquebusier.

[28] Beacon here cites Sir Henry Sidney's 1569 "Act for taking away [of] captainships and all exactions belonging thereunto from the lords and great men of this realm," see above, *Solon* I, note 6. Beacon's exact citation of fol. 168 provides almost certain evidence that his major source for Irish legislation is the 1572 edition of the statutes, sponsored by Sir Henry Sidney and printed in Dublin by Richard Tottle.

these statutes and recordes thus by you remembred, it seemeth that all the warres of *Salamina* did proceede from the greatnesse of the Nobles and Lordes. *Sol:* So much the recorde itselfe doeth report, whereas it^e is saide, that their greatnesse was such, as they did acknowledge no superiour, nor any obedience unto *Athens.* It is saide also that the might and greatnesse of *James* sometimes Earl of *Desmonde, Garralde FitzGarralde,* Earle of *Kildare,* and *Thomas FitzGarralde* his son, was the occasion of many rebellions, as by the recordes of *Salamina* more at large it may appeare. [*Anno 11. Eliz. cap.7. fol.168. Vid. Attay. of the earle of Kildare. acts 28. H.8.cap.1.*]^29 *Epi:* It seemeth also by the recordes of *Salamina,* by you now remembred, that the Nobles & Lords by their greatnes did mightily oppresse the commonalty, inforcing them to graunt ceases, benevolences, finding of men at armes, as horsemen, footemen, galloglasse, kearne, hasbutters, horses, horseboyes, huntes, studkeepers, officers, and adherents. *Sol:* Yes verily: for by way of protection and defence the nobility did levie exactions intollerable, so as they were forced to establish a law, that no man within the land of *Salamina* shall have any tribute, or exaction, or any other unlawful imposition of or uppon any subject within the same lande. *Epi:* Herein they were provident of the preservance and continuance of the estate of *Sa-*[K3]*lamina;* for nothing giveth greater occasion of declining then the oppression of the commonalty. For the *Israelites* beeing mightily oppressed by the *Ægyptians,* were thereby inforced to follow *Moyses,* by whom they were restored unto their libertie. The *Persians, Medorum imperio insensi,* were thereby induced to followe *Cyrus.* And the naturall citizens of *Rome,* being not defended from the oppression and furie of *Hanniball,* tooke occasion of revolting and rebelling.^30 How displeasing oppressions be everywhere unto the multitude, the same the people of *Salamina* have livelie witnessed, when as they tearmed sometimes the exactions of *Coiney* and *Liverie,* imposed by the nobility and Lordes of that land, by the name of grievous exactions: nay with great *Emphasies* they tearme it the frette of our times, and substaunce: nay yet with greater indignation car-

---

^29 See the "Act for the attainder of the earle of Kildare and others," *Stat. Ire., 10 Hen. VI–14 Eliz.,* fols. 37–42, and above, *Solon* II, note 19.

^30 Moses and Israelites, Cyrus and Persians, "rebellious against the empire of Medes": Telius, 29; *Principe* 6. Revolt against Hannibal: *Discorsi* 1.53.6.

ryed against this manner of oppression, they tearme it by the name of that horrible and most detestable custome of *Coiney* and *Liverie*, yea they terme it to be the very nurse, and teate, that gave sucke and nutriment to all disobedience, rebellions, enormities, vices, and iniquities of that realme over fowle and filthie, here to be expressed, and such as did justly provoke the wrath and vengeance of the almighty God uppon the people of that lande. The like oppression of the nobility over the meaner people, was sometimes the authour of many seditions in *Rome,* and provoked the people to demaunde Tribunes, which as arbitrators of the insolencie of the nobilty, might give them just defence from their oppression.[31] And this stirreth the people sometimes the better, to make their deliveraunce from the oppression of the mighty, with the consent of the forrain enemy, even to the invading and destroying of the people & country.

[K3v]

CAP. 6.

The meanes to withstande all occasions of de-
clining, growing unto the common-
wealth by the great-
nesse of the nobi-
litie.

SOL: Sith this seemeth to be a matter of so great importance, to defende the multitude from the oppression of the mighty, it shall be convenient that we now proceede unto the meanes whereby we may in such cases, as well abate the greatnes of the Lordes and Nobles, as also deliver the multitude from their oppressions and wrongs. *Epi:* The meanes are sundry. *Sol:* What be they? *Epi:* First we are to establish lawes, wherby as well the dignity of the Nobles, as the liberty of the people, may be preserved and defended, according to the example of all common-weales well governed. *Sol:* Herein *Salamina* is found inferiour to noe nation, especiallie for lawes, which respect the liberty and welfare of the people, the which is the matter nowe in deliberation. *Epi:* What be they? *Sol:* The lawes against

---

[31] Tribunes: *Discorsi* 1.3.3; 1.2.18.

Coiney and *Livery*, the lawes against Captainship, the lawes against taking of pledges contrarie to the common law, with many other lawes prohibiting unlawfull customes and exactions; so as it seemeth that good lawes are not sufficient to render a common-weale, happie and prosperous. *Epi:* Noe surely, no more then a medicine well prepared may cure the diseases of the body, if the same be not rightly applied: it resteth therefore, that governoures provinciall, doe diligently intend the observation of these lawes, in such sort, as they be inviolable, whereby in a short time they shall confirme the mindes of the multitude, and render them secure, quiet, and contented. *Sol:* This which you have saide, by sundry actes and recordes, nowe extant for *Salamina*, maie appeare: for there it is saide, that the people [K4] were not onlie drawne from rebellions and unlawfull attempts, by the extirpation of this exaction of *Coiney* and *Livery*, but they were sometimes by the due exaction of that lawe, stronglie indued to affect and imbrace justice and peace, so as al commaundementes by waie of justice are there obeied. Naie that which is more, in place of cursing and rebellions, there is founde joie, jolitie, and blessing of that goddesse *Minerva*, the protectour and defendour of *Athens*, by whose providence so great an evill was remooved. So as we maie conclude, that nothing doeth so much induce a nation or people, be they naturall subjects or gained by conquest, to imbrace that governement which is prescribed unto them by those which have rule, power, & authority over them, there is nothing (I say) so availeable to render them loyall subjectes, & willing embracers of governement, as a just defence given by due execution of profitable lawes from all oppressions and wronges. *Epi:* You have saide the trueth: for a nation conquered desire their former libertie, for no other cause so greatly, as thereby to possesse that which is their owne freelie and securelie; so as enjoying the same, they have attained the ende of their desires, and rest for the most parte contented with the governement. But on the contrarie, with the oppression of the mighty, the thoughtes and desires of their former libertie are daily kindled, in such sorte, as they sticke not to practise with forraine enemies the restitution thereof. It is necessary therefore in such countries, that the lawes for the defence of the multitude against oppressions bee holden inviolable, in such sort as everie one maie confidentlie saie with the governoures of *Darius*, it is the lawe of the *Medes* and *Persians* which maie not be broken. *Sol:* But some provinciall governoures of *Salamina*, have beene founde more studious with *Savanorola* in making of profitable lawes, then faithfull observers thereof, whereby the whole countrie of *Salamina* hath well neare perished: but I could wish, that with *Savanorola* at the least they might loose their honour and estimation amongest the *Florentines*:[32] for much evill ariseth unto *Salamina*, not onelie from the malice of the people, but by the negligence of Magistrates, in that they holde not their lawes inviolable; for the which causes they maye [K4v] never confirme the mindes of the multitude unto the state, nor render them quiet, and contented. But what other meanes is now left unto us to deliver the multitude from oppression? *Epi:* Commissioners in every of the several Provinces are to be constituted, which as judges shall restraine and suppresse the ambition of the nobles, and shall carefully defende the people from oppressors. Therefore wisely the king of *Fraunce* hath constituted a judge or arbitrator, which as a third person *sine regis invidia proceres cæderet, & tenuiores tueretur. Nihil melius, nihil sapientius hoc decreto esse potuit: nec regni aut ipsius regis potior securitatis causa.*[33] *Sol:* But what number of judges may suffice herein? *Epi:* You say well: for if one judge bee ordained, the mighty and great personages shall more easily corrupt him, then manie. Therefore the *Florentines* having entertained but one judge for the suppressing of the ambition of the nobility, whom they called *Capitaneum*, seeing him seduced by the nobilitie, in his place constituted eight judges or Commissioners. *Sol:* But in this second institution, they founde lesse security then in the first: for where a fewe are placed for the rule and governement, there they be founde commonly ministers and pleasers of the nobility, and contemners of the people; the which the *Venetians* wisely foreseeing, have not onely ordained their *Decemviri*, but also other magistrates, *quos Quarantos vocant*, & further for the same onely they have constituted *Concilium Prægium qui summus est magistratus*, to this ende, that neither judges nor accusers should be wanting for the suppressing of the ambition of the nobilitie.[34] *Epi:* As you have

---

[32] Savanarola: *Discorsi* 1.45.2.

[33] Telius, 121; *Principe* 19: "to crush the nobles and favor the weak, without bringing reproach on the king. There could be no better or more sensible institution, nor one more effective in insuring the security of the king and the kingdom" (Bull, 105–6).

[34] *Discursus*, 205; *Discorsi* 1.49.1–5: "Against this abuse the city of Venice has

saide, this must needes be the best forme of governement that may possibly be ordained in such cases; for many judges are not so easily corrupted as one: againe many are founde to be of greater strength and integritie to resist the displeasure of the nobilitie then fewe; and like as many eies discerne more perfectly then one, and that which escapeth or deceiveth one eie[f], maie be perceived and that without errour by many; so many wits judge more soundly and sincerely then one. Lastly, wee all obey more willingly the censures of many, then the judgements of a fewe, or one person whatsoever. *Sol:* But whither are we in such cases more to endevour the favour of the no-[L1]bility or the multitude? *Epi:* It is saide that a Monarchie governed popularlie is then secure and voide of perill: for in the multitude or people consisteth the strength and force of every kingdome; the which *Nabid* king of the *Lacedæmonians* well understanding, endevoured wholie the love and favoure of the people, so as with his proper forces hee was able to withstande and resist his enemies, without the aide of forraine princes. And *Appius Claudius* on the contrarie, neglecting the favoure of the people, did wholy cleave to the nobilitie, and lost thereby the principalitie and commaundement which then hee had obtayned.[35] *Solo:* It must be confessed that in common-weales gained by conquest, you shall advance your governement more assuredly by the favoure of the people, then by the might of the nobilitie; for nature itselfe by an inforcing necessitie hath taught the weaker part to adheare unto that which is the strongest; and for this cause the people diverse waies oppressed by the ambition of the mighty, are forced thereby to hasten and runne unto their conquerour, as unto a large palme tree, to bee defended from the stormes and violence of the mighty, so as delivering them from oppressions, they willingly yeelde their obedience; but of the contrarie the nobilitie are not so readily wonne nor so easily kept. Therefore the *Romaines* in all countries by them con-

---

safeguarded itself by having ten citizens who are empowered to punish any citizen without appeal; and, lest the ten should not suffice for the punishing of the powerful, though they have authority to do this, they have set up the tribunal of Forty and, yet further have decided that the Court of Rogation, which is the Greater Council, shall have power to punish them" (Walker, 232).

[35] Nabis, Tyrant of Sparta, 207–192 BC: *Discorsi* 1.40.11; Appius Claudius in deserting the populace and courting the nobles made a very obvious mistake: *Discorsi*, 1.40.10.

quered, did labour nothing more then to humble and deject the
mightie, & to protect and defend the feeble & weake, and deliver the
people from oppressions. The like order of governement did the *Græcians* observe, especially in provinces by them conquered, which dif-
fered in language and maner of living: for there the people, if they be
not carefully defended from the oppressions of the mighty, by these
outward differences as signes and badges of their former liberty, doe
hasten for the restitution thereof unto all rebellions, and doe provoke
some forraine enemy to invade. Farther in common-weales where
generally the manners of the people are found corrupted, there dangerous it is to advance the Lords & chieftaines, as it may appeare by
the statuts & records of *Salamina:* [*Anno: 11. Eliz. cap.7. fol.168.*][36] for
there it is declared that the Lords[g] and chieftaines of that land, in the
times of justice declination, by pretext of [L1v] defending the people
and their owne possessions, arrogated unto themselves absolute and
roiall authority within large circuites, by meanes wherof they grew
unto such greatnes, as they acknowledged no superior, nor obedience
unto *Athens,* they held for laws their owne willes and desires, and
finallie they assembled and led the people unto the accomplishing of
all actes offensive and invasive, without speciall authority, as before
we have at large discoursed. Therefore in *Salamina,* and in other common-weales gained by conquest, where the manners of the people
remaine corrupted, we are to give impediment (saith a learned
authour) unto all the meanes wherby the nobles may raise themselves
unto such greatnesse, as thereby they may become fearefull unto the
common-weale, and providently shall we favour and deliver the
people in such estates from oppression.[37] *Ep:* For this cause wisely
have the councel of *Salamina* suppressed and cut of al exactions and
tributes, by a firme and stable law before remembred, as the meanes,
whereby the nobles and cheifetaines did raise themselves unto such
greatnesse, as they became daungerous unto the common-weale. And
to the same purpose have they made another statute, wherby it is
ordained and enacted, that no Lorde nor gentleman of the said land,
retaine by liverie, wages, or promise, signe or token, by indenture or

---

[36] See above, *Solon* I, note 6.
[37] *Discorsi* 1.16.5–7.

otherwise, any person or persons, but onely such, as be or shalbe his officers, as baylifes, stewardes, learned counsels, receivers, and meni-all servantes, daily in householde, at the saide Lordes proper costes and charges entertained. [*Act Anno. H.7. 10. cap. 6.*][38] Thus if wisely we give impediment unto the meanes which raise the chiefetaines and nobles of *Salamina* unto this greatnes; if with *Pompey* we shall im-peach the forces of *Cæsar* by calling awaie two legions or regimentes; if with *Pompey* we shal withdrawe from *Cæsar*, *Labienus*, and other his friendes and commmaunders; if we shall cut off all exactions, and tributes, which *Cæsar* leavieth uppon the people; if we shall cut off all that infinite number of retainers, followers, and men which followe *Cæsar* more then his menial housholde according to the statute of retainers; if we shall suppresse all unlawfull authorities of Captain-ship and such like, which *Cæsar* chalengeth over the meaner people; if the great and large coun-[L2]tries which *Cæsar* possesseth, we shall part and dismember by drawing in the custome of Gavelkinde, by the which[h] pollicie, *Wales* was sometimes reformed, and brought in subjection; then *Cæsar* shall be no more able to rebell, and we shall rightly manage the state of *Salamina*.[39] *Sol:* Doe you thinke, that the statute against *Coiney* and *Livery*, is a sufficient barre against the Lordes and cheiftaines that they raise not themselves unto their for-mer greatnesse? *Epi:* No verily: for nowe they chalenge those exac-tions as lawfull services and reservations by the way of tenier[40] here-tofore reserved by their auncestors, & predecessors, & by these meanes holde the subject in servage, or otherwise they drive them to particular shiftes, which are tedious, infinite, and troublesome to the state, and the utter undoing of the subject; all which may well be

---

[38] The 1494 act against coyne and livery. See further, *Solon* I, note 5, and *Stat. Ire., 10 Hen. VI–14 Eliz.*, fols. 30–31.

[39] In discussing means to weaken the excessive power of the nobles, the author refers to the statutes against retainers and captainship. Beacon also advocates eliminating "Gavelkinde," a system of partible inheritance prevalent in Wales, as well as Tudor Kent, and Ireland, where it often resulted in the joint or equal division of a landowner's holdings among his male heirs. *Tudor Ire.*, 322.

[40] Coyne and Livery is here claimed as a condition of lawful tenure, i.e., a condition under which the land is held of the lord or one of the duties of the tenant to the lord. The term "tenier" (F. *tenir*), like "tener," "tenur," "tenuer," and "tenour," is an obsolete form of the more common "tenure."

appeased by way of composition betwixt the Lordes and tenantes:[41] and the better to enable us to make an equall compostion herein, we are to understande that these demaundes are of three sortes, and kindes: The one received his beginning by unlawfull meanes, namely by force and by violence, these are commonly called by the names of blacke rentes; such were the exactions which the *Obrians* sometimes levied upon the inhabitaunce of the countrie of *Limbricke*. Other demaundes there be, which did growe by way of giving protection and defence, from such as founde themselves oppressed with the power and might of others; such exactions sometimes have been yeelded by the inhabitants of the small countrie of *Limbricke*, unto the auncestors of the nowe Earle of *Kildare*, and such did *Mac Morris* sometimes yeelde unto the late Earle of *Desmond* attainted.[42] Lastly, other demaundes there be which did growe by way of tenier; these may easily bee discerned from the others, in that they be due unto the Lorde onely, from the handes of his proper tenantes or freehoulders, and the same commonly shall appeare to be so by writing or indenture. *Sol:* You have well disclosed the meanes whereby the greatnesse of the nobility and chiefetaines may be abated, and the people defended

---

[41] Beacon advocates the policy of composition, a "compounding" between the lord and his tenants for a regular and fixed rent instead of the variety of feudal and Gaelic duties owed to the lord and often exacted in an arbitrary and excessive fashion. The Munster attorney general witnessed such a compounding between the government and the lords, and the lords and their tenants, when Lord Deputy Sir John Perrot instituted composition in Connacht in 1589. Beacon favored the more moderate policy of composition with the nobles because, like Solon's "Seisachtheia," "it was effected with the consents of the subjects, and not forced and commanded." For a detailed discussion of composition see Brady 1986, 22–49; Cunningham 1984–85, 1–14; *Tudor Ire.*, 268–74, 284–88.

[42] "Blacke rentes" were rents forced from English settlers by neighboring Gaelic lords in return for protection, as in this example of money exacted from the inhabitants of Limerick by the O'Briens of Thomond. Similar monies were collected by the great Old English lords in return for protection from the Gaelic Irish, e.g., the dues collected by the Leinster-based Earls of Kildare, who held ancestral lands in Limerick, from the same area. Beacon adds to his list of feudal or semi-feudal exactions the traditional duties owed by the "Mac Morris" clan to their overlords, the Earls of Desmond. The author believes these exactions "unlawfull" and advocates their abolition because they were extorted from the less powerful by the violence of the "over mighty" as a means of extending their overlordship. Beacon holds these Gaelic-inspired duties as responsible for the excessive power of the Irish nobles and hence for the decline of English law and government in Ireland.

from the oppression of the mighty, in times peaceable, wherein lawe and justice doeth prevaile. It seemeth also that it is a matter of like necessitie that the good subject bee defended [L2v] from the oppression of the enemie or rebell: for the naturall subjectes of *Rome*, revolted unto *Hanniball*, when as they found themselves not defended from his oppression.[43] *Epi:* We must with *Fabius* providently from time to time sende aide sufficient to such as are our subjectes and friendes, whereby we shall still holde and keepe them in obedience and subjection. *Sol:* If this course had generally beene holden by some governours of *Salamina*, the rebellions had neither beene great, neither yet of long continuance; therefore wisely it is saide, *Qui non defendit nec obsistit si potest iniuriæ, tam est in vitio, quam si parentes aut patriam aut socios deserat:*[44] and after this manner speaketh a christian Doctor, saying, *Fortitudo quæ per bella tuetur â Barbaris patriam, vel defendit infirmos, vel â latronibus socios, plena iusticia est.*[45] By which course of governement, the *Romaines* almost conquered the whole worlde, as *Cicero* witnesseth saying, *Noster populus, sociis defendendis terrarum iam omnium potitus est.*[46] *Epi:* It seemeth also to bee a matter of like necessity, that the governours of *Salamina* doe with all care and indevour confirme the mindes of the subjectes by having a due regarde of their merites and services towardes the state, least otherwise when no

---

[43] Hannibal's defeat of Romans at Cannae: *Discorsi* 1.11.2; Hannibal & Fabius: *Discorsi* 1.53.5; unsuccessful revolt of Roman populace under Marcus Centenius against Hannibal: *Discorsi* 1.53.6.

[44] Lipsius, *Pol.* 5.4, citing Cicero, *De Officiis* 1; Lipsius 1590, 147; Lipsius 1594, 131: "For he that doth not resist, nor oppose himselfe against an iniurie if he may, is in as great faults, as if he did abandon his parents, his country, or his confederates."

[45] Beacon, like Sir William Herbert, takes this quotation indirectly from Lipsius, *Pol.* 5.4; Lipsius 1590, 147. Lipsius 1594, 131: "Yea a Christian Doctor saith to this purpose: that fortitude which by force of arms doth defend a man his countrey from barbarous people, or those that are weake and oppressed, or such as are entred into league with us, from the violence of theeves and robbers, is perfect iustice." Lipsius is quoting St. Ambrose (see Herbert 1992, edited by Keaveney and Madden, 139, note 24). Note the difference from the standard text of St. Ambrose, *de Offic.* 1.27.129: "Si quidem et fortitudo, quae vel in bello tuetur a barbaris patriam, vel domi defendit infirmos vel a latronibus socios, plena sit iusticiae" (as cited in Herbert 1992, 182).

[46] Lipsius, *Pol.* 5.4, citing Cicero, *De republica* 3; Lipsius 1590; Lipsius 1594, 131: "Our Nation in defending our confederates are become Lords of the whole earth."

estimation is had of their merites and publique services, they take occasion thereby of discontentment. For the slender care & estimation the *French* sometimes helde of the publicke merites of such as had well deserved, gave the first occasion of their expelling out of *Italy;* for so much doe their Cronicles and histories witnesse, where it is saide, that the nobility were not imbraced with that humanity they looked for, and much lesse had recompenses equall to their merites, yea they found manie difficulties to enter into the chambers and audience of the king. There was no distinction of persons, the merites and services of men were not considered, but at adventure, the mindes of such as were naturally estraunged from the house of *Arragon,* were not confirmed, many delaies and difficulties were suborned touching the restitution of the landes and goods of those that were of the faction of *Anjow,* and of the other Barrons that had beene banished by the olde *Ferdinando.* And lastly favoures and graces were imparted to such as procured them [L3] by corruption and meanes extraordinary, & not to such as had deserved the same.[47] Wisely therefore shall the governoures of *Salamina* confirme the mindes of such as are estranged from the house of *Arragon,* and coun-tenaunce such as were banished by *Ferdinando,* and lastlie if they shall imparte favoures and graces to such as have deserved the same, ac-cording to the advise of *Plinie,* which saith, *Tu largiere bellorum sociis, periculorum consortibus.*[48]

---

[47] the nobility ... and meanes extraordinary: Fenton, *Historie of Guicciardin* 2, 89. Words omitted from the passage in Fenton: "from many they took without iustice or reason, and to many, they gave without occasion or deserving." All references to disturbances and rapes in Fenton are omitted by Beacon.

[48] Lipsius *Pol.,* 4.8, citing Pliny, *Pane.;* Lipsius 1590, 82; Lipsius 1594, 76: "Bestow thou thy gifts upon thy companions in warre, and to them that are partakers of thy perils."

CAP. 7.

The occasions of declining, which usually arise unto the
state by the disorders and oppression
of the souldier.

EPI: Noe lesse occasion is offered of declining, when by the oppression of the souldier, the people remaine discontented. *Sol:* You saie truely: for the disorder and violence of the souldiers draweth with it a suspition of perpetual servitude, which caused the *Italians* to abandon the power of the *French*, for that they committed many disorders, and offered violence unto the people; so as that love, that desire, that affection, wherewith they honoured them before, had now taken contrary qualitie, and not only turned into hatred, conspiracie, and accursings against them, but also in the place of the malice they bare to the *Arragons*, there was new insinuation of compassion to *Ferdinando*, in such sorte, as all the kingdome with no lesse desire expected an opportunity, to repeale the *Arragons*, then a fewe monethes before they had desired their destruction.[49] *Sol:* The same historie doeth witnesse the like in sundry other places, saying, that garrisons governed with a desire to spoile, and pray, be the authoures of great discontentment: yet some there be carried with a contrary opinion, which give liberty unto the souldiers to oppresse and spoile the people, following the counsell of *Severus Imperator*, which sometimes he gave unto his children, saying, *Inter vos consentite, milites vitate, reliquos omnes spermite.*[50] *Epi:* This counsell of *Severus Imperator*, no Prince maie safelie put in practise, but [L3v] such as have a collected power and force into the strength of one entire armie, which shall farre exceede the force and strength of the people: as the *Sulthan*, the *Turke*, and such like kingdomes, which hath of footemen, twelve thousande in number, and sixteene of horsemen, for the garde of his person. These kingdomes and such like, shall more wisely favour and

---

[49] "that love ... Ferdinando": Fenton, *Historie of Guicciardin* 2, 89.
[50] Lipsius 4.7, citing "Severus Imperator apud Dionem in vita eius"; Lipsius 1590, 80; Lipsius 1594, 73: "Agree amongst your selves, enrich your men of warre, and make no reckoning of others."

enrich, rather the souldier, then the people.[51] But such Princes which have not a collected power, and force, and such as doeth farre exceede the strength and power of the people, are no farther to satisfie the souldiour then justice, his desertes, and the lawes of the lande shall require. Therefore *Carolus* passing manie countries, where the forces of his souldiers were inferiour to the people, did streightly commaunde, that they shoulde abstaine from committing of wronges and injuries.[52] *Sol:* This which you have saide agreeth with reason, but sometimes not with the necessity of times, which was never yet subject to humane discretion. *Epi:* It must be confessed, that the times of warres, and peace are not all one, but yet as well in the times of warres, as also in times peaceable, we ought to shew ourselves studious in delivering the people from oppression: For what hope may we have of those cities, *ubi milites in cives graviùs quam in hostes grassantur.*[53]

CAP. 8.

The readie waies and meanes to resist all occasions of declining, which maie arise by the oppression of the Souldiers.

S ol: Then we shall readily performe the same, if we shall remove the occasions which are in number two: namely the want of pay; and want of other discipline; for if the souldier were well paied, and offending by martiall discipline well punished, all disorders by these meanes would be easily reformed. *Epi:* You saie well: payment ought first to be made, and then discipline exercised, for *disciplinam, inquit Cassiodorus, servare non potest ieiunus exercitus, dum quod deest semper præsumat armatus.*[54] [L4] *Sol:* But ought this pay-

---

[51] "Turkes ... people": Telius, 133; *Principe* 19.

[52] "Therefore Carolus ... injuries": Fenton, *Historie of Guicciardin* 2, 89.

[53] "the tyme of warre and lawe are two thinges" (North, *Plutarch's Lives*, vol. 5, "Life of Julius Caesar," 310). Bodin, *De Republica* 6.2, 669: "Where the soldiers proceed more harshly against the citizens than they do against the enemy" (trans. Carroll).

[54] "disciplinam ... armatus": Bodin, *De Republica* 6.2, 670. "An army which wanteth food sayth Cassiodorus cannot keep discipline, because an armed man will presume most if any thing is wanting " (translation in Folger marginalia).

ment to be made at the charge of the Prince, or of the subjects?[i] *Epi:*
At the common charge of the subjects,[j] because it is a common safegarde and benefite[k] which equally redoundeth to all. *Sol:* You say
well: for garrisons are placed for naught else, but to garde the good
subject from the sodain invasion or oppression of the enemy or rebell,
and if they ought to defray the charge, that reape the benefite, then
every subject shoulde make equall contribution herein. *Epi:* Wee doe
agree herein, that payment ought to be made at the common charge
of the subject, but convenient it were that this charge were drawne to
a contribution certaine; for where the contributions are altogither
uncertaine by the waie of cease,[55] or otherwise, there the people are
usuallie oppressed, and the Prince wearied with complaints, or the
same rejecting, the people, take occasion thereby to mutinie and
rebell. Therefore wisely *Henricus secundus rex Francorum nostra ætate
tributum imperarat,* Anno. 1549. *Quod vulgus talionum appellavit, testatus
se id militum stipendio daturum, ne cum cæteris vectigalibus conturbaretur,
ut plebs ab iniuriis ac direptionibus militum tutæ esset.* At an other time,
payment was made by certaine citties for the maintenaunce of tenne
legions, *ut ab incensionibus ac direptionibus militum tutæ essent.*[56] In
like manner the counsel of *Athens* by receiving a composition certaine
from the handes of the subject, in liew of cease and duties uncertaine,
have thereby mightily quieted and pacified the subject, augmented
the publike treasury, and advaunced and reformed that governement.
Epi: Shew us I pray you the order and manner of the composition.
Sol: The first composition taken for the west partes, was framed after
this maner, as it may appeare by this president which I doe here
deliver unto you:

> By the Lorde President and
> Counsell of Mounster.

---

[55] As above, *Solon* II, note 10.

[56] Beacon finds discipline and regular pay recommended by Matthew Sutcliffe, *The Practise and proceedings, and lawes of armes* (London, 1593), cap. 2, 16–28,
as well as by Bodin, *De Republica* 6.2, 669: "Henrie the second in the yeare 1549,
did exact that extraordinarie tribute which they called Talion, he promised not to
employ that money to any other use, than to the entertainment of his men at
armes, and not to confound it with the ordinarie receits, that the subject might be
freed from the spoile of souldiers" (Knolles, 677).

Whereas *John MacConoghor* of *Corbally,* in the County of *Waterforde* gentleman complained unto us, that he holding and occupying two plough landes in *Corbally* aforesaide, the same being [L4v] charged with cease, and other impositions uncertaine, he desired to yeeld a yearely rent out of the same to her Majestie, in respect of the saide cease and other charges due, to the maintenance of the houshold of the Presidencie, or otherwise that by occasion may be imposed uppon the saide County; and therefore hath graunted and compounded for him and his heires, to pay to her Majesties use, yearelie out of the saide two ploughlandes, the summe of fortie shillings sterling; which being by us on hir Majesties part and behalfe accepted, We will and require you, and every of you, from henceforth in no wise to charge and impose or suffer to be charged, or imposed, the saide landes, or any part thereof, with any her Majesties cease of horsemen, horse boyes, kearne, galloglasse,[57] biefe, mutton, porke, corne, subsidie, or any other charge or provision whatsoever, tending or belonging to her Majesties service by waie of cease to be demaunded or challenged: In witnesse whereof, I the said *John* have to this parte of the Indenture remaining with the saide Lorde President set to my hand and seale, the xxvi of *October,* 1577.[58] *Epi:* I finde sundry matters observed in the making of this composition worthy to be commended. First for that the same was effected with the consentes of the subjectes, and not forced and commaunded, as sometimes the *Israelites* were by *Samuel,* which in his oration unto the people, saide, *Regem habituri estis, qui decimas fructuum vobis imperaturus est:*[59] neither here

---

[57] As above, *Solon* III, note 26.

[58] The provincial presidency of Munster (1570) was established by Sir Henry Sidney's effort to extend to Ireland this model of governing difficult areas which had been adopted successfully in England and Wales. While subordinate to the chief governor, the Presidents of both Connacht (1569) and Munster had full authority to extend English law in their areas. Sir William Drury (July 1576–Oct. 1579) was Lord President when this composition with John Mac Conogher of Corbally in Waterford was concluded. Although this is a good example of an agreement of composition, and one that relates to an area where Beacon eventually becomes a settler, its choice is not clear. Beacon did not gain an official position in the Munster provincial government until Dec. 1586, when he served in various commissions covering the issues of cess and noble exactions until 1591, yet he does not invoke this experience. *Fiants Ire., Eliz.,* 4949, 5297, 5536, 5561; and *NHI,* 9, 534–35.

[59] Bodin, *De Republica* 6.2, 657: "And when as Samuel prince of the Israelites

are they pressed by the authority of any duke of *Albane*, to render the tenth part of all things vendable, *Unde porro Belgarum ab Hispanis rebellantium orta seditio.*[60] *Sol:* I hold reasonable tributes to be a matter of so great importaunce and necessity, as Princes may lawfully commande and exact the same at the hands of the subject, and therefore saith one, *Quid enim restaret, quo princeps imperium tueri possit, sublatis portoriis ac tributis?*[61] And therefore when *Nero* offered to acquite and deliver the subject of all tributes and impositions, wisely the Senate after thankes rendred unto *Nero*, disswaded the fact, *Ne Respublica ære diruta, momento collaberetur;*[62] saying, though many seditious persons desirous of innovation have promised the people immunitie of all tributes and impositions, yet to graunt the same it were altogither unlawefull; and if [M1] it were lawful, yet ought you not to do the same for the safety of the common-weale, *Cum eo veluti firmamento Respublica nitatur.*[63] *Epi:* Be it so, that they may commaunde a matter so necessary for the sustaining and upholding of the common-weale; yet for the avoiding of sedition, and the discontentment of the people, their consentes are required, the time also is to bee regarded, the nature of the common-weale is to be respected, and lastly the imployment of those tributes ought to be unto publike uses. For Princes in the beginning of their governement are not to impose tributes, fearing least the ten tribes for this cause shall rebell, and that a new king be

---

spake unto the people, who demaunded a King of him, he added threats of bitter tributes, ... Therefore sayd he, you shall have a King which shall command the tenths of your fruits" (Knolles, 665–66).

[60] Bodin, *De Republica* 6.2, 657. "How comes it that the Netherlanders have revolted from the Spaniard" (Knolles, 666). The text gives the reason as excessive taxation: "but for that the Duke of Alva would exact the tenth pennie of everie thing which was sold, whereby he would have gathered an infinite treasor."

[61] Bodin, *De Republica* 6.2, 657. "to take away all impositions before the revenewes bee redeemed and the debts payd; it were not to repaire, but to ruine the state" (Knolles, 666).

[62] Bodin, *De Republica* 6.2, 657. "As Nero the Emperour would have done, who having wasted all the treasure, sought to abolish the tributes, whereof the Senate being advertised, they thanked him for his good will to the people, yet they dissuaded him from doing it, saying it would be the ruine of the Commonweale" (Knolles, 666).

[63] Bodin, *De Republica* 6.2, 657: "being as it were the ground and foundation of a Commonweale" (Knolles, 666).

chosen in the place of *Roboham*.[64] But at such times they shal more wisely with the French King being newly possessed of the *Duchey* of *Millaine,* acquit & discharge the people of al tributes, which did mightilie as then advance his conquest.[65] Againe, the nature and condition of the common-wealth is a matter no lesse worthy of consideration, then the time: for if the common-weale hath beene from time to time a free estate and not subject to others, as sometimes the *Romaines* were, to such estates all manner of tributes are grievous, and therefore not to be exacted, but uppon urgent causes, the which ceasing, the people ought to be delivered from tributes. But the people of *Florence* on the contrary, having alwaies lived in servitude, and as tributaries to others, admitte willinglye all sortes of impositions and tributes from time to time imposed uppon them by their duke:[66] and for this cause *Salamina* long ere this might have beene made profitable unto *Athens,* for that they have alwaies lived in servitude, and subject to all impositions and tributes, and many exactions have beene reared there by force and violence, to the maintenaunce of idle and evill disposed persons, the which being converted to private uses and not to publike services, have little profited the Citie of *Athens;* all which the recordes and statutes of *Salamina,* doe many waies witnesse, and especiallie the statutes against *Coiney* and *Liverie:* and therefore the last matter which is the imployment of tributes to publike uses, is not the least; wherein wee are to have diverse regardes: first, care is to bee had of the Prince and his family; secondarilie of the stipen-[M1v]dary souldiers, the which two matters are chiefely respected and regarded in the composition before remembred; thirdly of magistrates, which for want of their pay and stipend, doe more egerly sometimes then the souldiers rob and devour the people; fourthlie of such as have well deserved of the common-weale. Finallie care is to be had of the poorer subjects, least by want, and extreame povertie; they become

---

[64] Rehoboam: 2 Chronicles 10; *Discorsi* 1.19.2; Bodin, *De Republica* 6.2, 668.

[65] "The king receiving at Lyon the newes of so great a victory succeded with a speed swifter than his expectation, made way with great diligence to Millan, where, being received with a joye of the people, equal to the fortune of his victorie, he agreed to the deposing of divers tributes and imposicions, which as it is an action first requisite in Princes newly possessed of conquest, and a favour most plawsible to people altered" (Fenton, *Historie of Guicciardin* 4, 229–30).

[66] *Discorsi* 2.30.2–3.

movers of sedition. *Epi:* The charge being thus defrayed, to the ende exact paiment may be made, it were convenient that the souldiers were payed by the poule; for if paiment be made as now unto the Captaines, the souldier receiving not the same in due time, dareth not complaine against him, but is driven to seek his maintenance by oppressing of the people. Thus oftentimes the souldier is founde to hate his captaine which faileth to make paiment, and the captaine disliketh the souldier, because he faileth in order and government, so as by this private malice, impediment is given oftentimes unto publike services. The which mischiefe hath reigned long in *Salamina.*[67] *Sol:* Doctor *Sutliefe* that learned and skilfull writer hath discoursed hereof at large in his militarie workes,[68] and therefore we will proceede unto the other occasion of all the disorders in the men of garrison, which is the want of militarie discipline; for having neither a judge nor court martiall orderly kept for the due triall and punishment of offendours, the souldier for the most part receiveth no punishment for his offences, or being punished in courtes civill, they may well complaine of their manner of triall by the native borne people of the countrie. *Epi:* It is prohibited in all countries well governed to the men of garrison, to holde any affinitie, consanguinitie, contract, or bargaines, with the native borne people of the countrie, fearing least by this entercourse of friendshippe, the garrisons may be at the last corrupted: but greater occasion of corruption is there given in *Salamina*, where not onely these disorders are admitted by the negligence of Magistrates there placed, but that which is more, the native borne people are made tryers of the life and fortunes of the men in garrison: and may they boldlie prosecute in times of warres such as be enemies to the state, whome in times of peace they maie justlie feare as malicious tryers [M2] of their goods, life, and fortunes whatsoever. Therefore most necessarie it is, that a court martiall be established and orderly kept, as you have said, thoroughout the whole province of *Salamina*, for the reforming of disorders and mischiefes before recited.

---

[67] On the political and social impact of issues surrounding the pay and maintenance of the garrison in Ireland, and, particularly, in the Pale, see Ciaran Brady 1986, 11–32, and, *Solon* II, note 10.

[68] See Matthew Sutcliffe 1593.

CAP. 9.

Occasions of declining are then given, when Magistrates
placed for reformation of any Countrie or province,
are not supported and countenaunced during
the time of their governement.

SOL: There remain yet other occasions of the declining of common-weales, worthy of remembraunce. *Epi:* What maie the
same be? *Sol:* If Princes, Kings, and States, shall not publikely
grace, countenaunce, and support all governoures and Magistrates by
them placed for reformation of any province or nation during the
time of their governement, the subjects shal take thereby occasion of
rebelling. For the *Gaules* understanding that *Rome* did conspire to disgrace *Cæsar*, raised themselves forthwith in armes under the leading
of *Ambiorix*, and *Vercingentorix*, in such sort, as if they had not to hastily proceeded therein, they had put all *Italie* in as great feare and
daunger, as it was sometimes when the *Cimbri* came to invade their
cittie. *Epi:* Wee neede not search forraine examples herein: for *Salamina* by this errour committed was for many yeares vexed with the
rebellions of the *Burkes* and the *Orurkes*, until that famous knight Sir
R. *Bingham*[1] by his singuler art and skill in military discipline, as another *Cæsar*, suppressed at the last *Vercingentorix*, and the rebelling
Gaules.[69] *Sol:* What governoures were there, that were found so
unskilful in their charge? *Epi:* A late deputie of *Salamina*, whose name
here I passe over with silence, for that I may not say, *honoris causa no-
mino*.[70] But O you governoures, Princes, Kings, and Emperours,
[M2v] whatsoever, countenaunce all inferiour governoures and magistrates placed for the reformation of any nation or province: countenaunce *Pericles*, which beholdeth alwaies the *Amazon* holding his dart

---

[69] North, *Plutarch's Lives*, vol. 5, "Life of Julius Caesar," 296–99.

[70] Beacon's reference to Sir Richard Bingham's suppression of rebellions by
the Burkes and O'Rourkes in North Connaucht, in 1588–89, and in 1589–90, was
a subtle attack on the government of Sir William Fitzwilliam (reappointed
governor in Feb. 1588). The reference to the near-simultaneous rebellions suggests
that FItzwilliam was the governor responsible for these outbreaks, whose name
Beacon passed "over with silence." *Tudor Ire.*, 288–91, 297–98; and above, *Solon*
I, note 52.

with a hande stretched forth even in his face, with whome as with a deadly enemy hee must alwaies be fighting: countenaunce *Camillus,* which now is placed to reforme and suppresse the mutinous citizens, wherein if he fortune to be inferiour for want of your countenaunce and assistaunce, he shall be suppressed, condemned, and banished, or at the least hee must of force surrender his office of Dictator. Countenance *Pericles,* for otherwise he shall be as one that hath committed incest, he shal be a coward, the author of warres, yea of the plague, and of whatsoever else, which maie draw with it the hatred of all the citizens of *Athens.* Countenance *Camillus,* for there shall be a *Lucius Apulius,* which malitiously shall accuse him for stealing part of the spoile of the *Tuscans:* Lastly countenance this Magistrate placed for reformation: for with *David,* he is placed to fight with a beare after a lion, with a Giant after a beare, with a King after a Giant, and with the *Philistians* after a King.[71] They must fight with infamie after envye, with accusations after infamy, with condemnation after accusations, with judgement after condemnation, with imprisonment after judgement, with banishment after imprisonment, for *Simul ista mundi conditor posuit Deus, odium atque regnum.*[72] But if you shall not countenance them, the *Gaules* shall rebell against *Cæsar,* the citizens shall mutinie, but *Camillus* shall not be of force to suppresse them; yea this action of reformation shal fall to the ground, and the common-weale itselfe may not long continue.

---

[71] North, *Plutarch's Lives,* vol. 2, "Life of Pericles," 46, where the image of Pericles that Phidias carved on Pallas's shield is described: "he had cut out *Pericles* image, excellently wrought & artificially, seeming in manner to be *Pericles* self, fighting with an AMAZON in this sorte. The AMAZONES hand being lifte up highe, holdeth a darte before *Pericles* face." Camillus's suppressing the people: vol. 1, "Life of Camillus," 400. Lucius Apuleius's accusation of Camillus "for stealing part of the spoile of the Tuscans": vol. 1, "Life of Camillus," 362. Through the figure of Camillus, Beacon perhaps refers to himself as being accused of theft. Beacon also warns against lack of support for the governor, especially the current governor, Lord Russell.

[72] Lipsius, *Pol.* 4.6, citing Seneca, *Theb.*; Lipsius 1590, 77; Lipsius 1594, 71: "God the creator & maker of the world, coupled hatred and a kingdome together."

[M3]   CAP. 10.

Occasions of declining, which arise unto the common-
weale sometimes, by secluding a nation con-
quered, from bearing of offices,
and dignities.

S *ol:* Let us proceede unto other occasions of declining of estates and common-weales, which arise oftentimes by secluding a nation or people conquered from bearing of offices or dignity in the common-weale: for they remaine possessed with a desire to be restored unto their former liberty, for this cause especially, *Ut ipsis dominari, & publicis muneribus præfici liceat.*[73] *Ep:* And one the other side, no lesse occasion is given of declining, if you shall advaunce them unto the offices, and dignities of the common-weale. For did not *Salamina* decline sometimes by constituting *Garralde FitzGarralde* attainted, Lieuetenant of *Salamina?* did they not at other times decline by constituting *Thomas FitzGarralde* sometimes Lieuetenaunt of the severall provinces thereof? and at other times, by giving authority into the hands of *James* of *Desmonde?* all which, to them which shall viewe the severall recordes of their attainder, more at large may appeare. For the like causes, *Nec Achæorum merita in Romanos, vel Ætolorum unquam effecerunt, ut aliqua sibi imperii fieret accessio; nec Antiochi potentia fuerunt inducti, ut suo ipsorum consensu aliquam in ea provincia potestatem haberet.*[74] If the *Lacedæmonians* in their petition exhibited to the counsel of *Amphictyons,* held it convenient and necessarie, that the townes and Cities of *Greece,* which were not of the league with the *Græcians,* against the barbarous people, should be removed from the place of a councellour; then much more, those which are not onely, not parties with the *Græcians,* but of league with the barbarous people, yea their feeed and sworne servantes, are to be dismissed by the

---

[73] "It is permitted that they rule and be put in charge of the public duties." (trans. Carroll)

[74] Telius, 12; *Principe* 3: "Neither the merits of the Achaeans nor the Aetolians had any influence upon the Romans at any time so that they were not allowed an increase in authority, nor did Antiochus, despite controling power, by their own consent for some time in this province have power" (Bull, 39.)

counsell of *Amphictyons*;[75] for to such we shall more safely give offices of profite, then of commaunde-[M3v]ment, whereby the multitude shall rest pleased, and the state acquitted of peril and daunger: and if we shall give any higher places to anie then those of profite and gaine, let us then carefullie with *Antipater* make choise of such *Athenians*, as shall not be studious of any innovation.[76]

CAP. 11.

Occasions of declination, which arise sometimes
by the difference of lawes, reli-
gion, habite, and
language.

S OL: You have well discussed this matter: therefore let us proceede unto other occasions, amongst which I may finde none that doth more containe, and holde the subject of *Salamina*, in their disobedience and savage life, then the difference of lawes, religion, habite, and language, which by the eie deceiveth the multitude, and persuadeth them that they bee of sundry sortes, nations, and countries, when they be wholy togither but one body, as the same more at large appeareth by the statutes and records of *Salamina*, in the which a manifest proofe is alleadged of that which I have saide; for there it is affirmed, that those partes of *Salamina*, which embrace an uniformity[m] of lawes, religion, habite, and language, with the Cittie of *Athens*, are founde by daily experience, much more loyall, civill, and obedient, then all the other partes of *Salamina*, which are not as yet reduced unto so good an uniformity: for the which causes as wel the counsell of *Athens*, as of *Salamina*, have established certaine lawes for the uniformity of religion, lawes, habite, and language, and therby

---

[75] Amphictyons: North, *Plutarch's Lives*, vol. 1, "Life of Themistocles," 327–28.

[76] According to Canny the label "innovation" had a negative connotation in sixteenth-century New English circles in Ireland, particularly when applied to an opponent's writings or ideas. Any writer so identified was seen as challenging the social order, and being a follower of the republican and radical ideas of Machiavelli. See Canny 1987, 167. Antipater is negatively characterized by Plutarch, but his making the Athenians stick to their "auncient lawes" render his actions a fit allegory for Beacon's warning against innovation. See North, *Plutarch's Lives*, vol. 5, "Life of Phocion," 379.

have charged the subjects and governours of *Salamina* upon their due-
ties of allegeaunce, to holde throughout all the partes thereof, one
uniformity. [*Act. 28 H.8. cap.16.*][77] *Epi:* The Citties and townes which
the *Romaines* did not destroy, were permitted as free subjectes to live,
and to enjoy their owne lawes: and it is saide, the king of [M4]
Fraunce beeing taught by experience, that it was the most ready way
to win the affections of the people, to permit them as free subjectes to
live, and enjoy their owne lawes, did revoke & call home his deputy
from the governement of the Cittie of *Genuenses*, and permitted them
to make choise of their owne governour.[78] *Sol:* These objections
which you have made, doe receive severall aunsweres: and as for the
Romaines, they helde that course and order of governement by you
remembred, untill their power did extende beyonde the confines of *Italy*, but then they gave Prætors, and provinciall governours unto their
Citties. Againe, their lenitie by you remembred, did as much advance
their ambitious thoughts in conquering, as sometimes their knowledge in militarie discipline, so as it may be commended for a ready
way to conquere, but not as a safe waie to holde and keepe. And as
for the *French*, we may not safely followe their steppes as guides herein, for that they are deemed of all nations valiant conquerours, but
not provident defenders and keepers thereof, so as unto them we may
rightlie say, *Vincere scis Hannibal, sed uti victoria nescis.*[79]

CAP. 12.

The ready wayes and meanes to remoove al occasions of declining.

BUT now let us close uppe this long discourse with one pollicy
used by the *Romaines*, which being rightly applyed maie remoove
all occasions of declining: for after they had subjected *Macedony* unto

---

[77] "An act for the Englishe order, habit and language," *Stat. Ire.*, 10 Hen. VI–
14 Eliz., fols. 67v.–71.

[78] *Discorsi* 2.21.4.

[79] Livy 22.51.4: "You know how to gain a victory, Hannibal: you know not
how to use one." According to Livy, this is what Maharbal said to Hannibal after
he rejected his advice to march immediately upon Rome so as to take the city by
surprise. Hannibal's delay is said by Livy "to have saved the city." See also:
North, *Plutarch's Lives*, vol. 2, "Life of Fabius Maximus," 85.

their rule and governement, for the better preventing of all occasions of rebelling, they devided the kingdome into fower provinces, with a capitall punishment to be imposed uppon such, as should wander and travell from province to province, or should chaunge their habitation, or contract affinities, or use marchandise with those other provinces, by which course of governement, they did eftsoones remove all occasions of declining and rebelling for traytours and rebels having once incur-[M4v]red the penalty of lawes, may finde no safety but in wandering from province to province; their broken and decayed forces may not be repayred, but by contracting of affinities with such of other provinces, which they finde to be of strength and force; and sometimes under the coulour of merchandise, they transporte letters, importing and nourishing thereby a generall combination; by which meanes *Shane Oneile* attainted, sometimes laboured the corruption of all the West partes of *Salamina,* as in the statutes of his attainder it doth lively appeare: and by the like practises before remembred, did the late *Burkes* and *Orurkes* of *Conought* nourishe for a long time all their wicked rebellions.[80] And therefore *Mummius Consul Achæis victis, quo minus rebellarent, catibus ac societatibus interdixit, Corinthum quæ duo maria brevi terrarum intervallo iungebat, disturbavit.*[81]

CAP. 13.

*The subject and matter, as also the forme, from
whence every distemperature of this
pollitike bodie hath his
being and subsisting.*

SOL: But sith wee have discussed at large of the principall occasions of declining of estates and common-weales, and of the waies and meanes to suppresse the same, it remaineth that we intreat at large of the distemperature of this polliticke body: for it be-

---

[80] On the rebellion of Shane O'Neill, see above, *Solon* I, notes 3 and 4; and for the rebellion of the Burkes and the O'Rourkes, see above, *Solon* III, note 70.

[81] Bodin, *De Republica* 5.6, 587: "The Consul Mummius used the like policie, having subiected the estate of Achaia, he rased Corinth, and abolished the societies & communalities of Greece" (Knolles, 621).

hooveth princes not onely to foresee and prevent occasions of their declining, but also to knowe the nature of this distemperature, and howe it hath his subsisting and being, and by what meanes the same may be suppressed; for in vaine shall occasions offer themselves, where this distemperature is not kindled, or being kindled where it is suppressed. *Epi:* You have moved a matter of good importaunce, whereof the first is a distemperature of this politicke body, the which is nothing els but a decli-[N1]ninge from a just proportion eyther in obeyinge or governing the subjecte. This distemperature with all other thinges hathe his beeinge and subsistinge from his proper matter and forme: the matter also hath his beeing, eyther from a generall corruption of maners in the people, as in the times wherein *Galba*, and *Pertinax* lived and raigned, who though most just and upright kings, were notwithstanding slaine by their subjects; or els it proceedeth from a corruption in the heade onely, the which sometimes raigned in *Tarquine*; for if the people had then beene corrupted in maners, they could not have beene founde so constant defendors of their liberties, and so desirous of reformation.[82] The forme as in all other things, so unto this distemperature as unto his proper matter it giveth his subsisting & being, the which forme if we shal describe, it may be resembled to a faire cloake given to cover foule practises, shaped out by a cunning workeman, whereby the people oftentimes remaine deluded, and the common-weale subverted; for so ambitious persons desirous of innovation, have alwaies proceeded under an honest cloake and shew, to distemper and disquiet the common peace of the weale publike, and therefore it is truely saide, *Ambitio tam per virtutes quam per vitia nos oppugnat.*[83] *Epi:* But heere we are to observe this caution, that if this forme hath not his proper matter which is the corruption of manners in the people, wherein it maie make a deepe impression, the distemperature that groweth thereby, shall easilie be recovered: and for this cause the forme which *Tarquine* gave to his ambition, was easilie defaced by *Brutus*, and *Valerius*, for that the manners of the

---

[82] Galba & Pertinax: *Discorsi* 1.10.6–8; the Tarquins: Ibid., 1.17.2.

[83] "Ambition opposes us as much through virtues as through vices" (trans. Carroll). On blinding ambition see: *Discorsi* 1.42: "How easily men may be corrupted." Bodin 4.4: "Ambitious men never satisfied with honors, often times the cause of great trobles in a Commonweale" (Knolles, 481).

people were not then corrupted.[84] In like manner *Marcus Manlius*, and *Spurius Cassius*, had set downe unto themselves a forme of disturbing the peace of the common-weale, and for the advauncing of their owne ambition, but finding the manners of the people then uncorrupted, the matter wanting into which, the forme which they before had framed, might be received, they both failed of their purpose.[85] But otherwise it fareth with the common-wealth, when this forme hath founde his proper matter and embraceth the same, namelie the corruption of manners in the people; for in such a case there is kindled foorthwith [N1v] so mighty a distemperature, as without great resistaunce it maie not be quenched: and for this cause the forme of ambition which sometimes *Sylla*, *Marius*, and *Cæsar*, had framed unto themselves, meeting and concurring at once with the corruption of manners in the people as his proper matter, did assuredly advaunce their ambition, to the overthrow of that estate.[86] Therefore most false is that position, which affirmeth, that the people corrupted in manners, are more easily held in subjection, then a nation uncorrupted. The seconde caution to be observed, is the consideration of the sundry formes of disturbing common-weales, which usually doth advaunce her ambition not after one selfesame manner, but sometimes with a shew of profit, sometimes with the shew of magnanimitie, and at other times shee promiseth an alteration and chaunge of thinges to the contentment of al. After this last manner she presented herselfe sometimes unto the *Athenians*, and therefore it is saide, that notwithstanding the citizens of *Athens* observed and obeyed the lawes, which you *Solon* made for their reformation, yet they were found so corrupted in manners, partly by reason of their severall factions, and partly by idlenesse, wherewith the citie of *Athens* was well neare destroyed, as they desired nothing so much as a change and alteration of thinges, every man hoping thereby to be better then his adversaries.[87] Secondarily by a shew of magnanimitie, the people of *Rome* were sometimes induced so farre to imbrace the

---

[84] *Discorsi* 1.16.10.

[85] Mánlius Capitolinus, Spurius Cassius: *Discursus*, 477–78; *Discorsi* 3.8.1, 2.

[86] North, *Plutarch's Lives*, vol. 5, "Life of Julius Caesar," 267–69.

[87] Factions: North, *Plutarch's Lives*, vol. 1, "Life of Solon," 225, 227. Idleness: Ibid., 243. Change: Ibid., 255.

counsell of *Varro* for the resisting of *Hannibal,* as thereby they neare perished themselves and the common-weale. Finally, many are no lesse bewitched with a glistering shew of profit and gaine, the which *Pericles* wel understanding, did forthwith devide the enemies landes gayned by conquest, among the people, and did appointe them rewardes for all thinges, and did make large distributions among them, whereby at the last he did withdraw their obedience from the counsell *Areopagite,* unto his sole rule and governement: in like manner *Phillip* of *Macedonie* corrupted certaine tirauntes of the Ile of *Eubœa,* who with money in like sort corrupted the people, whereby they became rebels and traitoures to their countrie; after the same manner he corrupted and [N2] subdued the most partes of *Greece,* but shall not now the infinite calamities and miseries of the other partes of *Greece:* admonish us not to be deceived with this forme of ambition which *Phillip* of *Macedonie* hath now framed to our utter destruction?[88] O you *Grœcians,* let him not say as heretofore, with my treasure I have corrupted and subdued the most parts of *Greece,* & have found there no fort so strong, but that with an Asse laden with golde, I might enter the same, fearing in the ende hee make us his Asses and Mules, to carrie his silver & golde and not to use the same, or rather slaves to be committed to perpetuall bondage: but let us with the noble *Romaines,* refuse the money of *Spurius Cassius, Ne libertatem vendere eo pretio videamur;*[89] let us not give credit to his flattering orators the Jesuits, which bribed by *Polycarphon* laboure the destruction of *Athens;*[90] let us not be infamous with the *Neapolitanes* for unconstancie; let us not be led this day to affect the French, and tomorrow with a new insinuation of *Ferdinando;* for so it will be, when the yoke of the French shall once seeme heavie and untollerable unto our shoulders.[91] In vaine then with the labourer of *Phrygia,* shal we digge the

---

[88] Pericles: Ibid., vol. 2, "Life of Pericles," 50–51. Varro for resisting of Hannibal: *Discorsi* 1.53.5; Varro vs. Hannibal, foolhardiness of Varro, neither regarded wise counsel: North *Plutarch's Lives,* vol. 7, "Life of Annibal," 318–20. Phillip of Macedon and Ile of Eubœa: Ibid., vol. 5, "Life of Phocion," 362–63.

[89] *Discursus,* 477: "ne libertatem suam vendere eo praecio videretur"; *Discorsi* 3.8.1.: "That we may not be seen to sell liberty for a price" (trans. Carroll).

[90] In the allegory Polycarphon is the Pope; Phillip of Macedonie is Philip of Spain. Polycarphon was general of the army of the Macedonians and the enemy of Phocion.

[91] "The inconstancy of the Neapolitans, eager for the French regime, who at

earth, and searching say, we seeke for *Antigonus;* for such as governe, doe rule as tyrauntes and oppressors over us: in vaine with the worthy woman of *Megara,* shal we take up the bones of *Phocion* in the night, & give unto them the honorable ceremonies of buriall, for the affaires of the *Athenians* may not prosper, because *Phocion* is dead;[92] in vaine shal we then cry and say, O deare hearth & toombe, we pray thee faithfully to keep the bones of this honourable personage, until such time as the *Athenians* shal repent them of the many injuries and wrongs done unto him, for *Phocion* is now dead, and the affaires of the *Athenians* may not prosper: in vaine shall we make unto ourselves a costly stand or image in remembraunce of so worthy a personage, for the affaires of the *Athenians* shall not prosper, in that *Phocion* is dead. Let us therefore in time with the wise governour suspect the flattering of this our enemie, as the calmenes of the sea, which is naught else but a manifest token of a present and imminent tempest; and with *Cicero* and *Cato,* withstande in time the flatterie and ambition of *Cæsar,* least with the *Romanes* to late we repent the same:[93] let us not as men [N2v] overcome with the greatnes of the tempest, desperately seeke our safety in the middest of the rockes and sands, but rather let us fighting for our Prince and country, say, we will overcome, or die.

CAP. 14.

The sundry waies and meanes lefte unto us for the
suppressing of every distemperature
raigning in this polliticke
bodie.

S OL: But what meanes are left unto us to suppresse this distemperature? *Epi:* First we are to give impediment unto the forme and manner, and with *Valerius* deny the embassadoures of *Tarquine* to speake unto the people, least by flatterie they be deluded:

---

first overthrew Ferrando ... and then grew tired of the French, who abused their power and took the Neapolitans' land from them" (Fenton, *Historie of Guicciardin* 1, 70; 2, 88–89).

[92] Woman of Megara: North, *Plutarch's Lives,* vol. 5, "Life of Phocion," 392.

[93] Cicero, Cato, Caesar: Ibid., vol. 5, "Life of Caesar," 271–75.

with *Brutus* we are to condemne and execute even our owne sonnes, corrupted by *Tarquine:* and with *Valerius* we ought to deny the deliverie of *Vendicius* unto the traitoures: thus we must give impediment unto the forme, wherein this caution is to be observed, that the same be done in the beginning.[94] For the *Romanes* having sometimes laide a forme of their ambition for the disturbing and conquering of others, the same was at the first litle regarded, untill they had advaunced their ambition so highly, as to late their associates and neighboures did acknowledge their errour, and when they much desired, they founde themselves much unable[n] to suppresse the same. *Sol:* What other meanes remaine to suppresse this distemperature? *Epi:* First wee are to proceede by good and profitable lawes to the suppressing thereof: for the *Romanes* being given to understand, that forty several nations had combined for their ruine and destruction, they did forthwith create a Dictator to manage the affaires of their wars, unto whome they gave an absolute power;[95] all which, as well the manner of the creation, as his authority and continuaunce was established by lawes, fearing least when this distemperature should bee once thoroughly kindled in the bowels of the common-weale, [N3] they might want either time to effect the same, or that this innovation might then give occasion of mutiny. Secondly, we are to make preparation for the wars, and with *Themistocles* daily to arme and exercise the *Athenians,* to builde and vittaile our gallies, for the battaile of *Marathon* (saith he) will not give an end unto these warres, but rather it doeth foretell us of greater troubles.[96] Thirdly, we are to resist this distemperature by the force and strength of our alies, confederates, and associates: and herein above all others, we are highly to esteeme and regarde the confederation of free Citties and estates; for they doe not easily, or for light causes depart the same, in regarde they proceede judicially by voices, as well to establish, as to dissolve the same; the which caution *Tusci olim observabant,* and therefore it is saide, *Mul-*

---

[94] Ibid., vol. 1, "Life of Publicola": Valerius's denying the ambassadors of Tarquin, 263; Brutus's punishing his sons, 268; Valerius's protection of Vendicius who revealed the traitors' conspiracy, 266–67.

[95] Appointment of dictator: *Discorsi* 1.33.1.

[96] Themistocles and the battle of Marathon: North, *Plutarch's Lives,* vol. 1, "Life of Themistocles," 304–5.

tum negotii fuit populo Romano cum Tuscis hoc modo inter se confederatis:
by which observation they became as well by sea as by lande, mighty
commaunders; so as it is saide, *Quod ante tempora Romanorum. Tusci
potentissimi fuerint terra marique.* After this manner doe the *Helvetians*
at this day proceede in their warres: and in times past, *Achæi atque
Ætoli.*[97] In like manner the *Romaines* the better to overcome all difficulties in their warres, did make an association with other free Cities
and states, by the which manner of proceeding, they did everywhere
conquere and commaunde. But the *Lacedæmonians,* and the *Athenians,*
not making anie confederation, or association with other free Cities,
did not long continue their greatnes. Fourthly, wee must bee able at
all times to produce a collected power and strength of our proper
subjectes, well trayned and exercised in military discipline, for the
suppressing of this distemperature; for otherwise the *Thebanes* and the
rest of the Citties of *Greece,* shall decline and revolte from the *Lacedæmonians;* and *Italy* shall revolte from the *Venetians, Quoniam respublica
Spartanorum & Venetorum populum habuit imbellem;* therefore saith one,
*In promptu habeas exercitum egregium ad exemplum Romanorum, quo
motos liceat componere fluctus.*[98] Fiftly, necessarie it is, that we doe
possess all the strong fortes and holdes, the which although they shall
litle availe us against any general or strong assault made against
them, by such as commaunde the fielde, for that either [N3v] with the
forte or rocke of *Arazze,* they shall give place unto the furie of the ar-
tillerie, or with the towne and forte of *Avon* for want of succours, or
with the towne *Valencey* by the treason of *Donate Raffaguin;* yet they
beeing placed upon the confines of the countrie, may withstande all

---

[97] *Discursus,* 274; *Discorsi* 2.4.1–3: "The first was that which the Tuscans of old
adopted, namely that of forming a league consisting of several republics in which
no one of them had preference, authority or rank above the others; and in which,
when other cities were acquired, they made them constituent members in the
same way the Swiss act in our times, and as in Greece the Achaeans and Aetolians acted in olden times. Since many of the encounters of the Roman people
were with the Tuscans, allied in this way among themselves ... Before the
Romans established their imperium in Italy, the Tuscans were very powerful both
by sea and by land" (Walker, 283, emended by Carroll).

[98] *Discursus,* 38; *Discorsi* 1.6: "because the common-welth of the Spartans &
Venetians had but febble people ... Have a strong army in redines after the
example of the Romanes wherby thou mayst asswage the warres of sedition
when they shall arise" (translation in Folger marginalia).

sodaine attemptes, and give succour unto the wounded and dis-eased.[99] Sixtly, for the better suppressing of these distemperatures, we are to take hostages and pledges with king *Porsenna*,[100] from such persons as are likely to departe from their obedience, to the disturbance of the common peace, and tranquillity of the subjectes, by the which way hee suppressed the malice of the *Romaines;* then shall we safely with him dissolve our armie, and withdrawe our strength.[101] The people of *Salamina* hath in all ages beene founde so factious and rebellious, even in the times before *Athens* made their conquest over them, as the whole kingdome being then devided into foure serverall partes and provinces, which they tearmed kingdomes, yet all beeing commaunded by the king of *Ulster*, they did from time to time yeelde many of their best and chiefe personages, for pledges and hostages of their obedience unto the king of *Ulster:* if then their native borne kinges alied, fostered, maried, and continued even one in the others bosome, did yeelde pledges for their obedience, howe may we in this troubled age safely dismisse pledges, and set them at liberty? may we expect greater fidelity, then they bare sometimes to their native kinges? or doe these times offer more securitie? or doth this nation use more fidelitie? who so looketh into the histories and recordes of their newe and late warres, shall finde in them their olde disposition to rebell; and that this universall obedience which nowe they yeelde, is nothing but a sodaine heate or calme, which° is the true messenger of a tempestuous weather. The seventh caution observed for the suppressing of this distemperature, is speedily to disarme the people, and not suffer them at all to be trained or exercised in militarie discipline, especially where the people be not free, but obedient and tributaries unto us: for the use, knowledge, and exercise of militarie discipline, doeth render them bolde, turbulent, disobedient, and rebellious against us: for what boldnesse and disobedience raig-[N4]neth in the people of *Salamina*, by trayning and exercising them in the feates of warres, the same may lively appeare in their recordes and statutes, where it is saide, that diverse persons have assem-

---

[99] Fenton, *Historie of Guicciardin* 4, 224–25.
[100] Porsenna: North, *Plutarch's Lives*, vol. 1, "Life of Publicola," 286. Livy 2.13.
[101] Disarming subjects: *Principe* 20; *Discorsi* 1.6.

bled with banners displaied against the lieutenaunt and deputie of the saide lande, whereby many times the deputie hath beene put to reproch, and the common-weale set in adventure: [*Anno.10. H.7. cap.13*][102] for this cause it is saide, that *Veneti & Spartani opera plebis in bellis non uterentur;*[103] and more wisely the *Lacedæmonians* holding *Thebes* under their subjection and obedience, woulde not permitte that anie Cittizen of *Thebes* should be trained in the warres, but rather laboured to render them peaceable, and by ease and rest, soft and effeminate;[104] and there was no smith to be found through all the lande of *Israell*, during such time as the *Philistians* held them in subjection, least the *Hebrewes* make them swordes and spades, saie the *Philistians*. Let us then drawe the people of *Salamina* from the exercise of the warres; let us with *Numa* coole and pacifie the hoate courage of the *Romaines* to fight, by the daily use and exercise of religion, prayer, and devotion;[105] and let us with the ancient kinges of *Athens*, draw them unto planting, sowing, & ploughing the land; and let us there advance and shewe forth the olive tree unto the judges; let us there from henceforth honor the Godesse *Pallas,* and not *Mars* or *Neptune,* as heretofore; for she of right ought there to prevaile, and have preheminence; for she it is that shall cause the people to imbrace with all humility and obedience the governement of kinges. Put that great number of *Heilotes* to laboure, and plough the grounde, and let no man be trained but the free Citizen, saieth *Lycurgus*, let them yeelde unto us *magna vactigalia,* and let us give unto them *magnum & egregium exercitum,* if nede shall require.[106] Lastly, let us advance all occupations and sciences with the counsel *Areopagite,* that thereby they may be drawen from the study and thoughts of innovation and

---

[102] This is a reference to the 1494 "Act that no person stirre any Irysherye to make warre," *Stat. Ire., 10 Hen. VI–14 Eliz.,* fol. 29.

[103] *Discursus,* 36: "si aut Venetos aut Spartanos imitaretur: vel sicut illi, opera plebis in bellis non uterentur. *Discorsi* 1.6.5: "either to emulate the Venetians and not to employ its plebs in wars, or like the Spartans, not to admit foreigners" (Walker, 121). Beacon does not distinguish between Venice and Sparta.

[104] On how the Spartans made the conquered Thebans effeminate see North, *Plutarch's Lives,* vol. 3, "Life of Pelopidas," 9–10. See also *Discorsi* 1.21.3.

[105] Numa: see above, *Solon* II, note 41.

[106] "*magna vactigalia . . . magnum & egregium exercitum*": plenty of victuals . . . a great and excellent army.

change, for *difficilis res est*, saith a learned writer, *innumerabilem multitudinem a principe vel a paucis coerceri, nisi plebs operibus intenta quæstum faciat.*[107] Therefore wisely did sometimes *Pericles, Vespasianus, Augustus*, and nowe the *Venetians*, holde the mindes and thoughts of their Citizens alwaies occupied and imploied in [N4v] labours, occupations, and sciences.[108] *Sol:* There are which finding this politicke body distempered, have devided the same into partes and factions, whereby as a smoke parted into many rivals it looseth his principall force: for with the aide and assistance of the weaker parte, they have suppressed the stronger, and then easily commaunded the weaker; and for this cause it is saide, that the kinges of *Ægypt* have heretofore devided their regions and kingdomes by factions, *Ne unquam conspirare inter se Ægyptii omnes possent.*[109] *Epi:* This course of governement is never to be embraced, but upon a great extremitie, when as neither there remayneth counsell, nor forces, which otherwise may suppresse this distemperature: for thereby foure mischiefs shall arise unto the state; first the rentes, revenewes, customes, compositions, tributes, escheates, and other profites annexed unto the crowne, shall thereby cease; for it is saide, the *Florentines* by their civill factions, that first received their beginning of the disorders which were in the governement popular, were rendred as well unable to pay the *French* king the residue of the money which had beene lent them by the Duke of *Millaine*, as also to defray the ordinarie charges of the warres with *Pisa*. The like mischiefe did arise unto the severall townes of *Romagna*,[P] from their severall factions and disorders;[110] but why doe we seeke forraine examples? did not all compositions, customes, rentes, revenewes, tributes, and other escheates, and profits, for a long time cease by the extreame povertie of the subjectes of *Salamina*, which did first arise unto that countrie by reason of their severall factions? as it

---

[107] Bodin, *De Republica* 6.2, 670. "it is a hard thing for the multitude to be kept in awe of a prince or few, unless they may make some gaine by their work" (translation in Folger marginalia). Compare to *Discorsi* 1.6.: "Whether in Rome a Form of Government could have been set up as would have removed the Hostility between the Populace and the Senate" (Walker, 118).

[108] Bodin, *De Republica* 6.2; Knolles, 678.

[109] "Nor were all the Egyptians able to conspire among themselves" (trans. Carroll).

[110] Fenton, *Historie of Guicciardin* 5, 254.

may appeare by the statute of Captaineship, where it is declared, that in the time of justice declination, the Lords and chiefetaines fell into much strife for greatnesse of rule and governement, by reason where-of they drewe unto them other inferiour states to be of their severall factions, whereby the countrie was drawen into that povertie, as for a long time, all rentes, revenewes, and other profits there ceased, and more then that, a newe charge and trouble did growe unto *Athens* for the appeasing of those disorders.[111] Againe, the honour of well governing and commaunding is hereby lost, which is a second mischiefe that ariseth unto us herein; for *ob discordias ci-[O1]vium accidit, ut undus imperio non pareant, sed in diversas partes divisa regio nullis principibus parere cogatur.*[112] All which did sometimes lively appeare in *Salamina,* when as the Lordes and chieftaines of that land, by drawing all other inferiour states unto their severall factions, did thereby withdraw the feare, obedience, and attendance of the subject of *Salamina,* due unto the state of *Athens,* and wholy converted the same unto themselves, as in the statute of Captainship more at large may appeare. [*Act of captainship. 11. Eliza. cap.7. folio 168*] Thirdly by factions and discordes there groweth a neglect of al publike affaires; for it is truely saide, that in the civill discords of the *Florentines,* no man having a sound care of the affaires publike, & many of the principal citizens being suspected, either to frend the *Medices,* or as men that desired another forme of governement, things were overruled more with confusion then with counsel.[113] Lastly, greater mischiefe then any before remembered, ariseth by factions and discordes; for in such cases a third person shall easily atchieve unto the principallity, & suppresse either faction at his pleasure; for so *Clearchus* by the assistance of the faction of the nobility, was inabled to hold the place & kingdome, as wel against the people as nobles, which were then the two factions that raigned & disturbed the politike body:[114] & it is also said, the particular factions of the citizens of *Millaine* drawing to

---

[111] See above, *Solon* I, note 6.

[112] "On account of the discords of the citizens it happened that they would not obey any authority, but a territory divided in different factions is constrained to obey no princes" (trans. Carroll). The threat of factions: Discorsi III.27.5.

[113] Fenton, *Historie of Guicciardin* 5, 254.

[114] Clearchus: *Discorsi* 3.6.31.

privat counsels, did immediatly conspire & take armes against *Lodo-wicke Sforce,* in such sort, as he was forced thereby to make his present departure with his wife & children, at which instant the citizens of *Millain* with francke & ready goodwil received the enemy:[115] & have not several factions of *Salamina,* offred themselves with francke & ready goodwill to receive the enemy? hath not *James* sometimes Earle of *Desmond* sent unto the french king, & by al means excited & provoked him to send an army for the invading of *Salamina,* the which conspiracy did not then take his desired effect, by reason of a peace then immediatly concluded betwixt King H. the 8. & the french King? againe being frustrate of that hope, hath he not many waies provoked the emperour, to send an army for the invading & posses-sing of *Salamina?* in like maner hath not *Thomas FitzGarrald* addressed his letters unto the Bishop of *Rome,* as also unto the Emperor, by one *Gale* in *Granyll,* otherwise, called *Charles Raynold* Archdeacon of *Kelles,* [O1v] for the invading of *Salamina?* all which in the act of the attain-der more at large may appeare. [*Act. 28. H.8. cap.1.*][116] And hath not *Oneile,* who by sufferaunce and tollerance, long supported his faction against the state, sometimes addressed his letters unto several forraine Princes, for the drawing in of straungers to invade and possesse *Sala-mina,* the which were publikely intercepted by the Lorde Deputie? &c. All which may evidently appeare in the statutues of his attainder.[117] Againe did not the faction of the ancient *Brittains* lay open a gap unto *Cæsar* his invasion, and did hee not by the aide of one faction of the *Gaules* subdue the rest, and them also in the end?[118] Was not the Duke sometimes of *Valentinois,* emboldened to invade the dominion of the *Florentines,* with a weake and slender armie, by the feare, suspi-tion, and great disagreement, that then possessed them, for that he

---

[115] Fenton, *Historie of Guicciardin* 4, 228.

[116] This is another reference to the "Act for the attainder of the Earle of Kildare and others," *Stat. Ire., 10 Hen. VI–14 Eliz.,* fols. 37–42; and above, *Solon* II, notes 18–21.

[117] Beacon again refers to the "Act of attainder of Shane Oneile and thectin-guishment of the name of Oneile," *Stat. Ire., 10 Hen. VI–Eliz.,* fols. 156–65; and above, *Solon* I, notes 3 and 4.

[118] North, *Plutarch's Lives,* vol. 5, "Life of Julius Caesar": his journey to England, 295; "how Caesar made allegiances with certain Gaules and played one tribe against another," 289–92, 296–98.

had in his army *Vitellozze*, and the *Ursins*, and for that also *Peter de Medicis* was abiding at *Loiana* in the countrie of *Bollognia* at his direction? for it is saide that hee did entertaine *Peter de Medicis, Vitellie,* and the *Ursins*, not with a minde or desire to advaunce them, for nothing more then that could be farther from his thoughtes, but to augment the mutinies and disagreementes of the *Florentines*, by the which he hoped to urge them either to better conditions, or be able to occupy some place of importance in their jurisdiction.[119] And did not the *Megarians* during the uproares raised by the severall factions then maintained by the issue of *Cylon*, and the offspring of *Megacles*, take from us the haven of *Nysea*, and the ile of *Salamina*?[120] then wee may rightly conclude, that so long as we have an enemy, which raiseth himselfe against us, so long we ought for the safetie of the whole, strongly to suppresse all factions whatsoever: for factions breede an unsetled minde in the people, and doth nourish this desire of chaunge and alteration; the which did livelie appeare in the people of *Athens*, during the continuance of the severall factions, then entertained betwixt the people of the valley, sea-cost, & mountaine; for not withstanding they al kept & observed the laws made by you *Solon*, for their reformation, yet there was none founde but gaped for a change, and desired to see thinges in another state, either parties hoping their condition & state of life [O2] would amend by chaunge, and that every of them should be better then their adversaries. There

---

[119] *Discorsi* 3.27.6. Fenton, *Historie of Guicciardin* 5, 253–54.

[120] North, Plutarch's *Lives*, "Life of Solon," 225–26. Nicaea was a Greek colony, and Megacles was head of the faction known as Paraloi in opposition both to the Pedieis led by Lycurgus and to the Hyperakrioi or Diakrioi. At first Megacles joined with Lycurgus to expel Pisistratus, who had made himself tyrant. Then Megacles helped Pisistratus to a second tyranny in return for the promise of his daughter's hand. The marriage led to a further quarrel, and Pisistratus again retired under the opposition of the other two factions. Cylon was an Athenian nobleman who married the daughter of Theagenes, tyrant of Megara, and with his help seized the Acropolis at Athens with a view to becoming tyrant. The masses, however, did not rally to him. He was besieged but escaped; his friends surrendered, and suppliants were killed. Those responsible for the murder of the suppliants were blamed, especially Megacles. See *OCD* This example cautions against factions. Megacles may possibly stand for Lord Grey as head of the English army at Smerwick (the Haven of Nicaea), which fought against the Italian and Spanish papal forces (Megarians). Grey executed hostages, just as Megacles killed the surrendering suppliants.

remaineth now that we deduct[121] colonies, which is the last, but not the least meanes to suppresse this distemperature, which of all others is the most beneficiall for the containing of a nation conquered in their duty and obedience; wherein foure matters are worthily considered: first the necessitie of deducting colonies; secondarily the benefite that redoundeth thereby unto common-weales; thirdly what order and manner in deducting colonies is to bee used and observed; lastly, the impedimentes which are usuallie given unto the deducting of colonies. *Sol:* Shew us the necessitie of collonies. *Epi:* A nation conquered may not be contained in their obedience without the strength of colonies or garrisons: for may we be induced to beleeve, that that people or nation, who daily bewaileth & accuseth his present state and condition, may persist therein longer then they be pressed thereunto by necessitie? and more then this in the act of *Absentes, [28. H.8. cap.3.]*[122] the meere native borne people of *Salamina*, are tearmed to be mortall and naturall enemies unto their conquerour and all his dominions. After this sort did the citizens of *Cremona* affect the *Venetians;* and the *Pisans*, the *Florentines:* but now to suppresse this distemperature, if wee shoulde give unto them garrisones, and *Præsidia perpetua, nihil isto intollerabilius est,* saith a learned writer, *quia tantum abest ut victi vincentium imperiis assuescere condiscant, ut non prius a novandis rebus conquiescant, quam aut præsidia interemerint, aut arces ceperint, aut finitimos principes ac populos ad bellum accerserint;*[123] whereof we neede not search forraine examples, when the daily calamities of *Salamina* doe witnesse the same, which happened since the times,

---

[121] deduct: to lead forth or establish a colony (L. *deducere*).

[122] See *Stat. Ire., 10 Hen. VI–14 Eliz.,* fols. 46–49; and above, *Solon* II, note 5.

[123] Bodin, *De Republica* 6.2, 644; Folger marginalia: "perpetual aide nothing is more hard to be born then this because it is so far that they which are overcome would learne to accustome themselves unto the governments of them which do overcome then they will cease from making of a change no longer they shall take away their help or take the towers or send for the princes about them & the people to make war." Here Bodin warns against perpetual garrisons as an impediment to successful rule of a conquered territory. "Nothing is more intolerable than perpetual garrisons ... because it is so necessary that those who have been conquered accustom themselves to the rule of those who have conquered them, since at first they will not be content with new things, so much more if garrisons are acquired or castles or citadels arise, or the princes prohibit the people from going to war" (trans. Carroll).

wherein we gave unto them *præsidia perpetua:* for how many waies did this people incite the French King, how oft have they provoked the Pope to invade this lande of *Salamina*? Againe the Emperour and all other Princes and Potentates, what fortes and holdes have they not taken, and how many of our garrisons have they most cruelly slaine and murdered, the same, in the several actes of Attainder of *Shane Oneile, Garralde FitzGarralde, James of Desmond,* and by severall other recordes, may appeare at [*28. H.8. cap.1.*][124] [O2v] large. Neither doth this forme of governement drawe with it a perpetuall discontentment onelie, but also an infinite and continuall charge in maintaining these severall garrisons, as well to the Prince, as to the subject; for so in the act of subsidie and other recordes it may appeare. Neither be these all the discommodities that perpetual garrisons drawe with them, for these notwithstanding, we have beene forced to send at sundry times armies roiall to supresse disorders and rebellions, as the same more at large may appeare in the act of restraining of tributes; [*28. H.8. cap.11.*][125] so as wee may conclude, that where colonies are not strongly and faithfully deducted, there the ende of the first warres, is but a beginning of the second more daungerous then the first; the which maie appeare by the recordes of *Salamina:* for no sooner were the people or sects, called *Omores, Odempseis, Oconores,* and others, expelled by great forces and strengthes, to our great charges, out of the severall countries of *Liece, Slewmarge, Irry, Glimnaliry, and Offaile,* but eftsones for that we deducted not colonies, they traiterouslie entered the said countries by force, and long detained the same, untill they were with greater forces expelled, all which more at large may appeare in the act made for the deviding of countries, into shiere groundes, [*Act. An.3.4. Phil.& Mariæ c.2. folio.145*][126] so as we

---

[124] Beacon refers again directly to the "Acte for thattainder of thearle of Kyldare and others," *Stat. Ire., 10 Hen. VI–14 Eliz.,* fols. 37–42; and above, *Solon* II, note 18. He also indirectly refers to the "Act of attainder of Shane Oneile," *Stat. Ire., 10 Hen. VI–14 Eliz.,* fols. 156–65.

[125] "An Acte restrayning trybutes to be geven to Irishe men," *Stat. Ire., 10 Hen. VI–14 Eliz.,* fols. 56–56v.; for a more detailed discussion of these tributes or blackrents, see above, *Solon* III, note 42.

[126] The 1557 "Acte for the disposition of Leice and Offalie" and the "Acte whereby the King and Queene be intituled to the countries of Leice, Slewmarge, Irry, Glinmaliry & Offaile & for making the same countries shire grounds" were the basis for the plantation of the O'More, O'Connor and O'Dempsey lands in

may conclude, that it is not for wise Princes to persevere in that course of governement, which doth nourish as it were a perpetuall interest in troubles, charges, and expenses: for the which causes chiefely did the *Venetians* willingly abandon the governement of *Bybienna* and *Pisa*, and wee of *Athens*, *Salamina*, the which did chiefely arise unto us, for that insteede of planting of colonies, we placed garrisons.[127] Now then if we be willing to cast of our former and manifolde troubles, if we be desirous to dismisse ourselves of these infinite and perpetual charges, and lastly if we indevour to be strong against the invaders, and such as shall contend to occupie *Salamina* by force, let us loose no opportunity of deducting of colonies, for they be deducted and maintained with small or no charges, & with no great offence, but onely to such whose landes and houses they possesse, the which remaine for the most part pacified, in that they enjoy their life which stoode in the handes of the Prince, as well as [O3] their landes to dispose, for their offences: and if they should remaine discontented, for that having respect to the whole kingdome they be but a handfull, and also dispersed and poore, they may never be able to hurt or disturbe the state, & all others which finde themselves free from their losses, shall rest pacified, partely fearing, least they commit anything rashly or foolishly, and partly doubting, least the like befalleth them as to those which remaine spoyled for their offences. Againe, being thus deducted with small or no discontentment, and maintained with far lesse charge, they bee founde also more faithfull and stoute defendours of the confines of the country then garrisons, and therefore it is saide by a man of great understanding, *Si reges nostri capto Ludovico 12. rege Insubriae, Colonias eo misissent, ut quondam Celtarum reges fecisse dicuntur, Insubria a Francorum ditione ac potestate non tam facile defecisset: nec vero Hispani præsidiis militaribus nulla Colonia deducta perpetuum eius regionis imperium tuebuntur, sed ab imperio subditi arrepta occasione desciscant oportet; non aliter quam Belgæ, quos iam pridem coloniis Hispanorum ad imperium retinendum coniungi necesse fuis-*

Laois and Offaly. These plantations were not effectively established until the 1560's, and even then suffered from ongoing O'More and O'Connor resistance. See *Stat. Ire., 10 Hen. VI–14 Eliz.*, fols. 124–26; Beacon's reference to fol. 145 is apparently a mistake.

[127] Bibbiena: Fenton, *Historie of Guicciardin* 4, 217–18.

set, quoniam nec ulla vis diuturna esse potest, & pessimus diuturnitatis custos est metus:[128] in like manner *Salamina* notwithstanding the strength of garrisons, doth daily take all occasions of declining, but in former times, after colonies were deducted, then *Salamina* continued for many ages in their obedience, in such sorte, as none durst beare uppe heade, but lived as vassals and obedient people, untill partly by the iniquity of the times, partly by our domesticall factions, and lastly by a negligence and security then found in these colonies, they were overthrowne and expelled by the native borne people of that lande, all which in the act of attainder of *Shane Oneile* more at large may appeare, as also in the statutes of *Absentes*. *Sol:* Nowe sith the necessity of colonies doeth manifestly appeare by unfallible proofes and examples, let us proceede unto the profite and benefite that groweth thereby. *Epi:* The benefites that hereby arise to the common-weale, are sundry and diverse: first the people poore and seditious which were a burden to the common-weale, are drawen forth, whereby the matter of sedition is remooved out of the Cittie; and for this [O3v] cause it is said, that *Pericles* sent into the country of *Cherronesus,* a thousand free men of his Cittie there to dwell, and to devide the landes amongst them; five hundreth also into the Ile of *Naxus,* into the Ile of *Andros* others, some he sent to inhabite *Thracia,* and others to dwell with the *Bisaltes;* as well thereby to ridde the Cittie of a number of idle persons, who thorough idlenes began to be curious and to desire chaunge of thinges, as also to provide for the necessity of the poore towns-men that had nothing, which being naturall Citizens of *Athens* served as garrisons, to keepe under those which had a desire to rebell, or to attempt any alteration or change:[129] secondly by trans-

---

[128] Bodin 6.2, 645. Folger copy marginalia: "if our Kings (Lewes the 12 king of Insubria bing taken) had sent the Colonians thither as the kings of the Scotts did in tymes past Insubria had not so easily departed from the government & power of the French men: neither the Spaniards shall defend or keep the government continually by the help of the souldiers having lead forth no Colonie, but the subiects when they shall see any occasion must needs depart from the government no otherwyse then the men so called when it was necesary to be ioyned to the townes of the Spaniards so called to reteine their government, because no force can be ever lasting and feare is the worst keeper of continuance as may be." Machiavelli, like Bodin, recommends settlements; the passage preceding the quotation from Bodin almost exactly translates *Principe* 3.

[129] North, *Plutarch's Lives,* vol. 2, "Life of Pericles," 18.

lating of colonies, the people conquered are drawen and intised by little and little, to embrace the manners, lawes, and governement of the conquerour: lastly the colonies being placed and dispersed abroade amongest the people, like Beacons doe foretell and disclose all conspiracies, and as a garrison also are wont to suppresse the mutinies of such as are desirous of alteration and change; and to this effect it is saide, in the statute of *Absentes*, that the colonies, which were sometimes deducted for the defending of the confines of *Salamina*, then and many ages after abiding in the saide lande, did nobly and valiantly defende the same against all enemies whatsoever, as also kept the same in such tranquillity & good orders, as the kings had due subjection of the inhabitance, the lawes were well obeyed, and of all the revenewes and regalties they were duely aunswered as in any place whatsoever: lastly, they yeelde a yearely rent, profite, or service unto the crowne for ever; for these causes above rehearsed it is saide, *Romani victis hostibus Colonias deducebant:* and the French conquering *Lombardy,* did chase out the auncient inhabitants, and in their dwelling placed colonies: in like manner the Emperour of the Turkes from time to time, of Christians whome then he reduced in servitude, deduceth colonies,[q] so as it is saide, that *Carolus* 5. *imperator debellatis Peruanæ regionis gentibus, eadem quam Turcarum rex, in coloniarum translatione, ratione usus est.*[130] *Sol:* Nowe sith as well the necessity as the profite of deducting colonies doth sufficiently appeare unto us, let us proceede unto the manner and order of translating of colonies, as [O4] the thirde matter woorthy of consultation. *Epi:* In the order and manner of deducting collonies, certaine rules are to bee observed: first that the lands be so devided, as strengths by great numbers may be deducted, and therefore *Duo cuique iugera tributa sunt;* but not long after, *Prolatis finibus, lege Licinia septem iugera cuique civi assignata legimus,* the which order was observed by the *Romaines*. But otherwise the Emperour of the Turkes, *iugera quindecim cuique attribuit.*[131] The

---

[130] *"Romani … deducebant":* The Romans having conquered their enemies deducted colonies. Bodin, *De Republica* 6.2, 645. "The Emperour Charles 5, having conquered Peru … just as the king of the Turks, found means to enrich his treasure by means of Christian slaves, which he sent in Colonies into conquered countries" (Knolles, 656).

[131] Bodin, *De Republica* 6.2, 639, 645: "for the division of two journeys or acres continued a long time … But since the law *Licinia*, everie citizen was allowed to

Romaines laboured to deduct colonies by great numbers, especially out of the confines of *Italy*, to the ende that by the proper strength and forces of colonies, they might easilie defende the confines of their dominions, and suppresse al such as were founde desirous of innovation. Secondly we are to plant and place our colonies in the most rich and fruitfull landes, *Ut in eo civibus numero auctis alimenta suppetant, potentiaque, auctæ huius modi novæ urbes, omnem internam vim propulsare atque etiam opprimere queant.*[132] Thirdly, such as are to be deducted in the number of colonies, we shall wisely make them but proprietaries of the landes, during life onely, *Ut fructuarii occasu fructus in ærarium cogerentur, quoad principis beneficio alius succederet, quemadmodum Amurates cum Timariolis egit:*[133] by which constitution three matters beneficiall to the weale publicke shall arise; first opportunity shall be lent from time to time, to recompence servitours by these casuall profites that shall arise, without imposing any newe charge upon the common-weale; secondly by the death of this tenaunt for life, the profites thereof growe unto the prince untill the landes be newly disposed by him; thirdly, the prince or state being to dispose these landes at his or their pleasure, shall with this rewarde binde the proprietarie of the lande during life, in all services to be loyall and faithfull; lastly, by holding this course, sundrie inconveniences shall be eschewed which usually followe such as graunte these landes in perpetuity; for in such cases they have beene founde in *Salamina*, especially after two or three descentes, to inter-marry and foster with the meere native people, and by that occasion decline sometimes from their obedience; at

---

have seven journies or acres of land ... Yet wee find, that *Sultan Mahumet* king of the Turkes, found meanes to inrich his treasure by meanes of Christian slaves, which hee sent in Colonies into conquered countries, giving to every one fifteene acres of land" (Knolles, 650–651; 656).

[132] *Discursus*, 8; *Discorsi* 1.1: "it is necessary to avoid sterile places and for cities to be put in very fertile places where, when expansion has taken place owing to the fruitfulness of the land, it may be possible for them both to defend themselves against the attack and to overcome any who stand in the way of the city's greatness" (Walker, 102).

[133] Bodin, *De Republica* 6.2, 645. "Amurath the first dealt more mildly with the Timariots, giving them certayne lands and rents, to some more, and to others less, upon condition they should attend him in the wars when they were called, with a certayne number of horse: and if the Timariots chanced to die, the fruits should acrue unto the Prince, untill that hee had aduaunced some other, by way of gift" (Knolles, 656).

other times they are founde to make leases of their landes, or to make
a grant over of their estates unto such as are not [O4v] well affected
unto the governement, to the overthrowe of themselves and common-
weale, as it may appeare in the statute of Absentes, where it is saide,
that the colonies being possessed of their landes, did make leases of
diverse of their holdes and manners unto the late Earle of *Kildar* attainted, by occasion whereof the same came to the possession of
Thomas FitzGarralde, his sonne and heire, who intending a daungerous
rebellion, was aided, assisted, and maintained against the state, by the
inhabitants, & occupiers of the saide lande, so as the state was compelled of force to sende thither an army royall for the better suppressing of those disorders and rebellions; lastly, these colonies must
unite and gather themselves together into places of strength, walled
or intrenched for their better defence against sodaine incursions, and
never be destitute of provision sufficient for their defence: for such of
our auncient colonies in *Salamina,* which in times peaceable suffered
their townes, holdes, and castles to decay, and neglected the main-
teining of such garrisons, as of right appertained unto them to maintain, were in difficult times exiled, bannished, or put to the sword,
onely such remained and prevailed, which with a collected power
and strength, did inhabite places walled or intrenched, and were not
founde destitute of sufficient provision for the wars, as it may more
at large appeare in the act of *Absentes.* Therefore of late daies two
worthy Knightes, Sir *Henry Walloppe* Treasurer,[134] and Sir *Nicholas
Bagnole* Knight Marshall,[135] being the principall personages of the

---

[134] Sir Henry Wallop (1540–1599), Vice-Treasurer of Ireland, was one of the
most prominent New English government officials in Ireland in the period of
Beacon's stay there. Wallop was one of the strongest advocates of the plantation
of Munster, participating in its development as joint Lord Justice between 1582
and 1584, and as Vice-Treasurer until 1599. Beacon's not very specific praise of
Wallop may have been occasioned by their friendship and by the latter's presence in England prior to and during the publication of *Solon.* See *DNB; Tudor Ire.,*
284, 286–88, 329, 331.

[135] Again Beacon generally praises the activities of one of the longest serving
New English officials in Ireland, Sir Nicholas Bagenal, who had been Marshal of
the army in Ireland and chief commissioner for the government of Ulster. Since
the aged Bagenal had passed on his responsibilities to his son Sir Henry (1556–
98) in 1590, it is not clear what military actions "of late" Beacon is referring to
when he introduces Wallop and Bagenal. For Bagenal, see *DNB; Tudor Ire.,* 229,
231, 252, 270, 298.

late deducted colonies, for the better strengthening of the confines of *Salamina*, have not dispersed their forces but wisely collected them into one place of strength, whereby they have repelled from time to time, all internall forces or sodaine incursions. *Sol:* You have at large described unto us the necessity, the profite, and the order and manner of deducting of colonies, you shall orderly proceede, if you nowe intreate of the impedimentes which usually are given unto such actions. *Epi:* The impediments are sundry and diverse: the first is given by such as usually oppose themselves against all newe orders, for that they reape a benefite by the olde disorders. The second is equall with the first, and proceedeth from a generall incredulitie ingrafted in [P1] all sortes of persons, which never yet have given affiance or confidence unto newe attemptes, be they never so profitable. The thirde impediment ariseth greater then the rest, when the authours of these new orders, shall become faint defendors thereof, and shall give leave and waye to others, which give impediment thereunto. The last impediment is the great trouble and charge, which followeth such as shall inhabite landes farre removed; with the consideration whereof, the *Romaine* Cittizens were sometimes withdrawen, and discouraged from the inhabiting of the lands removed out of the confines of *Italy*, and the same also doeth not a little withdraw the newe colonies from inhabiting *Salamina*: But *Muhamedes* the Emperour sometimes of the *Turkes*, contending to remove this impediment, *Cuique coloniæ duos bubulos ac sementem dedit.*[136] *So:* Now you have at large discoursed of a reformation of declined common-weales, declare unto us what you intende by the subsequent words which followe in your generall and first description, where you tearme it an happie restitution unto his first perfection.[137] *Epi:* I have tearmed it an happy restitution, when the same is effected without bloud-shed and spot of tyranny, or cruelty; but yet it must be confessed that where *sanandi medicina* may not prevaile, there *execandi*, is rightly used;[138] neither is nature saide

---

[136] Bodin, *De Republica* 6.2, 645. "*Muhumet* king of the Turkes ... giving to everyone ... two oxen and feed for one yeare" (Knolles, 656).

[137] ricorso: Machiavelli, *Discorsi* 3.1.

[138] Cicero, *Letters to Atticus* 2.1: tamen non minus esset probanda medicina, quae sanaret vitiosas partes rei publicae quam quae exsecaret [still a remedy which cures the diseased parts of the State should be preferable to one which amputates them].

to hate those members and partes, which shee cutteth of for the pres-
ervation & safety of the whole body: and by this word perfection, I
intend nothing but that good, which even from the first institution we
did aime & shoote at, *Nam omne principium bonum aliquod spectabat*,[139] and this is the ende and scope of al reformations: as for example, when *Athens* had first conquered *Salamina*, they labored nothing more, then to conteine the subject in his obedience unto the Cittie
of *Athens* under good & profitable lawes, & that the people might
more assuredly be drawen thereunto without any great grievance or offence, they strongly deducted colonies into all parts of *Salamina*, and
established there many and profitable lawes, the which were truly and
justly observed by many ages, and so continued their obedience from
time to time, until these colonies were by the iniquity of times exiled.
Let then our second reformation be like unto the first, for *Omne principium bonum aliquod spectabat*:[140] [P1v] so as I may ende like as I began
this discourse, saying, that a reformation of a declined common-weale
is an happy restitution unto his perfection. *Sol:* You have wisely discoursed of all the partes of this general description, and happily have
made an ende thereof, for beholde my messenger hasteneth unto me
more then with an ordinary expedition. *Nuncius:*ʳ My Lord and generall
Solon, the *Megarian* army approacheth neare at hand; for nowe standing
upon the pinnacles of the temple of *Venus,* we did plainly discover their
ships. *Solon* then turning himselfe unto *Epimenides* saide, I go armed
against the *Megarians* with the wisedome of *Epimenides;* in such sorte, as
with *Numa* I may safely sacrifice when as they remaine in armes, in
requitall of which good counsell from henceforth I shall confesse to
holde my life from *Epimenides. Epi:* These meane lightes which I have
given for the reformation of *Salamina,* with the wisedome of *Solon* as
with the beames of a bright sunne, remaine extinguished, so as there
restesth nothing but our former goodwill which may tie you to make
acceptance thereof. *Sol:* And the same may never die but with *Solon;*

---

[139] Folger marginalia: "for every beginning did tend to some good end." Cf.
Discursus, 420: "Principia enim cum Sectarum, tum Republicarum atque Imperi-
orum, omnia aliquid boni habent." *Discorsi* 3.1.2: "For at the start religious
institutions, republics and kingdoms have in all cases some good in them"
(Walker, 386).

[140] See above, *Solon* III, note 139.

farewell then *Epimenides. Epi:* And you *Solon* in like manner adue. Then with the great noise and clattering of the weapons, and armour of the souldiers, I sodenly awaked, and remained for a small time amazed with the event of so weighty and great matters, but at the last my drousie sence being newly refreshed, I might beholde, all was sodenly vanished and nothing left in place but a vision or dreame, the which according to my small skill, and understanding, I have heere expressed in pelting prose and not in heroicall verse; wherewith *Solon* as then it seemed to me, did much commende and grace the matter, which then he ut- tered unto *Epime- nides.*

FINIS.

TEXTUAL NOTES

Book I

a. *pœnam*] *pænam Hn*
b. disorders] discorders *Hn*
c. feare,] feare *Hn*
d. *pœnæ*] *pænæ Hn*
e. *Cæsar*] *Cesar Hn*

Book II

a. [D4]] [C4] missigning in *Hn*
b. tooke] tooke, *H* (comma inked in)
c. *Epi:*] not in *Hn*
d. sorte] sote *Hn*
e. extraordinary.] extraordinary, *Hn*
f. much as] muchas *Hn*
g. speciallie] especiallie *Hn* (s appears to be printed over e)
h. F1v misnumbered as p. 32 should be p. 42
i. (as Plutarch witnesseth)] as (Plutarch witnesseth) *Hn*
j. principalitie] prncipalitie *Hn*
k. *Epi:*] not in *Hn*
l. *Sol:*] *Sol. Hn*
m. Ubi] Vti *Hn*
n. Sol:] Sol. *Hn*
o. with all] withall *Hn*
p. pœnas] pænas *Hn*
q. writtes: end of H1v reads writes top of H2 reads writtes *Hn*
r. institution.] institution? *Hn*
s. asunder] a sunder *Hn*
t. honors,] honors *Hn*

Book III

a. fourthly,] fourthly *Hn*
b. so much] somuch *Hn*
c. the] the the *Hn*
d. legs] legges, K1 *Hn;* legs K1v *Hn*
e. it] it it *Hn*
f. eie] eie ! written in ink *Hn*
g. Lords] L: *Hn*
h. which] whch *Hn*
i. subjects?] subjects. *Hn*
j. subjects,] subjects? *Hn*
k. safegarde and benefite *BL1*] safegar benefite *Hn.* "de and" are blotted out in *Hn,* an offset from the deleted blot on [L4v]: other charges due *BL1*] other ~~his wives~~ charges *Hn*
l. Sir R. Bingham] Sir B. Bingham *Hn*
m. uniformity] uinformity *Hn*
n. unable] nable *Hn,* u dropped to line below
o. which] wich *Hn*
p. Romagna] Bomagna *Hn*
q. colonies] co-*lonies Hn*
r. *Nuncius:*] *Nuncius. Hn*

SELECTED BIBLIOGRAPHY

I. Manuscript Sources

a. Chatsworth House, Derbyshire

Lismore MSS
"Boyle Patent Book"
(Consulted in Unpublished Typescript of Michael MacCarthy-Morrogh)

b. Public Record Office, London

State Papers, Ireland, Elizabeth.
S. P. 63/131–S. P. 63/205.

c. British Library, Department of Manuscripts

Additional MS: 34.
"A collection of treatises on the rebellion in Ireland, 1594–1603 [G. Carew, 1617]."

Additional MS: 4728.
"A journal or diary of all the passages and accidents ... during the government [of Ireland] of Sir William Russell, June 1594–May 1597."

Harleian MS: 35, fols. 145–78.
"A discourse of the realme of Ireland contayninge the ancient civill warrs thereof, the incursions of the Scotts, and a platforme how to reduce the Irish to civill government."

Harleian MS: 3292, fols. 5–18v.
"Sir John Perrot's discourse for repressing the rebellions stirred up in Ireland by the earl of Desmond and Visc. Baltinglas and for reforming the realm."

II. Printed Primary Sources

A. M. *The Successe God Gave Unto . . . Soldiours.* London, 1581. No. 541 in *The English Experience: Its Record in Early Printed Books Published in Facsimile.* New York: Da Capo Press, 1972.

Agricola, Rudolf. *De Inventione Dialectica.* Louvain: Theodoricus Martinus, 1515.

Aristotle. *Politics.* Trans. H. Rackham. The Loeb Classical Library [Greek Authors]. London: Heinemann, 1959.

———. *The Nicomachean Ethics.* Trans. H. Rackham. The Loeb Classical Library [Greek Authors]. London: Heinemann, 1926.

Ascham, Roger. *Toxophilus, The Schoole of Shootynge Conteyned in Two Bookes.* London: Edward Whytchurch, 1545.

———. *The Scholemaster* (1570). English Linguistics 1500–1800, A Collection of Facsimile Reprints. Ed. R. C. Alston. Menston: The Scolar Press, 1967.

Beacon, Richard. "From *Solon His Follie,*" in *The Field Day Anthology of Irish Writing.* Ed. Seamus Deane. Derry: Field Day Publications, 203–10.

Bodin, Jean. *De republica libri sex, Latine ab autore redditi: Multo quam antea locupletiores.* London: Iacobus Du-Puys, 1586.

———. *Les Six Livres de la République.* Paris: Fayard, 1986.

———. *The six bookes of the commonweale.* Trans. Richard Knolles. A facsimile reprint of the English translation of 1606, corrected and supplemented. Ed. Kenneth D. McRae. Cambridge: Harvard Univ. Press, 1962.

Browne, Nicholas. "The means how to keepe the provynce of Munster and suche as are of anye force thearin from being able to raise any power," in *Cork Historical and Archaeological Society Journal* 12 (1907): 253–68.

Calendar of the Carew Manuscripts Preserved in the Archiepiscopal Library at Lambeth, 1515–1624. Ed. J. S. Brewer and William Bullen. 6 vols. London: Longmans, Green, Reader, & Dyer, 1867–1873.

Calendar of Patent and Close Rolls of Chancery in Ireland, Henry VIII-Elizabeth. 2 vols. Dublin: Thom & Sons for H. M. Stationary Office, 1861–62.

Calendar of the Manuscripts of the Marquis of Salisbury at Hatfield House. 24 vols. London: Historical Manuscripts Commission, 1883–1976.

Calendar of State Papers, Domestic Series, of the Reigns of Edward VI, Mary, Elizabeth, and James I, 1547–1625. Ed. Robert Lemon. 12 vols. Nendeln: Kraus Reprint, 1967.

Calendar of the State Papers Relating to Ireland, of the Reigns of Henry VIII, Edward VI, Mary and Elizabeth, 1509–1603. Ed. H. C. Hamilton, E. G. Atkinson and R. P. Mahaffy. 11 vols. Nendeln: Kraus Reprint, 1974.

Cambrensis, Giraldus. *The English Conquest of Ireland, A. D. 1166–1185 from the "Expugnatio Hibernica."* Ed. Frederick J. Furnival. E. E. T. S., O. S., No. 107. London: Trench, Trubner, 1896.

Campion, Edmund. *A Historie of Ireland* (1571). Introduction by Rudolf B. Gottfried. New York: Scholar's Facsimiles & Reprints, 1940.

Campion, Edmund. *Two Bokes of the Histories of Ireland* (1633). Ed. A. F. Vossen. Assen: Van Gorcum, 1963.

"Chronicles of Ireland from 1594 to 1613". Ed. C. L. Falkiner. *English Historical Review.* 22 (1907): 104–30, 527–52.

Cicero, Marcus Tullius. *Somnium Scipionis ex libro sexto de Repub.* Ed. Erasmus. Paris: Thomas Richardus, 1557.

———. *Letters to Atticus.* Trans. E. U. Winsted. 3 vols. The Loeb Classical Library [Latin Authors]. London: Heinemann, 1912–1918.

———. *De oratore.* Ed. and Trans. Edward Sutton and Harris Rackham. 2 vols. The Loeb Classical Library [Latin Authors]. London: Heinemann, 1959–1960.

Collins, Arthur, ed. *Letters and Memorials of State. . .written and collected by Sir Henry Sidney. . . , Sir Philip Sidney, and his brother Sir Robert Sidney. . . .* 2 vols. London: for T. Osborne, 1746.

Davies, John. *A Discovery of the True Causes why Ireland was never Entirely Subdued* (London, 1612). Introduction by John Barry. Dublin: Irish University Press, 1969.

Derricke, John. *The Image of Irelande with a Discourse of Woodkarne* (1581). Introduction, transliterarum and glossary by David B. Quinn. Belfast: Blackstaff Press, 1985.

The Description of Ireland: and the state thereof . . . in anno 1598. Ed. Edmund Hogan. Dublin: M. H. Gill, 1878.

Dimock, John. "A Treatise of Ireland." In *Tracts Relating to Ireland,* edited by Richard Butler. Vol. 2. Dublin: Irish Archaeological Society Publications, 1842.

De L'Isle and Dudley. *Report on the Manuscripts of Lord De L'Isle and Dudley Mss.* 6 vols. London: Historical Manuscript Commission, 1925–66.

E. C. S. *The Government of Ireland Under Sir John Perrot, 1584–8.* London: A. Matthews for T. Walkley, 1626.

Elyot, Sir Thomas. *The Boke Named the Governour.* London: Thomas Berthelet, 1537.

Fiants. "Calendar to fiants of the reign of Henry VIII . . ." [etc.] Reigns of Henry VIII to Elizabeth in *Seventh* to the *Twenty-Second Report of the Deputy Keeper of the Public Records in Ireland.* Dublin, 1875–90.

Four Masters. *Annala Rioghachta Eireann: Annals of the Kingdom of Ireland by the Four Masters, from the earliest period to 1616.* Ed. and trans. John O'Donovan. 7 vols. Dublin: Hodges, Smith, 1856.

Foxe, John. *Actes and Monuments of these latter and perillous days, touching matters of the church.* London: John Day, 1563. *Newly recognised and inlarged.* 2 vols. 1570, 1576. *Newly revised and recognised partly also augmented, and now the fourth time published,* 1583.

———. *The acts and monuments of John Foxe: with a life of the martyrologist, and vindication of the work, by George Townsend.* New York: AMS Press, 1965.

Fraunce, Abraham. *The Lawyers Logicke.* London: W. How, 1588.

Gainsford, Thomas. *The true exemplary and remarkable history of the Earl of Tyrone.* London: G. Purslow, 1619.

The Geneva Bible, A facsimile of the 1560 edition. Ed. Lloyd E. Berry. Madison: University of Wisconsin Press, 1969.

Guicciardini, Francesco. *The Historie of Guicciardin* conteining the warres of Italie and other partes, continued for many yeares under sundry kings . . . with a table at large. Reduced into English by Geoffrey Fenton. London: Thomas Vautroullier for W. Norton, 1579.

Harrington, Sir John. "A Short View of the State of Ireland written in 1605." In *Anecdota Bodleiana.* No. 1. Ed. William Dunn Macray. Oxford, 1879.

Harvey, Gabriel. *Letter-book of G. Harvey (1573–1580)*. Ed. from original, Sloane MS. 93 by E. J. L. Scott. *Camden Society Publications*, New Series, No. 33. 1884.

Herbert, Sir William. *Croftus, Sive de Hibernia liber*. Ed. W. E. Buckley. London: Roxburghe Club, 1887.

———. *Croftus sive de Hibernia liber*. Ed. Arthur Keaveney and John A. Madden. Dublin: Irish Manuscripts Commission, 1992.

Holinshed, Raphael. *The ... Chronicles of England, Scotlande, Irelande.* Ed. John Hooker and others, 3 vols. London: H. Bynneman for J. Harrison, 1577, 1587. Reprint. Ed. Henry Ellis, 6 vols. London: J. Johnson [etc.], 1807–8.

Hooker, John. "Diary of 1569–71 parliament." *Procedings of the Royal Irish Academy*. 25 sect. c (1904–5): 563–66.

———. "An account of the Session of 1569." Reprinted in *Irish Historical Documents, 1172–1922*. Ed. Edmund Curtis and R. B. McDowell. London: Methuen, 1968, 89–96.

Lee, Thomas. "A Briefe Declaration of the Government of Ireland ... in the government of Sir William Fitz-Williams (1588–94)." In *Desiderata Curiosa Hibernica*, edited by John Lodge. vol. 1. Dublin: David Hay, 1772.

"A Letter sent by T. B. gentleman ... wherein is conteined a large discourse of the peopling and inhabiting the Cuntrie called the Ardes ... taken in hand by Sir Thomas Smith(London, 1571)." In *Historical Account of the MacDonnels of Antrim*, edited by George Hill. Belfast: Archer & Sons, 1873.

Lipsius, Justus. *Politicorum sive civilis doctrinae libri sex. Editio altera, quam auctor pro Germana fide agnoscit*. London: George Bishop, 1590.

———. *Sixe Bookes of Politickes or Civil Doctrine*. London, 1594. Trans. Jones. The English Experience Its Record in Early Printed Books Published in Facsimile, No. 287. Amsterdam: Theatrum Orbis Terrarum, 1970.

Livius, Titus. *Livy*. Trans. B. O. Foster. 14 vols. The Loeb Classical Library [Latin Authors]. London: Heinemann, 1919–59.

Machiavelli, Niccolò. *De Principe libellus*. Trans. Sylvestrus Telius. Basel, 1560.

———. *Disputationum de republica quas discursus nuncupavit, Libri III. Quomodo in Rebuspub. ad antiquorum Romanorum imitationem aciones omnes bene maleve instituantur. Ex Italico Latini facti.* Mompelgarten: Iacobus Foilletus, 1591.

———. *The Discourses of Niccolo Machiavelli.* Ed. Leslie J. Walker. 2 vols. London: Routledge & Kegan Paul, 1950.

———. *The Discourses of Niccolo Machiavelli.* Ed. with an introduction by Bernard Crick and trans. by Leslie J. Walker. Harmondsworth: Penguin, 1988.

———. *Istorie fiorentine.* Ed. Franco Gaeta. Milan: Feltrinelli, 1962.

———. *The Prince.* Trans. George Bull. Harmondsworth: Penguin, 1975.

———. *Il Principe e Discorsi sopra la prima deca di Tito Livio.* Ed. Sergio Bertelli. Milan: Feltrinelli, 1983.

Macrobius. *Commentary on the Dream of Scipio.* Trans. and Ed. William Harris Stahl. New York: Columbia Univ. Press, 1952.

Mayor, J. E. B., ed. *Early Statutes of the College of St. John the Evangelist.* Cambridge: Cambridge Univ. Press, 1859.

Moryson, Fynes. *An itinerary containing his ten yeeres travell* ... 3 pts. London, 1617. Reprint. 4 vols. Glasgow: J. MacLehose & Son, 1907–8.

O'Rahilly, Alfred. "The Massacre at Smerwick (1580)." *Cork Historical and Archaeological Society Journal.* 2nd Series. 42 (1937): 1–15; 65–83.

Payne, Robert. *A Briefe Description of Ireland 1590.* Ed. Aquilla Smith. Dublin: Irish Archeological Society, 1841.

Perrott, James. *A Discoverie of Discontented Minds.* Oxford: Joseph Barnes, 1596.

———. *The Chronicle of Ireland, 1584–1608.* Ed. Herbert Wood. Dublin: Irish Manuscripts Commission, 1933.

Plutarch. *The Lives of the Noble Grecians and Romanes, Compared together by that grave learned Philosopher and Historiographer, Plutarke of Chaeronea: Translated out of Greeke into French by Iames Amyot ... and out of French into English by Thomas North.* London: Thomas Vautroullier, 1579.

———. *The Lives of the Noble Grecians and Romanes, Compared together by that grave learned Philosopher and Historiographer, Plutarke of Chaeronea: Translated out of Greeke into French by Iames Amyot ... and out of French into English by Thomas North.* Boston and New York: Houghton Mifflin, 1928.

Privy Council. *Acts of the Privy Council of England,* 1542–1631. 46 vols. London: Eyre and Spottiswoode for H. M. Stationery Office, 1890–1964.

Rawlinson, Richard. *The History of that most Eminent Statesman Sir John Perrott.* London, 1728.

Rich, Barnabe. *Allarme to England.* London: C. Barker, 1578.

———. *Greene's News.* London: T. Adams and J. Oxenbridge, 1593.

———. *A Short Survey of Ireland.* London: N. O[kes] for B. Sutton and W. Barenyr, 1609.

———. *A New Description of Ireland.* London: W. Jaggard, 1610.

———. *A True and Kinde Excuse, Written in Defence of that Booke Intitled, 'A Newe Description of Ireland'.* London: T. Dawson for T. Adams, 1612.

———. *The Irish Hubbub, or the English Hue and Crie.* London: G. Purslow for J. Marriot, 1618.

Sidney, Sir Henry. "Sir Henry Sidney's Memoir of His Government of Ireland." *Ulster Journal of Archaeology.* vol. 3 (1856): 33–52, 85–109, 336–57; vol. 5 (1857): 299–323; vol. 8 (1860): 179–95.

Sigonio, Carlo. *Opera omnia.* Ed. Ludovico Muratori. 6 vols. Milan: Palatinus, 1732–37.

Smith, Sir Thomas. *De republica Anglorum, the maner of government or policie of the realme of England.* London: Henry Middleton for George Seton, 1583. *De republica et administratione Anglorum: Olim Thomae Smithi, ... Nunc primum Ioannis Buddeni ... in Latinum conversi.* Marburg: P. Egenolphus for [W.?] Norton, London, 1610.

———. *A Discourse of the Commonweal of This Realm of England, Attributed to Sir Thomas Smith.* Ed. Mary Dewar. Folger Shakespeare Library. Charlottesville: Univ. of Virginia, 1969.

Smith, William. *The Particular Description of England.* 1588. Ed. Henry B. Wheatley and Edmund V. Ashbee. London: S. Austin & sons, 1879.

Spenser, Edmund. *The Works of Edmund Spenser: A Variorum Edition.* Ed. Edwin Greenlaw, C. G. Osgood, F. M. Padelford. 9 vols. Baltimore: Johns Hopkins Univ. Press, 1932–49.

Starkey, Thomas. *A Dialogue of Cardinal Pole and Thomas Lupset.* Ed. T. F. Mayer. London: Royal Historical Society, 1989.

Statutes, Ireland. *In this volume are contained all the statutes* [10 Hen. VI–14 Eliz.] *made in Ireland.* Dublin: R. Tottle, 1572.

Sutcliffe, Matthew. *The practice, proceedings and laws of arms*. London, 1593.

"A Treatise for the Reformation of Ireland, 1554–55." Ed. Brendan Bradshaw. *Irish Jurist* 16 (1981): 299–315.

Tudor Royal Proclamations. Ed. P. L. Hughes and J. F. Larkin. 3 vols. New Haven: Yale Univ. Press, 1964, 1969.

Walsh, Edward. "Edward Walsh's 'Conjectures' Concerning the State of Ireland [1552]." Ed. D. B. Quinn. *Irish Historical Studies* 5 (1947): 303–22.

Walsingham, Sir Francis. *The Walsingham Letter-book or Register of Ireland, May 1578 to December 1579*. Ed. James Hogan and N. MacNeill O'Farrell. Dublin: Irish Manuscripts Commission, 1959.

White, Rowland. "Rowland White's 'Discourse touching Ireland,' c. 1569." Ed. Nicholas Canny. *Irish Historical Studies* 20 (1977): 439–63.

———. "Rowland White's 'The Dysorders of the Irisshery' (1571)." Ed. Nicholas Canny. *Studia Hibernica* 19 (1979): 147–60.

Wilson, Florence. *Scholia seu commentariorum epitome in Scipionis Somnium ad egregium adolescentem*. London: R. Redman, 1535.

———. *De animi tranquilitate dialogus*. Edinburgh: Hamilton, Balfour and Neill, 1751.

Wilson, Thomas. *The Arte of Rhetorique*. London: Mense Inaurii, 1553. No. 206 in *The English Experience Its Record in Early Printed Books Published in Facsimile*. Amsterdam: Da Capo, 1969.

Wright, Robert, ed. *Funebria nobilissimi ac praestantissimi Equitis, D. Henrici Untoni*. Oxford: Joseph Barnes, 1596.

III. Secondary Sources

Anglo, Sydney. "A Machiavellian Solution to the Irish Problem: Richard Beacon's *Solon His Follie* (1594)." In *England and the Continental Renaissance*, edited by Edward Chaney and Peter Mack. Woodbridge: Boydell Press, 1990.

Armitage, David. "The British Empire and the Civic Tradition 1656–1742." Ph.D. diss., Cambridge Univ., 1991.

Bagwell, Richard. *Ireland Under the Tudors*. 3 vols. 1885–90. Reprint. London: Holland Press, 1963.

Baker, D. J. "Some Quirk, Some Subtle Evasion: Legal Subversion in

Spenser's *A View of the Present State of Ireland.*" *Spenser Studies* 6 (1985): 147–63.

Baker, Thomas. *History of the College of St. John the Evangelist, Cambridge.* Ed. John. E. B. Mayor. Cambridge: Cambridge Univ. Press, 1869.

Bauckham, Richard. *Tudor Apocalypse.* The Courtenay Library of Reformation Classics. Appleford: Sutton Courtenay Press, 1978.

Bindoff, S. T., J. Hartfield and I. C. H. Williams, eds. *Elizabethan Government and Society: Essays Presented to John Neale.* London: Athlone Press, 1961.

Binns, J. W. *Intellectual Culture in Elizabethan and Jacobean England: the Latin Writings of the Age.* ARCA Classical and Medieval Texts, Papers and Monographs. Leeds: Francis Cairns, 1990.

Bradbrook, M. C. "No Room at the Top: Spenser's Pursuit of Fame." In *The Artist and Society in Shakespeare's England: the Collected Papers of Muriel Bradbrook.* Vol. 1. Brighton, Sussex: Harvester Press, 1982.

Bradshaw, Brendan. "Cromwellian Reform and the Origins of the Kildare Rebellion, 1533–34." *Transactions of the Royal Historical Society* 27 (1977): 64–95.

———. "Sword, Word and Strategy in the Reformation in Ireland." *Historical Journal* 21 (1978): 475–502.

———. *The Irish Constitutional Revolution in the Sixteenth Century.* Cambridge: Cambridge Univ. Press, 1979.

———. "The Elizabethans and the Irish: A Muddled Model." *Studies: An Irish Quarterly Review* 70 (1981): 233–44.

———. "Edmund Spenser on Justice and Mercy." In *The Writer as Witness: Literature as Historical Evidence,* edited by Tom Dunne. Cork: Cork Univ. Press, 1987.

———. "Robe and Sword in the Conquest of Ireland." In *Law and Government Under the Tudors,* edited by Claire Cross et al. Cambridge: Cambridge Univ. Press, 1988.

Brady, Ciaran. "Faction and the Origins of the Desmond Rebellion of 1579." *Irish Historical Studies* 22 (1980–1): 289–312.

———. "The Killing of Shane O'Neill: Some New Evidence." *The Irish Sword* 15 (1982–83): 116–23.

———. "Conservative Subversives: The Community of the Pale and the Dublin Administration, 1556–86." In *Radicals, Rebels and Establishments,* edited by P. J. Corish. Belfast: Appletree Press, 1986.

———. "Spenser's Irish Crisis: Humanism and Experience in the 1590's." *Past and Present* 111 (1986): 16–49.

———. "Reply to Nicholas Canny." *Past and Present* 120 (1988): 210–15.

———. "Court, Castle and Country: The Tudor Framework of Government in Tudor Ireland." In *Natives and Newcomers: Essays on the Making of Irish Colonial Society, 1534–1641,* edited by Ciaran Brady and Raymond Gillespie. Dublin: Irish Academic Press, 1986.

———. *The Chief Governors: The Rise and Fall of Reform Government in Tudor Ireland, 1536–1588.* Cambridge: Cambridge Univ. Press, 1994.

Brady, Ciaran, and Raymond Gillespie, eds. *Natives and Newcomers: Essays on the Making of Irish Colonial Society 1534–1641.* Dublin: Irish Academic Press, 1986.

Canny, Nicholas. *The Elizabethan Conquest of Ireland: A Pattern Established, 1565–76.* Totowa: Barnes & Noble, 1976.

———. "Edmund Spenser and the Development of an Anglo-Irish Identity." *Yearbook of English Studies* 13 (1983): 1–19.

———. "Identity Formation in Ireland: the Emergence of an Anglo-Irish Identity." In *Colonial Identity in the Atlantic World,* edited by Nicholas Canny and Anthony Pagden. Princeton: Princeton Univ. Press, 1987.

———. *From Reformation to Restoration: Ireland, 1534–1660.* Dublin: Helicon, 1987.

———. "Debate: Spenser's Irish Crisis: Humanism and Experience in the 1590's." *Past and Present* 120 (1988): 201–9.

———. *Kingdom and Colony: Ireland in the Atlantic World, 1560–1800.* Baltimore: Johns Hopkins Univ. Press, 1988.

Carroll, Clare. "Representations of Women in Some Early Modern English Tracts on the Colonization of Ireland." *Albion* 25, 3 (1993): 379–94.

Collinson, Patrick. *The Religion of Protestants: The Church in English Society 1559–1625.* Oxford: Clarendon Press, 1982.

———. *The Elizabethan Puritan Movement.* Oxford: Clarendon Press, 1990.

Cooper, Charles Henry, and Thompson Cooper. *Athenae Cantabrigienses.* Cambridge: Deighton Bell & Co., 1858–1913.

Coughlin, Patricia, ed. *Spenser and Ireland.* Cork: Cork Univ. Press, 1989.

Cox, Virginia. *The Renaissance Dialogue.* Cambridge Studies in Renaissance Literature and Culture 2. Cambridge: Cambridge Univ. Press, 1992.

Cunningham, Bernadette. "Composition of Connacht in the lordships of Clanricard and Thomond, 1577–1642." *Irish Historical Studies* 24 (1984): 1–14.

Curtis, Edmund and R. B. McDowell, eds. Reprint. *Irish Historical Documents, 1172–1922*. London: Methuen, 1968.

Deakins, Roger. "The Tudor Dialogue as Literary Form." Ph.D. diss, Harvard Univ., 1964.

——. "The Tudor Prose Dialogue: Genre and Anti-Genre." *Studies in English Literature* 20 (1980): 5–23.

Dewar, Mary. *Sir Thomas Smith: A Tudor Intellectual in Office*. London: Athlone Press, 1964.

Dunlop, Robert. "An Unpublished Survey of the Plantation of Munster in 1622." *Journal of the Royal Society of Antiquaries of Ireland* 54 (1924): 128–46.

Ehrenberg, Victor. *From Solon to Socrates: Greek History and Civilization during the sixth and fifth centuries B. C.* London: Methuen, 1968.

Ellis, Steven G. "Tudor Policy and the Kildare Ascendancy in the Lordship of Ireland, 1496–1534." *Irish Historical Studies* 20 (1976–77): 235–71.

——. *Tudor Ireland: Crown, Community and the Conflict of Cultures 1470–1603*. New York: Longman, 1985.

Elton, G. R. *Reform and Renewal: Thomas Cromwell and the Common Weal*. Cambridge: Cambridge Univ. Press, 1973.

——. *The Tudor Constitution: Documents and Commentary*, 2nd ed. Cambridge: Cambridge Univ. Press, 1982.

Empey, C. A. and K. Simms. "The Ordinances of the White Earl and the Problem of Coign in the Later Middle Ages." *Proceedings of the Royal Irish Academy* 75 C (1975): 250–64.

Falls, Cyril. *Elizabeth's Irish Wars*. New York: Barnes & Noble, 1970.

Frame, Robin. *Colonial Ireland, 1169–1369*. Dublin: Helicon, 1981.

Fellheimer, Jeannette. "Geoffrey Fenton's *Historie of Guicciardini* and Holinshed's *Chronicles* of 1587." *Modern Language Quarterly* 6 (1945): 285–98.

Ferguson, Arthur B. *The Articulate Citizen and the English Renaissance*. Durham: Duke Univ. Press, 1965.

———. *Clio Unbound: Perception of the Social and Cultural Past in Renaissance England.* Duke Monographs in Medieval and Renaissance Studies 2. Durham: Duke Univ. Press, 1979.

Firth, Katharine R. *The Apocalyptic Tradition in Reformation Britain 1530–1645.* Oxford: Oxford Univ. Press, 1979.

Foster, Joseph. *Alumni Oxoniensis: The Members of the University of Oxford 1500–1714.* 8 vols. 1887–92. Reprint. Nendeln: Kraus, 1968.

Gerber, Adolph. *Niccolò Machiavelli, die Handschriften, Ausgaben und Übersetzungen seiner Werke im 16. und 17. Jahrhundert.* Torino: Erasmo, 1962.

Gottfried, Rudolf. "Geoffrey Fenton's *Historie of Guicciardin.*" Indiana University Humanities Series 3 (1940): 5–42.

Grafton, Anthony and Lisa Jardine. *From Humanism to the Humanities: Education and the Liberal Arts in Sixteenth-Century Europe.* London: Duckworth, 1986.

Greenblatt, Stephen. *Renaissance Self-Fashioning: From More to Shakespeare.* Chicago: Univ. of Chicago Press, 1980.

Greenlaw, Edwin. "The Influence of Machiavelli on Spenser." *Modern Philology* 7 (1909): 187–202.

———. *Studies in Spenser's Historical Allegory.* Baltimore: Johns Hopkins Univ. Press, 1932.

Guy, John. *Tudor England.* Oxford: Oxford Univ. Press, 1988.

Heale, Elizabeth. *"The Faerie Queene": A Reader's Guide.* Cambridge: Cambridge Univ. Press, 1987.

Henley, Pauline. *Spenser in Ireland.* Dublin: Univ. of Cork Press, 1928.

Hulse, Clark. "Spenser, Bacon, and the Myth of Power." In *Historical Renaissance,* edited by Heather Dubrow and Richard Strier. Chicago: Univ. of Chicago Press, 1988.

Jardine, Lisa. "Humanism and the Sixteenth Century Arts Course." *History of Education* 4 (1975): 16–31.

———. "Mastering the uncouth: Gabriel Harvey, Edmund Spenser and the English experience in Ireland." In *New Perspectives on Renaissance Thought: Essays in the History of Science, Education and Philosophy,* edited by John Henry and Sarah Hutton. London: Duckworth, 1990.

Jenkins, Raymond. "Spenser with Lord Grey in Ireland." *PMLA* 52 (1937): 338–53.

Judson, Alexander C. *The Life of Edmund Spenser.* Baltimore: Johns Hopkins Univ. Press, 1945.

———. "Spenser and the Munster Officials," *Studies in Philology* 44 (1947): 157–73.

Kearney, Hugh. *The British Isles: A History of Four Nations.* Cambridge: Cambridge Univ. Press, 1989.

———. *Scholars and Gentlemen: Universities and Society in Pre-Industrial Britain,* 1500–1700. London: Faber & Faber, 1970.

Kinney, Arthur F. *Humanist Poetics.* Amherst: Univ. of Massachusetts Press, 1986.

King, John N. *English Reformation Literature: The Tudor Origins of the Protestant Tradition.* Princeton: Princeton Univ. Press, 1982.

———. *Tudor Royal Iconography: Literature and Art in an Age of Religious Crisis.* Princeton: Princeton Univ. Press, 1989.

———. *Spenser's Poetry and the Reformation Tradition.* Princeton: Princeton Univ. Press, 1990.

Kruger, Steven. *Dreaming in the Middle Ages.* Cambridge Studies in Medieval Literature, 14. Cambridge: Cambridge Univ. Press, 1992.

MacCaffrey, Wallace T. *The Shaping of the Elizabethan Regime.* Princeton: Princeton Univ. Press, 1968.

———. *Queen Elizabeth and the Making of Policy: 1572–88.* Princeton: Princeton Univ. Press, 1981.

———. *Elizabeth I: War and Politics, 1588–1603.* Princeton: Princeton Univ. Press, 1992.

MacCarthy-Morrogh, Michael. *The Munster Plantation.* Oxford: Clarendon Press, 1986.

McConica, J. K. *English Humanists and Reformation Politics under Henry VIII and Edward VI.* Oxford: Clarendon Press, 1965.

MacCurtain, Margaret. *Tudor and Stuart Ireland.* Dublin: Gill and Macmillan, 1972.

Madan, Falconer. *The Early Oxford Press: A Bibliography of Printing and Publishing at Oxford 1468–1640.* Oxford: Clarendon Press, 1911.

Maley, Willy. "Edmund Spenser and Cultural Identity in Early Modern Ireland." Ph.D. diss., Cambridge Univ., 1989.

———. "Spenser and Ireland: A Select Bibliography." *Spenser Studies* 9 (1991): 225–42.

———. "The Supplication of the Blood of the English Most Lamentably Murdered in Ireland, Cryeng Out of the Yearth for Revenge (1589)." *Analecta Hibernica* 36 (1994): 3–92.

Mendle, Michael. *Dangerous Positions: Mixed Government, the Estates of the Realm, and the Making of the 'Answer to the xix propositions.* University: Univ. of Alabama Press, 1985.

Mueller, Janel. "Contextualizing Milton's Nascent Republicanism." In *Of Poetry and Politics New Essays on Milton and His World,* edited by Paul Stanwood. Medieval & Renaissance Texts and Studies 126. Binghamton, NY: 1995.

Miller, Edward. *Portrait of a College, A History of the College of St. John.* Cambridge: Cambridge Univ. Press, 1961.

Moody, T. W., F. X. Martin and F. J. Byrne. *A New History of Ireland: Vol. III. Early Modern Ireland 1534–1691.* Oxford: Clarendon Press, 1976.

———. *A New History of Ireland: Vol. IX. Maps, Genealogies, Lists.* Oxford: Clarendon Press, 1984.

———. *A New History of Ireland: Vol. II. Medieval Ireland, 1169–1534.* Oxford: Clarendon Press 1987.

Morgan, Hiram. "The Outbreak of the Nine Year's War: Ulster in Irish Politics, 1585–96." Ph.D. diss., Cambridge Univ., 1986.

———. "The End of Gaelic Ulster: A Thematic Interpretation of Events between 1534 and 1610." *Irish Historical Studies* xxvi, no. 101 (1988): 8–32.

———. *Tyrone's Rebellion: The Outbreak of the Nine Years War in Tudor Ireland.* Woodbridge, Suffolk: Boydell Press, 1993.

Neale, J. E. *Queen Elizabeth I.* New York: Harcourt Brace, 1934.

Nichols, Kenneth W. *Gaelic and Gaelicised Ireland in the Middle Ages.* Dublin: Gill and Macmillan, 1972.

Ong, Walter J. *Ramus, Method, and the Decay of Dialogue.* Cambridge: Harvard Univ. Press, 1958.

O'Rahilly, Alfred. "The Massacre at Smerwick (1580)." *Journal of the Cork Historical and Archeological Society.* 2nd series 42 (1937): 1–15; 65–83.

Orsini, Napoleone. *Studi sul Rinascimento Italiano in Inghilterra.* Firenze: G. C. Sansoni, 1937.

Oxford Classical Dictionary. *The Oxford Classical Dictionary.* Ed. N. G. L. Hammond and H. M. Scullard. 2nd ed. Oxford: Clarendon Press, 1970.

Pawlisch, Hans. *Sir John Davies and the Conquest of Ireland: A Study in Legal Imperialism.* Cambridge: Cambridge Univ. Press, 1983.

Peltonen, Marku. "Classical Republicanism in Tudor England: The Case of Richard Beacon's *Solon his Follie*." *History of Political Thought* 15, 4 (1994): 469–503.

Pocock, J. G. A. *The Machiavellian Moment: Florentine Political Thought and the Atlantic Republican Tradition*. Princeton: Princeton Univ. Press, 1975.

Porter, H. C. *Reformation and Reaction in Tudor Cambridge*. Cambridge: Cambridge University Press, 1958.

Quinn, David Beers. "The Bills and Statutes of the Irish Parliaments of Henry VII and Henry VIII." *Analecta Hibernica* 10 (1941): 71–169.

———. "A Discourse of Ireland (circa 1599): A Sidelight on English Colonial Policy." *Proceedings of the Royal Irish Academy* 47, sect c (1942): 151–66.

———. "Sir Thomas Smith (1513–77) and the Beginnings of English Colonial Theory," *Proceedings of the American Philosophical Society* 89, 4 (1945): 543–60.

———. *Raleigh and the British Empire*. 2nd edition. London: English Universities Press, 1947.

———. "Ireland and Sixteenth-Century European Expansion." *Historical Studies* 1 (1958): 20–32.

———. *The Elizabethans and the Irish*. Ithaca: Cornell Univ. Press, 1966.

———. "The Munster Plantation: Problems and Opportunities," *Cork Historical and Archaeological Society Journal* 71 (1966): 19–40.

———. "Renaissance Influences in English Colonization." *Transactions of the Royal Historical Society* 26 (1976): 73–93.

Raab, Felix. *The English Face of Machiavelli, a Changing Interpretation, 1570–1700*. London: Routledge & Kegan Paul, 1964.

Sheehan, Anthony J. "Official Reaction to Native Land Claims in the Plantation of Munster." *Irish Historical Studies*. 23, no. 92 (1983): 297–318.

Shire, Helena. *A Preface to Spenser*. London: Longman, 1978.

Simms, Katherine. *From Kings to Warlords: The Changing Political Structure of Gaelic Ireland in the Later Middle Ages*. Woodbridge: Boydell Press, 1987.

Skinner, Quentin. "Moral Ambiguity and the Renaissance Art of Eloquence." *Essays in Criticism* 44, 4 (1994): 267–92.

Stephen, Leslie and Sir Henry Lee, eds. *Dictionary of National Biogra-*

phy: From the Earliest Times to 1900. Reprint. Nendeln: Kraus, 1968.

Strong, Roy. *The Cult of Elizabeth.* Berkeley: Univ. of California Press, 1977.

Treadwell, Victor. "The Irish Parliament of 1569–71." *Proceedings of the Royal Irish Academy* 65, c, no. 4 (1966): 55–89.

Van Dorsten, J. A. *Poets, Patrons, and Professors: Sir Philip Sidney, Daniel Rogers and the Leiden Humanists.* Leiden: Sir Thomas Brown Institute, 1962.

Venn, John, and J. A. Venn. *Alumni Cantabrigienses.* 10 vols. Cambridge: Cambridge Univ. Press, 1927–54.

Wells, Robin H. *Spenser's "Faerie Queene" and the Cult of Elizabeth.* Totowa: Barnes & Noble, 1983.

Williams, Penry. *The Tudor Regime.* Oxford: Clarendon Press, 1979.

Wilson, K. J. *Incomplete Fictions: The Formation of English Renaissance Dialogue.* Washington, D.C.: Catholic Univ. Press, 1985.

Yates, Frances. *Astraea: The Imperial Theme in the Sixteenth Century.* London: Routledge & Kegan Paul, 1975.

The Renaissance English Text Society was established to publish literary texts, chiefly nondramatic, of the period 1475–1660. Dues are $25.00 per annum ($15.00, graduate students; life membership is available at $500.00). Members receive the text published for each year of membership. The Society sponsors panels at such annual meetings as those of the Modern Language Association, the Renaissance Society of America, and the conference at Kalamazoo. Inquiries should be addressed to the president, Arthur Kinney, Department of English, University of Massachusetts, Amherst, Mass. 01002, USA.

Copies of volumes X–XII may be purchased from Associated University Presses, 440 Forsgate Drive, Cranbury, NJ 08512. Copies of earlier volumes still in print or of later volumes from XIII on may be ordered from MRTS — LNG 99, SUNY, Binghamton, NY 13902–6000.

Recently published volumes:

VOL. X. *Two Early Renaissance Bird Poems,* edited by Malcolm Andrew, 1984.

VOL. XI. *Argalus and Parthenia* by Francis Quarles, edited by David Freeman, 1986.

VOL. XII. Cicero's *De Officiis,* trans. Nicholas Grimald, edited by Gerald O'Gorman, 1987.

VOL. XIII. *The Silkewormes and their Flies* by Thomas Moffet (1599), edited with introduction and commentary by Victor Houliston, 1988.

VOL. XIV. John Bale, *The Vocacyon of Johan Bale,* edited by Peter Happé and John N. King, 1989.

VOL. XV. *The Nondramatic Works of John Ford,* edited by L. E. Stock, Gilles D. Monsarrat, Judith M. Kennedy, and Dennis Danielson, with the assistance of Marta Straznicky, 1990.

Special Publication. *New Ways of Looking at Old Texts: Papers....* edited by W. Speed Hill, 1993.

VOL. XVI. *George Herbert, The Temple: A Diplomatic Edition of the Bodleian Manuscript (Tanner 307),* edited with introduction and notes by Mario A. Di Cesare, 1991.

VOL. XVII. *The First Part of the Countess of Montgomery's Urania by Lady Mary Wroth.* Ed. Josephine Roberts. 1992.

VOL. XVIII. *Solon His Follie by Richard Beacon,* ed. by Clare Carroll and Vincent Carey. 216 pp. 1993.